D1578381

INTERNATIONAL YEARBOOK COMMUNICATION DESIGN 2011/2012

[Editor PETER ZEC]

INTERNATIONAL YEARBOOK
COMMUNICATION
DESIGN 2011/2012

[Editor PETER ZEC]

reddot design award
communication design

VOL **1**

Contents

editorial

Communication with added value. Holistic and effective editorial designs – paired with distinction and high recognition value – allow companies to stand out from the competition.

posters

Creative and strong in concept. Poster design is one of the supreme disciplines in the world of design – a challenge with each new design.

illustrations

Print and digital media achieve a distinctive identity through illustrations that emerge from a wealth of outstanding ideas and a passion for imagery and storytelling.

magazines & daily press

Make it rustle, smell it, feel it. Be it a newspaper or magazine design: sophisticated typography, unusual motifs and surprising colour concepts are convincing.

typography

Triggering the imagination. Text is not only a means of communication, it is also an important design element.

designer portraits

In the portraits the designers and design studios whose extraordinary and creative design achievements convinced the jury are introduced with vita, interview and photo.

index

Peter Zec
Initiator and CEO of red dot

Preface
Peter Zec

The history of the "red dot award: communication design" goes back a long way. It began as Grafik Design Deutschland, a competition organised by the German design association Bund Deutscher Grafik-Designer. In 1993, the Design Zentrum Nordrhein Westfalen took over as organiser, renaming it Deutscher Preis für Kommunikationsdesign. In 2001, the competition was integrated into the red dot design award and ever since went on to write a unique success story.

Each year, the competition attracts a growing number of submissions and increasing international attention. Today, designers, agencies and companies from 40 countries participate in the "red dot award: communication design". Due to its challenging yet fair selection process, the competition is well respected both domestically and abroad and is widely considered to be one of the best competitions of its kind across the world.

Over the years, the red dot design award as a whole has undergone several changes. For example, the competition now has 24 different categories, up from only 10 in 2001. At that time, digitalisation was still in its infancy, and CD-ROMs, screen and website design, digital interfaces and navigation systems were all grouped into the single category "multimedia". Despite the broad scope of that category, the number of submissions was still at a manageable level, so there were accordingly few awards in that field. And not only the competition itself, but also designers, agencies, companies and, not least, the jurors were not yet familiar with this new, unknown and unaccustomed category. With simply no previous models to rely on and no prior experience to build on, the aesthetic and functional design of digital applications was initially approached with the same, long-time established, principles as classic graphic design. I remember very well the kind of discussion held among the jurors at that time. And, genuine enthusiasm about the "new" digital world was relatively rare. Instead, the jurors tended to bemoan the decline of traditional techniques and technologies and warned against the "disastrous repercussions of digitalisation on the profession and field of communication design". So it is little wonder that the early stages of the competition still focused on more traditional design disciplines such as illustration, book design and poster design. Thanks to this learning curve, the competition now offers many new award categories, allowing us to promote design quality in digital media. Despite these incentives, jurors have noted a lag in the development of more universal design principles in this field. One explanation is that designers in new media tend to focus exclusively on what is technically feasible. Whether developing digital games, online communication or interface design, most designers appear to cave into the immediate pressure of delivering peak technological performance. Under these circumstances, design tends to fall on the back burner. The resulting delay in integrating design is even more pronounced when contrasted with the breathtaking speed at which communication on the Internet is continually accelerating. Yet, the "red dot award: communication design" was created precisely to address this widening gap and to contribute to establishing appropriate guidelines for design quality in the digital technology sector.

»6,468 works were entered in the 24 categories.«

entries in total

Once again this year we are pleased that the number of works submitted to the competition has increased, as it has each year. A total of 6,468 works were entered in the 24 categories of the competition. Submission numbers have increased significantly in the categories of online communication and event design, reflecting a growing awareness and appreciation for design in these areas and confirming that we were on the right track when we added these new categories. In order to stay on that track, we will continue to monitor the communication design market and respond to newly emerging branches and applications in communication design with new categories. Although the large number of competition categories may strike some as bewildering or superfluous, we are convinced that this degree of differentiation is necessary to provide participants with the right framework for submitting their works. After all, what's the use of comparing apples to oranges? Instead, our goal is to arrive at fair and comprehensive evaluations of individual works on the basis of appropriate, detailed observations. It is only through this type of evaluation that the competition will be able to contribute to the orientation and development of communication design in the long term.

»What matters is simply the design quality of the work itself.«

the jury of the red dot design award

One crucial element in the quality of a competition is always the jury. Who exactly are these people who dare to judge the works of others? What authority do they have to deem something to be poor, insufficient, good, better or best? Apart from demonstrating professional competence, jurors must be able to respect a work regardless of its quality. This means they have to recognise the effort that goes into each work and appreciate it for what it is. Only then can they make an appropriate assessment. Since the value of design cannot be counted or measured, and because there is no "absolute truth" to refer to, we can never really arrive at a wholly objective evaluation. Thus, decisions in design will always be subjective to some degree and, rather than binary, may be ranging anywhere on the broad spectrum from clear-cut validation to rejection.

Yet, this is exactly why we need design competitions in the first place and what makes the whole endeavour so exciting! Still, despite the subjective nature of design, a competition jury has to demonstrate an utmost degree of fairness and exacting rigour. Otherwise, the competition will be of no value to the participants. The successful execution of a design competition requires mutual trust and respect between the participants and the jurors. Participants entrust their work to the jury and have confidence in the competence and fairness of the jurors, while jurors respect the participants' work and commit to judge it according to the best of their knowledge and ability. At the "red dot award: communication design", each submitted work is examined, analysed and evaluated by a minimum of three jurors. These jurors then discuss and compare their views, a process during which they reach their final consensus on whether to issue, or not, a "red dot", a "red dot: best of the best" or a "red dot: grand prix".

A red dot is granted when at least two of the three jurors consider the quality of a work to be very high. However, it happens that the jurors tend to unanimously agree on the evaluations. In determining whether or not to award a red dot, the jurors consider each work solely on its own merit, not in comparison to other submissions. What matters is simply the design quality of the work itself, not how it compares to other works or to a certain task. Once the jury has finished issuing the red dot awards for a certain category, it will proceed with the task of awarding up to three of the red dot awarded works with the "red dot: best of the best" distinction. Next, if the design quality of one of these three works stands out significantly from those of the other two, the jury will grant a "red dot: grand prix".

Thus, in order for a work to earn a "red dot: best of the best", it must stand out from a multitude of other works that have already received a red dot. This may be achieved with an especially intelligent solution to a particular challenge, with the successful implementation of an outstanding design idea, with the precise execution of a design idea, or with any combination of these, for example a symbiosis between superb craftsmanship and an ingenious solution to a design problem.

»outstanding design quality«

red dot: best of the best & red dot: grand prix

A "red dot: best of the best" and "red dot: grand prix" can

also be awarded on the grounds of the special impact or significance a communicative statement has. When issuing one of these two highest awards, unanimity among the jury has also been the rule rather than the exception, not only with regard to the overall decision that a work should receive this award, but also with regard to the specific reason why.

It should be noted that the jury may also decide to issue neither of these special awards if the jurors feel that none of the red dot awarded works stands out significantly from the others. Moreover, all jurors agree on the need for stringent evaluation criteria in their search for high and highest design quality. Given this common ground, the process of awarding the best works of a given year with a red dot occurs independently of the tastes or predilections of the individual jurors.

In 2011, the jury awarded 608 works with a red dot, which constitutes less than 10 per cent of all submissions. Furthermore, 80 were honoured with a "red dot: best of the best" and only 10 of them with the "red dot: grand prix". Thus, less than half of the 24 categories received a "red dot: grand prix", demonstrating the jury's commitment to quality and rigour and cementing the reputation of the "red dot award: communication design" as the most critical competition of its kind worldwide. So, not least because of that, congratulations to all winners of a red dot award for your extraordinary achievement!

»upcoming designers«

red dot: junior award

Participation in the competition for the "red dot award: communication design" has always been open to junior designers, including students and young professionals. New talents have the opportunity to compare themselves with the best in their field. To highlight the accomplishments of junior designers, the competition also issues the "red dot: junior prize", which comes with a 10,000 euros cash prize. Year after year, a huge number of emerging designers from all over the world participate in the "red dot award: communication design" in order to vie for this prestigious distinction. To be eligible, a work must already have been awarded a "red dot: best of the best". This year, 17 of the 80 "red dot: best of the best" works were considered "junior works" and entered into the competition for the "red dot: junior prize". To determine the winner, the

jurors of each category involved always engage in an initial discussion and decision-making process. This year, that process resulted in shortlisting 3 of the 17 qualified works for a final round. These were the following:

"Dirt Devil – Exorcist", a commercial by Andreas Roth from Germany;
"QR Type", an information design work by Kyuha Shim from the USA; and
"Aufschwung durch Ableben" (Economic revival through death), an annual report by Martina Morth from Germany.

After intense discussion, the jury arrived at the unanimous verdict that the "red dot: junior prize" should be granted to Martina Morth for her annual report on, as juror Jean Jacques Schaffner put it, "the profitable balance of death". On over 200 pages, partly manually designed, death is depicted as a listed company that is raking in record profits for the fiscal year 2009/2010.

The work provides a macabre, bizarre and superbly insightful look into a sensitive subject and stands out not only for its content but also for its exquisite craftsmanship and design. Jury member Jean Jacques Schaffner praised the annual report, saying: "This is the kind of work that makes jurors envious of not having come up with the idea themselves. (...) The subject and its interpretation are headstrong, and the texts and illustrations demonstrate virtuosity and mastery." Martina Morth is a worthy award winner, who has accomplished an exceptional design achievement with her annual report "Aufschwung durch Ableben" (Economic revival through death).

»red dot: client of the year«

AUDI AG

In 2010, the "red dot award: communication design" introduced a new honorary title – "red dot: client of the year" – for which participants do not apply directly but are automatically entered when they participate in the competition. The award honours the special involvement and commitment of a company that demonstrates a track record with regard to design and sets new standards within its field. When AUDI AG received this award in 2010, Lothar Korn, Head of Marketing Communications at the company, solemnly announced that he would defend the title again next year. AUDI AG clearly didn't take that pledge lightly, and Korn lived up to his word. Last year's and this year's "red dot: client of the year" is AUDI AG. In striving to position itself as the world's most successful automobile brand, the company has demonstrated an impressive level of competence, determination and quality in its communication design. Audi managers orchestrate collaborations with diverse design and creative agencies throughout the world, which they hand-pick according to the task in question. An achievement that remains unravelled in the world of communication design.

»red dot: agency of the year«

Beetroot Design Group

The "red dot award: communication design" also issues the honorary title "red dot: agency of the year". Presented along with the travelling Stylus trophy, this honorary title is the highest possible distinction granted by the competition. The "red dot: agency of the year 2011" – Beetroot, from Greece – has been successfully participating in the "red dot award: communication design" for several years and has received multiple "red dot: best of the best" awards. Beetroot was founded in 2000 by Vangelis Liakos, Alexis Nikou and Yiannis Charalambopoulos and employs eleven employees. Despite the company's relatively small size, Beetroot Design Group is active in nearly all fields of communication design, such as poster and book design; branding campaigns; web, video and TV productions; and a variety of installations and exhibitions. Its client list includes numerous companies, both Greek and foreign, including several public organisations. In 2010, Beetroot Design Group received the "red dot: grand prix" for its poster "Romeo & Juliet". Based in Thessaloniki, this unique agency is certainly a deserving recipient of the "red dot: agency of the year" award.

Putting the excitement of awards and distinctions aside for a moment, I would also like to take this opportunity to pay tribute to the life's work and legacy of Kurt Weidemann, one of the most significant and prolific designers of our time. In addition to being a famous designer, he was a long-time companion and juror at red dot, and a personal friend and mentor of mine. Although he reached the proud age of 88 years, on 30th March 2011, in the small

community of Sélestat in Alsace, Kurt Weidemann left us much too soon. We will always remember him, not only as a typesetter, graphic designer, typographer and brilliant expert in his field, but above all as a shrewd and critical thinker, a sophisticated mind, a highly articulate and quick-witted speaker, and a man with an extraordinary zest for life. He will be deeply missed. This year's yearbook pays tribute to him and his achievements with a special photo series.

»red dot goes berlin«

red dot gala & Designers' Night

This year, for the first time in the history of the competition, the award ceremony of the "red dot award: communication design" took place not in Essen, but in Germany's capital city, Berlin. More than 1,400 designers and creatives from all over the world flocked to the glamorous event, which continued up until the early hours of the morning. Held in the Konzerthaus Berlin and the Alte Münze, the event was marked by enthusiasm and passion for the field of communication design, and of course by praise and acclaim for the award winners. With the images included in this book, we hope to impart a sense of just how special the evening was.

In closing, I would like to once again express my sincere thanks to all the designers, agencies and companies who participated in this year's competition, and to congratulate all the winners on their success. And finally, to the readers of this yearbook: we hope you enjoy reading it as much as we enjoyed creating it!

Yours,
Peter Zec
Essen and Berlin, October 2011

Obituary for Kurt Weidemann

Kurt Weidemann was not only one of the formative and leading international designers of the 20th century, he was also a prophet, pundit and, in particular, a lateral thinker. His work was furthermore not only of seminal importance to the design world, but also to the Design Zentrum Nordrhein Westfalen. Aside from the countless hours we spent with this witty, astute and distinguished jurist, we also are grateful to him for the important impulses for the "red dot award: communication design" he gave as a long-standing companion and valued friend. As recently as December 2010, Kurt Weidemann delighted guests at one of our events with his inimitable quick wit and impressed them with the high degree of competence with which he has guided our communication design competition since its inception in 1993. We shall never forget his alert, critical mind, unsparing truthfulness, tireless commitment to the essential and, last but not least, his practical, clear and logical approach to design.

The series of images on the following pages show Kurt Weidemann as a juror of the "red dot award: communication design" as well as at our award ceremonies.

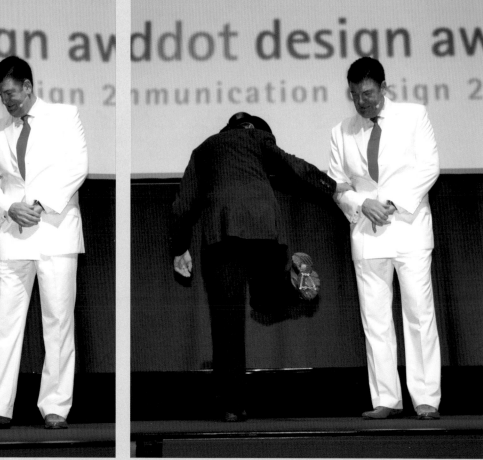

»You always need to have fun, otherwise you are not good at all.«

Kurt Weidemann

6,468

entries in total participated in the
"red dot award: communication design 2011".

The award by the numbers

608

works were honoured with a red dot by this years' international jury.

1.2

per cent of all entries were awarded the "red dot: best of the best".

10

outstanding works were conferred the "red dot: grand prix".

350

cm high – the Minotaur rises out of the special exhibition by the "red dot: agency of the year 2011".

240

bottles were used as motif for the opener site of the yearbook capture "packaging design" (in Vol. 2).

2009/10

was the most successful and flourishing year for the Grim Reaper – this stated the annual report, which was awarded the "red dot: junior prize".

29

stairs led the laureates and guests to the glamorous red dot gala at the Konzerthaus Berlin.

1,400

guests attended the award ceremony and the Designers' Night.

55

years! At the stroke of midnight, Peter Zec also celebrated his 55th birthday with all guests at the Designers' Night.

THE BEST AGENCY IN 2011 is named after a very healthy vegetable: Beetroot from Thessaloniki, Greece, is the "red dot: agency of the year 2011". Since 2000 the design group has been seeking new ways of expressing creativity and providing design solutions: all team members are design enthusiasts with expertise and skills in various creative fields. The agency, consisting of real all-rounders, works on projects in all media where graphic design is conceivable and applicable.

At the glamorous award ceremony in the Konzerthaus Berlin, Beetroot received the honorary title "red dot: agency of the year" and, accordingly, the challenge cup Stylus for its outstanding achievements in communication design. This unique trophy – exclusively designed for red dot by Simon P. Eiber, by order of the Gebrüder Niessing jewellery manufacturer in Vreden – was passed from BBDO, last year's recipient of this highest distinction, to Beetroot.

AGENCY
OF THE
YEOR

Beetroot Design Group – "red dot: agency of the year 2011":
Ilias Pantikakis, Kostas Kaparos, Yiannis Charalambopoulos,
Vangelis Liakos, Karolos Gakidis, Michalis Rafail, Haris Matis,
Kostas Pappas, Alexis Nikou

BEETROOT DESIGN GROUP

How do three extremely creative minds come to their ideas? Vangelis Liakos, Yiannis Charalambopoulos and Alexis Nikou give insights in their reasoning, acting, decision making and in their projects that are featured in all media, where graphic design is conceivable and applicable – thus in print, branding and also in web, TV, installations and exhibitions.

Why do you call yourselves "Beetroot"?

Vangelis Liakos: The name is due to the American writer Tom Robbins. When we were younger, we liked his books very much. One of them is called "Jitterbug Perfume", where he wrote a lot about the beetroot. It's a colour and a substance that you cannot entirely reproduce with technical means: beetroot is stainless and very unique.

Yiannis Charalambopoulos: We are more inspired by the fact that it can't be reproduced than by the colour itself.

Before the name, there was the plan for the three of you to join together. Can you tell me something about your history of origins?

Alexis Nikou: The three of us are old friends. We visited high school together and didn't plan to team up later. Initially, everybody went in different directions, but we then got more or less the same academic qualification. When we came back to Thessaloniki, accidently at the same time, we realised that we had similar future plans.

What was the original idea behind your venture? Is its present form exactly what you had in mind when you started your business?

Yiannis Charalambopoulos: It is characteristic for us that we grew along with the company. When the need arose, we tried to hire people in specific areas, like photography. We started as three graphic designers and the final outcome is quite a prosperous company with 12 people covering a lot of disciplines.

Alexis Nikou: The majority of our colleagues have been collaborating with us for many years. For most of them, this was their first job. So we had the chance to build them up and are able to communicate with each other on the same level. We have established an efficiently working and close team.

»Collaboration is the magic word.«

Vangelis Liakos

How did you achieve this, and what's the secret of this team spirit?

Vangelis Liakos: Collaboration is the magic word. Everybody needs each other. To be honest, there's only one girl at our agency. But since we also need the female perspective, she's very much sought after; we ask her opinion on all Beetroot works.

Yiannis Charalambopoulos: It's always beneficial to include her viewpoint. Quite often she can give us solutions that work. It's just a coincidence that we are not working with more female designers at the moment – but there's always hope.

»If you are too explicit, ironically, you won't catch the meaning. If you go too far, then you lose it. If you're too gentle, it becomes boring.«

Vangelis Liakos

Museum of Photography Thessaloniki (Corporate Identity)
The two eyes of a photographer while
taking a picture as a highly symbolic logo.
red dot: best of the best 2010

»If you are too explicit, ironically, you won't catch the meaning. If you go too far, then you lose it. If you're too gentle, it becomes boring.«

Was there any kind of work that was a breakthrough experience for you?

Vangelis Liakos: Different works give you different experiences. Years are passing by and bigger and bigger projects are coming your way. But it's primarily important to maintain standards, no matter how big the project is. Just then you realise that you have the experience to manage everything. Every project is a learning procedure. That's the most interesting part in succeeding.

Is there a certain trend within Beetroot towards a specific technology?

Alexis Nikou: We are just talking about mediums. We have to decide what would be the best solution for the client, and then we have to choose the adequate software or platform.

Yiannis Charalambopoulos: We aren't really driven by technology, though. I agree with Alexis: we would rather try to locate the project's needs and decide then what medium is the right one.

»Keep the balance in every aspect of graphic design.«

Yiannis Charalambopoulos

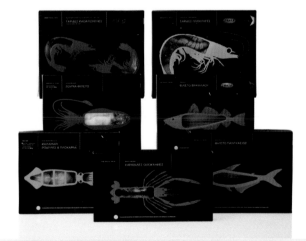

Trata On Ice (Packaging Design)
A high-quality packaging series with a strong element branding and recognition value for frozen seafood.
red dot 2011

»The variety keeps us alive. The ever-changing projects are our hybrid motor.«

Yiannis Charalambopoulos

Is there something that Beetroot is famous for?

Yiannis Charalambopoulos: We are famous, if that's the word, for various reasons to different people. There are some who associate us with web design, others with illustrations or packaging design. But we try to keep the balance in every aspect of graphic design.

Looking at your red dot-winning designs, this huge variety in your work becomes clear. You have done films, corporate, exhibition or packaging design... Is there anything you like to do most?

Yiannis Charalambopoulos: The variety keeps us alive. The everchanging projects are our hybrid motor.

As further proof of your variety, you also did a corporate design for a museum. Is it, in your opinion, different to the corporate design of a more commercial client?

Alexis Nikou: I don't think that this is a different process, because at the end you have to communicate something to an audience. The starting point is always the same: you are servicing people. The whole process is similar, but the outcome of a campaign for cultural institutes can be completely out of the expected context, which may elicit amazement and further inspiration.

Vangelis Liakos: Sometimes it is easier to work for a cultural client. There is much more freedom. While the museum likes to have more excited visitors, a commercial client, for example, often only wishes to increase sales.

It seems as if you have a rather semiotic approach in your designs, as you don't often use naturalistic environments.

Yiannis Charalambopoulos: That's right. It's a semiotic approach, but not a symbolical one. It's deeper than that.

Vangelis Liakos: We like to create realities that can be cognised by the clients' target groups. So we try to generate sceneries that foster constructive reception. All in all, we're positive and provide optimistic expressions.

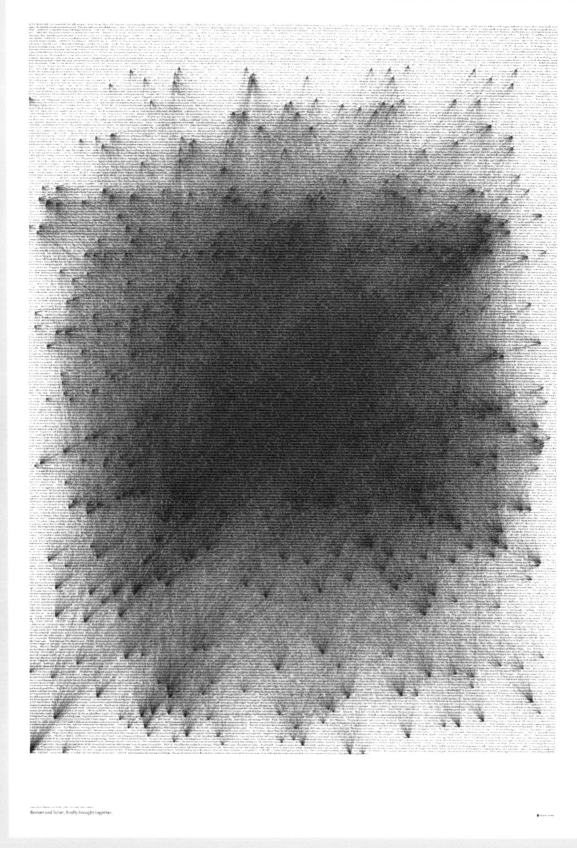

Romeo & Juliet (Poster)
The secret and tragic love story with deadly ending
visualised by a network of red lines.
red dot: grand prix 2010

What are the key mistakes an agency could make at this point?

Vangelis Liakos: You need a balance. If you are too explicit, ironically, you won't catch the meaning. If you go too far, then you lose it. If you're too gentle, it becomes boring.

Yiannis Charalambopoulos: It's all about proportions. Sometimes the recipients might not understand the key message because of a tiny detail or a way-too-strong exaggeration. We're working with connotations rather than sledgehammer methods. When they get the message unconsciously, we've done a good job.

So, if you have achieved a good job – will that always be beneficial for the client?

Alexis Nikou: Yes. You always have to keep in mind the commercial aspect. It's not something for you to show off.

Vangelis Liakos: That's why we use semiotics. People understand something because they recognise it. If, of course, semiotics are changing, you have to create something new. But recognising a first element in a campaign as something familiar opens the door to creative and commercial success.

»You always have to keep in mind the commercial aspect.«

Yiannis Charalambopoulos

You said that you are "positive". However, your ingenious and bloody work "Romeo & Juliet" that was awarded with the "red dot: grand prix" in 2010, doesn't create a positive scenery.

Yiannis Charalambopoulos: That's true. This isn't a positive scenery. But that's the only way "Romeo & Juliet" can come together after all. Obviously, it's not an optimistic story at all. So the bloody image fits to the context. This was an experimental project for us. In this case, we were the clients.

Are there techniques that you use to arrive at these ideas?

Alexis Nikou: We have this thing in the office where we brainstorm when we pass by each others' screens. Then we start to talk to each other and the inspirations follow automatically.

The Modern Arab World (Poster)
A provocative exhibition poster inspired by the burqa for changing perspectives – and against the stereotypic view on the Arabic world.
red dot 2009

How would you characterise yourself – from the communication designers' point of view?

Yiannis Charalambopoulos: Probably we are the most reasonable creatives. That's a communication designer's point of view who has been a guest to many red dot galas.

Vangelis Liakos: We are three founders and CEOs, and we are completely different. Besides that, I think that a designer has to adapt to any situation, if it's necessary. Whether you are communicating with another person or through your work, you have to adjust all the time, depending on the clients' and projects' needs.

Is it difficult for you to adjust to a client who has, let's say, a distinctive artistic preference for the works he wants you to create?

Yiannis Charalambopoulos: You have to adapt to every situation and communicate with all different sorts of clients. You can make a creative work, but at the end of the day, it has to communicate the message. So it is not art.

45th Dimitria Festival (Illustration)
A fitting visual identity for a large cultural festival visualised by 16 promotional characters.
red dot: best of the best 2011

It can be at the border of art. At latest, you have to keep in mind that you have a commercial job. And that's an amazingly convincing statement to the client when it comes to arguing about artistic preferences.

What's your relationship to the client's demands?

Vangelis Liakos: If the briefing is very well placed, everything is easier. There are people complaining, "the client doesn't allow me to do this or that". But you need the client. You have to involve him in the procedure, so that the outcome will spawn the best result. The strategy will arise from the collaboration.

Yiannis Charalambopoulos: We try to design everything for a reason. The strategy maybe arises from this procedure. During the creative process, there is a strategy without even knowing it. We always try to include the clients. In a way, you are responsible for these guys' future: economically, in terms of prestigious appearance, and in terms of future advantages for them.

It sounds like Beetroot's success derives from a strong bond to the customers.

Alexis Nikou: Not necessarily. There are clients who don't want to be included. Sometimes not being included is exactly what they want.

Yiannis Charalambopoulos: It becomes difficult when the strong bond leads to them associating their sales with your work. If they fail, they blame it on you. If they are successful, they ascribe it to their own capabilities.

How do you feel about pitches?

Yiannis Charalambopoulos: We try not to be involved in them too often. But, of course, we know the procedure.

Vangelis Liakos: We are careful and try to participate in small pitches. When it's completely open, it isn't worth it.

Yiannis Charalambopoulos: We have an unofficial rule. If there isn't a pitch fee, we won't take part. If the project opens a new market for us, we'll consider it. We usually don't like to present semi-finished work. Maybe, after all, you aren't able to imagine the whole work. That's very tricky. We might invest a great deal of time presenting a work when maybe it won't be chosen in the end. Many agencies taking part deal with the project for just one day, and if they get it, they got it. But that's not our philosophy: fooling the client with some kind of "blah, blah" and with unrealistic promises. That doesn't work for us.

**How do you feel about the crisis in Greece?
Is it something that you feel in your work in terms of the flow of offers to you?**

Yiannis Charalambopoulos: One of our biggest clients went bankrupt. This was a challenge to us. In general, everybody is lowering budgets in terms of advertising and communication design. Sometimes that is ridiculous, because they are cutting necessary things. But I think we live in a time where everything bounces back. We have had to find ways to design stuff that works, but with low costs. In every crisis you can see the bright side.

The economic crisis in Greece and the EU is mainly perceived as a political problem. How has your experience been with politicians as clients?

Vangelis Liakos: Politicians normally have opinions on things that they shouldn't have. And that's the problem. Concerning good communication design, they can't possess expertise. Though I am sure that they do so in many other fields.

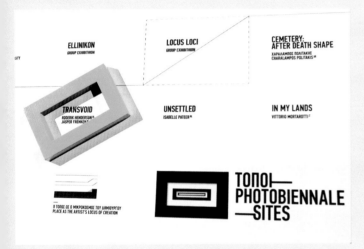

Photobiennale – Sites (Interactive Installation)
A retrospective presentation of the Photobiennale Topos festival by a gesture-responsive grid system which, when pointing a specific topic with a frame, starts a synthesised slideshow.
red dot 2011

Are there any international, non-Greece projects that you have realised?

Vangelis Liakos: Yes, of course. For example, our participation in the Biennale in Venice. We also did the video for Corbis in London. Corbis provides exceptional commercial and editorial photography and illustrations. Slowly, people are beginning to understand that Greek agencies can provide and export good design.

Nowadays, especially younger people can't seem to live without social networks. How do you rate this development?

Vangelis Liakos: This shows that younger people in general have a strong need for communication. Through Facebook they are starting revolutions. It's up to us to realise that this is not only a commercial need. We need to use this knowledge to make good communication design and not only to make money.

Alexis Nikou: For many people, it is much easier to communicate through Facebook or SMS, because it's easier to say that you dislike somebody when you don't see him. For me, it's not a sign of progress when there's no longer a need to speak face to face.

Vangelis Liakos: In the past, you made appointments with a friend and you had to be there, otherwise you couldn't find each other. Technology offers many advantages in the way we communicate with each other.

Yiannis Charalambopoulos: You can use the technology, but you shouldn't replace your personal contacts. Most people choose written speech first when contacting their families and friends. That's not originally a Facebook thing, but a thing of the "new" communication channels, also including SMS and e-mail.

What does the Beetroot future look like?

Vangelis Liakos: We are looking for a united Europe. By that, I don't only mean economic aspects. It would bring us closer together if everyone could work anywhere he wanted. We design labels for wine, cheese and vegetables, for example. This is how our design is exported from our country. But we can also export "pure" design. For instance, we can export our services directly. This is something for the future. Orders do not matter anymore; Internet matters.

Yiannis Charalambopoulos: But you still need the face-to-face contact. The clients need to know that you are there. This way they feel much more secure.

»It's only good communication design that matters.«

Yiannis Charalambopoulos

You are the "red dot: agency of the year 2011". How do you feel about that?

Yiannis Charalambopoulos: It's an honour to us and we are really, really happy and also a little bit surprised. It's also a very special accolade, because you can't apply for it.

Vangelis Liakos: When we saw last years' winners, we turned to each other and wished that the Stylus would one day come to our office. But then we started laughing. We are a small agency in a small country. But now we realise that the number of clients or employees doesn't matter; it depends on the services you provide. red dot is able to see this.

Beetroot Design Group – "The Greek Monsters"!
Yiorgos Lemonidis, Haris Martis, Karolos Gakidis, Spyros Vlahopoulos,
Kostas Pappas, Yiannis Charalambopoulos, Evi Blazou, Michalis Rafail,
Alexis Nikou, Kostas Kaparos, Ilias Pantikakis, Vangelis Liakos

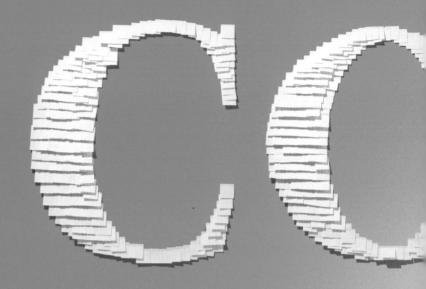

DIFFERENTIATION THROUGH IDENTITY. Recognition leads to renown: corporate design is the public face of every company. It encompasses all visually perceivable elements, from the logo to holistic concepts. Good corporate design communicates the key aspects of a company's activities in an easy-to-remember form. Depending on the image, target group and branch of industry it takes on either a colourful or restrained, playful or reduced design.

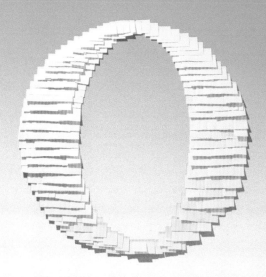

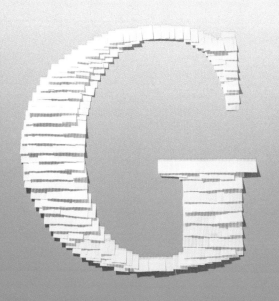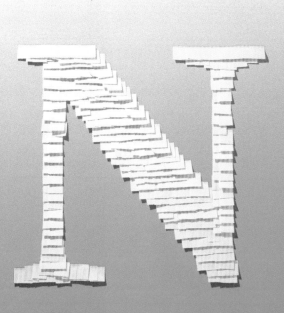

red dot: grand prix

Alex Poulsen Arkitekter

[Corporate Identity]

Alex Poulsen Arkitekter (APA) was founded in 1944 by Danish architect Alex Poulsen, one of the most progressive architects of his time. Since Poulsen was appointed as supervising architect of the Danish Justice Department, the studio has developed particular expertise in creating governmental architecture. The new corporate identity was developed with the aim of both communicating the studio's rich history and background, including their Nordic values and traditions, and lending it a professional, modern as well as innovative appearance. The new visual identity is based on space and building elements: the letters of the logo are transformed into individual building blocks with the letters themselves combined in such a manner as to create an austerely clear yet playful form. The new corporate identity thus gains an overall self-explanatory character, as it visualises the significance of architecture without the need to name it in words.

Statement by the jury

»The corporate identity of this architecture studio does not only represent typically Danish graphic design, characteristical for being clear, logical and reduced to the essential. It is also intelligent: it combines the letters of the studio into a minimalist arrangement, so that their form visualises a kind of brick, the classical structural element. Thus architecture does no longer have to be explained, but instead is illustrated through typography.«

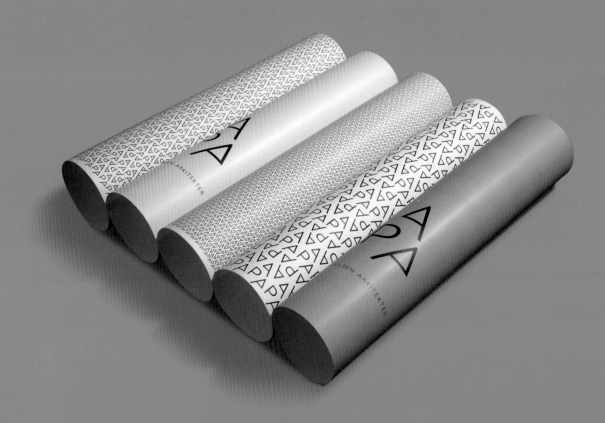

client
Alex Poulsen Arkitekter,
Copenhagen

design
Re-public, Copenhagen

art direction
Romeo Vidner

graphic design
Romeo Vidner

strategic planning
Morten Windelev

web design
Christoffer Hald

designer portrait
→ Vol.1: p.498

Leica S2

[Product Identity]

The Leica S2 camera system sets new standards in professional photography through ease of handling and an outstanding image resolution. The high quality of this camera, which was launched true to its slogan of "Loud and Proud", is reflected by the visual presentation of the product identity. The Leica S2 takes centre stage aesthetically in all product photographs for use in advertisements, brochures and POS materials and is presented against an elegant background of grey and silver shades highlighting the model designation "S2". This distinctive typographical icon is the key component in the corporate design and features on the packaging, for instance, a skilful play with the similar yet mirrored curvatures of the "S" and the "2", which wrap around the edges both upright and sideways.

Statement by the jury

»The product identity of the Leica S2 illustrates that the company remained faithful to itself both in terms of industrial design and technology, as well as in its visual communication. This is demonstrated in the stringently designed appearance. Both the photographic and typographic quality is very high – a convincing example that it pays off to consistently stick to one's own design language.«

client
LFI – Leica Fotografie
International

design
Tom Leifer Design, Hamburg

creative direction
Tom Leifer

art direction
Alessandro Argentato

concept
Tom Leifer,
Alessandro Argentato,
Johannes Hermann

graphic design
Alessandro Argentato,
Johannes Hermann

photography
Frank Hülsbömer

designer portrait
→ Vol.1: p.487

Israeli Cultural Institute Budapest

[Visual Identity]

The challenge behind the development of the corporate design for the Israeli Cultural Institute in Budapest, one of the first of its kind in Europe, was to create an identity that was neutral, highly expressive and easy to understand at the same time. In addition, it needed to be easily adaptable to the three languages Hungarian, Hebrew and English. The solution that integrated all these requirements was to use the millennium-old symbol of Judaism, the Star of David, which has the shape of a hexagram consisting of two intertwined equilateral triangles. The basic design principle started with the triangular structure of this star and complements it with elements generated through the help of a digital algorithm. The result were ever-changing patterns that do not only allow for a variety of configurations, and thus make the logo suitable for various different formats, they also help create a playful identity of high flexibility, in both form and colour, which communicates freshness and lightness.

Statement by the jury

»This visual identity is an excellent example of a new approach in interpreting corporate design concepts. It playfully improvises on a broadly defined basis consisting of forms, colours, imagery and text, so that even single elements can easily be associated with the whole. This creates a constantly changing appearance that nonetheless is fully consistent with the overall identity.«

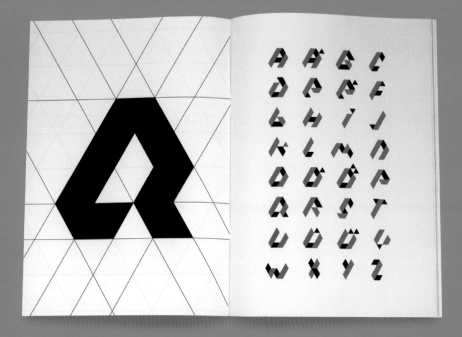

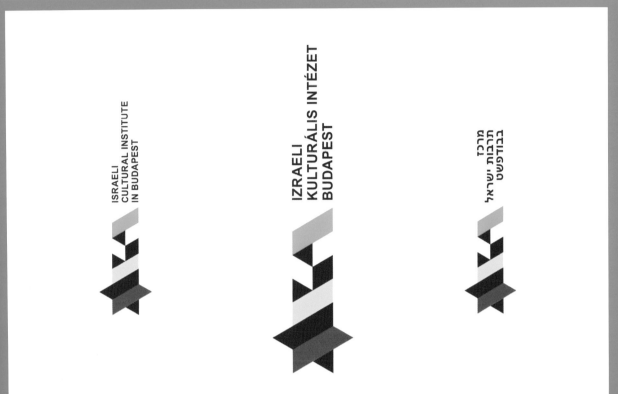

client
Israeli Cultural
Institute Budapest

design
Imre Lepsenyi

branding
Agnes Keltai

art direction
Imre Lepsenyi

graphic design
Imre Lepsenyi,
Aaron Fabian

printing
MPB Hungary

designer portrait
→ Vol.1: p.485

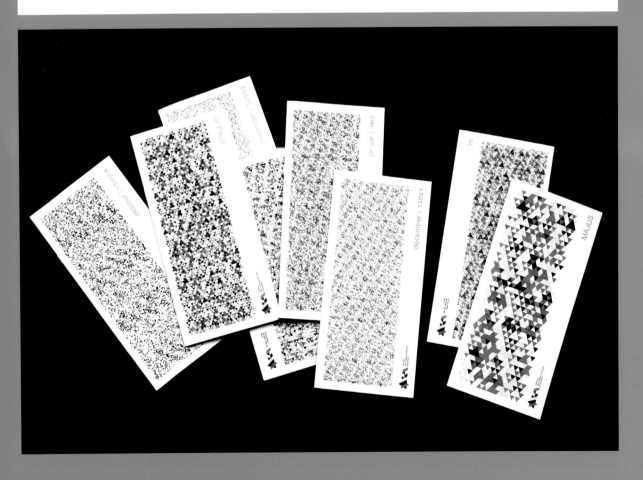

MKO Season 10/11

[Corporate Design]

For the 2010/2011 season of the Münchener Kammerorchester (Munich Chamber Orchestra), the design task was to create programme brochures, posters and other promotional material under the season's theme of "Architecture". The design specifications included the creation of a non-representational design aesthetic appropriate to the topic. The implementation visualises various elements that play with the concepts of sound, space and light in order to achieve an array of highly differentiated results and effects. The resulting season appearance thus is easily recognisable and yet leaves leeway for variations when adapting it to individual applications. The twenty seasonal motifs were created by taking photographs of abstract, handmade objects and changing the colour and light atmosphere of the photographs through technical processes, such as flash lighting, inversion and digital colour processing.

Statement by the jury

»This visual appearance is remarkable because it does not rely on classical representations of music, but instead uses an imagery composed of abstract rhythms, three-dimensional surfaces and light/shade effects. Furthermore, the communication takes place on a parallel basis, via a superimposed clear typographic language. The design thus is able to play with colours and motifs that never resemble themselves, and thereby to differentiate the Münchener Kammerorchester from competitors in the culture scene.«

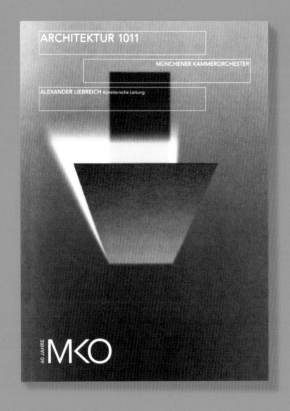

client
MKO, Münchener Kammer-
orchester, Munich

design
Schmidt/Thurner/
von Keisenberg, Munich

graphic design
Prof. Gerwin Schmidt

designer portrait
→ Vol.1: p.501

red dot: best of the best

AND market

[Branding]

"AND market" is a newly developed brand of Japan's first smartphone retailer, which operates entirely independently from major mobile phone companies. Alongside the brand name, the corporate design includes the visual identity, website, stores and promotion handouts. The brand emphasises its independence from conventional retail business and conveys the message that it provides only what customers really need. Accordingly, the brand concept was subsumed under the term "neutral" and thus integrates all designs and strategies based on this unique position in the market. "Neutral" consequentially aims at an appearance that does without any colour highlights, yet is neither explicitly in black and white; instead, the essence of the brand is expressed through a well-balanced ratio of different shades of black and white. The playful approach to typography is marked by the use of a large "&" character turned into a bird, thus lending this corporate design a humorous appeal and a high degree of recognition.

Statement by the jury

»This work places typography centre stage and boldly does without anything non-essential. Thus, the all too often desperate search for an artificial logo was no longer called for and this instead made pragmatism come to the fore. The reduced colourfulness further underlines the typographic play with the inside and outside spaces of the letters.«

client
NEC Mobiling,
Ltd., Tokyo

design
Hakuhodo Inc.,
Tokyo

head of marketing
Seiichi Nishikawa

creative direction
Atsushi Muroi

art direction
Kimitaro Hattori

motion design
Yu Maruno

space design
Atsushi Muroi,
Kazuma Nakai

designer portrait
→ Vol.1: p.479

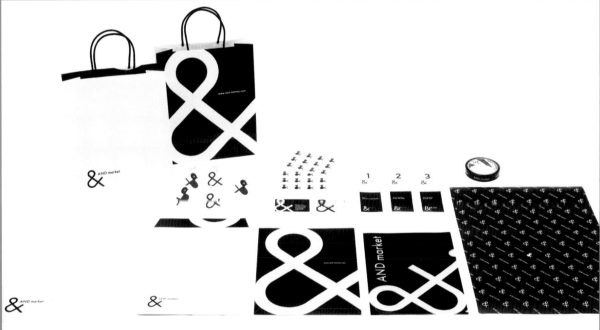

Weingut von Othegraven

[Corporate Design]

On the occasion of a change in ownership, the von Othegraven winery received a new corporate appearance. To emphasise brand character, the label was designed in a clear, striking colour composition, with the new company emblem – an "O" crowned by a "V" – elevated to a distinctive key visual. An elegant cursive script was selected for the vintage wines, while the young MAX wine collection features a fine banderole. Both the website and the brochure communicate current issues in an expressive visual language.

client
Weingut von Othegraven,
Kanzem

design
die Medienagenten OHG,
Bad Dürkheim

creative direction
Christoph Ziegler

graphic design
Alexander Bechtloff

text
Judith Eckfelder,
Christoph Ziegler

project management
Christoph Ziegler

photography
Andreas Durst

programming
Jochen Stange

VON OTHEGRAVEN
KANZEM AN DER SAAR

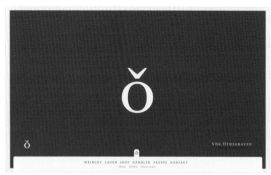

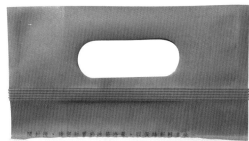

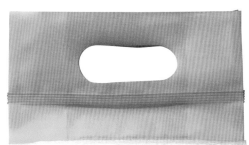

SUNSUIVI

[Logo Design]

The primary colour of the rectangular logo for this Chinese rice brand is green, symbolising square rice fields. The white words, displayed both in Chinese and Latin characters, mean "They humbly receive nourishment from the earth". The third word "rice" is written in vigorous calligraphy, and its shape means that the rice field is cultivated criss-crossly. The round red stamp visualises an ancient Chinese word for "goodness". Two additional types of rice feature orange and violet versions of the logo respectively, which can be applied either horizontally or vertically.

client
Shan Shui Rice Enterprise Co., Ltd.

design
Creative-E Design Studio., Taichung

creative direction/art direction
Wen Chun Fong

calligraphy
Kuo Shu Huang

customer advisory service
Tung-Chao Lee (Chairman), Shu-Huie Yeh (President), Shan Shui Rice Enterprise Co., Ltd.

strategic planning
Tung Liang Chen

project management
Evonne Lin

Gize
Corporate Design
[Bottle, Burgopak, Brochure,
Brand Book]

client
C.M.W. Canadian Mineral Water
Development S.A., Luxembourg

head of marketing
Dominique Khoilar

marketing/communication
Claudia Schneider

design
Werbeagentur Zweipunktnull
GmbH, Föhren/Germany

creative direction
Reiner Rempis

graphic design
Achim Bach

text
Frank Jöricke

The integrated corporate identity concept for Gize, a gold-filtered mineral water from Canada, emphasises the unique character and exclusivity of this luxury brand. Glass bottle, packaging, brochure and brand book feature an elegant white/gold/grey colour scheme. The extraordinary shape of the glass bottle is distinguished by its clear lines and understated elegance. Both packaging and brochure are produced from high-quality white matte cardboard – elegant and pure, with a great deal of white space. Moreover, print varnish has been applied to sections of the image brochure to highlight the exclusivity of the brand.

Victor Russo's Osteria

[Corporate Identity]

client
Victor Russo's Osteria, Leiden

design
Total Identity, Amsterdam

creative direction
Felix Janssens

graphic design/illustration
Maarten Brandenburg

customer advisory service
Bob van der Lee

project management
Annemarie van Noort

As an importer of Italian wines and delicacies, Victor Russo has introduced a new franchise system in the Netherlands with his Osteria gastronomy concept. In addition to the existing shop and wholesale business, the first Osteria restaurant was opened in the city centre of Leiden. The aesthetically appealing corporate design features a sense of ornamental symbolism, while 18th-century engravings are reminiscent of the fruit and vegetable portraits of late Renaissance painter Arcimboldo. The central logo supports the monochrome visual language and can be flexibly adapted to each franchisee. In addition to corporate stationery, various advertising materials – including menus, a newsletter, flyers and a website – have been developed.

21 Tea House

[Corporate Identity]

The aesthetically appealing corporate design of this Taiwanese tea brand contrasts calligraphy elements with a harmonious colour scheme. The logo shows a new tea sprout with two light-green leaves unfolding. The design concept for the 21 Tea House brand is also inspired by the number "21" and toys with its manifold meanings. Immersion in the aroma of tea causes the world to split into a moment of duality – in this dimension, only the soul and the taste of the tea exist, thus symbolising the Zen of tea as a moment of unity.

client
Wen-Cheng Tea Farm

design
Magic Creative, Taipei

Beryozka
Petrol Stations

[Corporate Identity]

The Russian petrol station chain Boryozka demonstrates that a service brand with a pronounced Russian character can be contemporary and, at the same time, coherent and distinctive. Conveyed are values of hospitality. The fresh and striking visual design, meant to enliven the conservative and faceless Russian petrol station market, exhibits broad appeal and has been inspired by the term "Berezka" (birch tree). In addition, stylised plant motifs underline the technologically advanced and eco-friendly style of the company.

client
Totaloil, LLC, Moscow

design
PLENUM Brand Consultancy, Moscow

head of marketing
Tanya Haritonova

art direction
Egor Myznik

text
Nadya Yurinova

strategic planning
Katya Palshina

designers
Lena Ledkova, Olga Balina

Weingut
Dr. Corvers-Kauter

[Corporate Design]

The Dr. Corvers-Kauter winery
is associated with the slopes of
wine-growing families steeped
in tradition and plays a pioneering role: the objective of the new
identity concept is to target new
groups of aficionados beyond
the region and to market the
Rheingau as an attractive and
multifaceted wine-growing area.
The corporate design comprises
a wine classification system and
corporate stationery, but also
packaging design and a website,
presenting the Corvers-Kauter
brand as contemporary, clear
and distinguished by high quality
– above and beyond an old-fash-
ioned fetishisation of wine.

client
Weingut Dr. Corvers-Kauter,
Oestrich-Winkel

design
Fuenfwerken Design AG,
Wiesbaden/Berlin

holyfields

[Corporate Identity]

The corporate design for the Holyfields restaurant chain aims at a personal overall identity by avoiding anything that appears standardised, noisy or hasty. Illustrations express a contemplative style that is enhanced by a timeless serif typeface. Witty, playful stories are told on advertising materials, screens and packaging. And with the appealing dictum "time to eat", customers are invited to linger and savour in these hectic times. The restaurants' elegant interior design is highlighted by large-scale illustrations on the walls.

client
Holyfields Restaurant GmbH & Co. KG, Düsseldorf

design
loved gmbh, Hamburg

creative direction
Mieke Haase, Judith Stoletzky

art direction
Christiane Eckhardt

layout
Tilo Pentzin

illustration
Jeanne Detallante

account director
Peter Matz

Schloss Hohenkammer

[Corporate Design]

client
Schloss Hohenkammer GmbH,
Hohenkammer

design
Keller Maurer Design, Munich

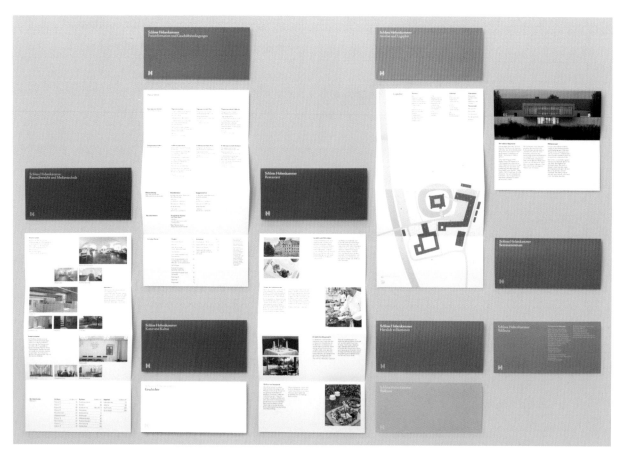

Schloss Hohenkammer
Seminarzentrum

Schloss Hohenkammer
Restaurant

Schloss Hohenkammer
Gut Eichethof

The seminar centre Schloss Hohenkammer boasts a refurbished 17th-century castle, a modern guest house, a restaurant and an organic agricultural estate. The corporate identity merges a contemporary design approach with references to traditional aesthetics. The combination of a renaissance antiqua word mark with a clean sans-serif typeface is visually complemented by fresh colours and innovative production techniques. A specifically designed system allows flyers, brochures and folders to be combined individually. The website features inspiring photographs and a highly functional layout, communicating current events and information in a clear and appealing manner. The packaging for Gut Eichethof, the manor of Schloss Hohenkammer, playfully extends the corporate design to a wide range of quality products.

MIES_container

[Corporate Design]

client
MIES_container, Daegu

design
MIES_container Design Team,
Daegu; JUN Cooperation, Daegu;
IRU Adcom, Daegu

creative direction
Chang Hee Lee

art direction
Jong Eun Ahn

graphic design
Jong Eun Ahn

photography
Yong Han Lim

designer portrait
→ Vol.1: p.489

MIES_container

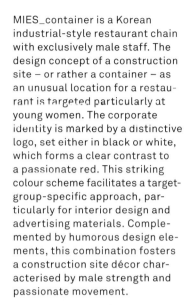

MIES_container is a Korean industrial-style restaurant chain with exclusively male staff. The design concept of a construction site – or rather a container – as an unusual location for a restaurant is targeted particularly at young women. The corporate identity is marked by a distinctive logo, set either in black or white, which forms a clear contrast to a passionate red. This striking colour scheme facilitates a target-group-specific approach, particularly for interior design and advertising materials. Complemented by humorous design elements, this combination fosters a construction site décor characterised by male strength and passionate movement.

Love Meat Tender
[Branding]

client
Love Meat Tender, Guimarães

design
Mola Ativism, Linda-a-Velha

creative direction
Rui Morais

graphic design
Rui Morais

strategic planning
Vasco Durão

project management
Ligia Mateus

industrial design
Carlos Cardoso

Creating a restaurant dedicated to the preparation of finest steaks, Mola has cooked a recipe with the three secrets passion, exclusivity and exigency so that the steak is truly juicy and full of tenderness. The visual identity of this fast food restaurant focuses on the impact of its catchy logotype. Alluding to a classic by Elvis Presley, the restaurant name Love Meat Tender conveys the pleasure of indulging in an excellently prepared steak. The logo has the three-dimensional silhouette of a steak and is applied in either black-and-white or red-and-white. When it comes to further advertising material, the company name is invoked as a claim, printed in capitals that look like flames or steaks.

Laib und Seele

[Brand Relaunch,
Brand Communication]

The corporate design for Laib und
Seele unites craftsmanship and
lifestyle. The powerful typography employed provides a down-
to-earth appearance, while the
use of intense colours appeals
to lifestyle-oriented tastes.
Illustrations inspired by the art
of pastry-making underline the
creative facets of this handicraft,
conveying an appealing overall
look. The unique design parameters pervade the brand's entire
communication range – from
interior design, external communication and staff uniforms to
menus, coffee-to-go cups, cof
fee tins, paper bags and pastry
boxes.

client
cyclos design GmbH,
Münster

design
cyclos design GmbH,
Münster

designer portrait
→ Vol.1: p.469

roter hamm Produktserie / *roter hamm product line*

[Corporate Design, Branding]

The roter hamm brand comprises products made of apples from a workshop for mentally disabled people. The visually appealing design emphasises the pure character of the products and distinguishes the brand from health-food shops, organic markets and beverage stores. The subheading "Manufaktur für Gutes aus Äpfeln" (Manufacturing good things made of apples) communicates sustainable quality standards, which are further underlined by the label design. The varied colouring of the labels aids the disabled workers in distinguishing and labelling the products and in assembling deliveries.

client
Frankfurter Verein für soziale Heimstätten e.V., Frankfurt/Main

design
Impulslabor, Frankfurt/Main

graphic design
Ulrike Gauder, Uwe Tischer

text
Cora Walker

photography
Andreas Reeg

Madam Sixty Ate
[Corporate Identity, Brand Story]

The objective here was to create a strong brand based on the restaurant name Madam Sixty Ate, a word play on the address 60 Johnston Rd, Shop 8. The corporate identity is centred on a mythical character whose open world view is reflected in the style of the food. Illustration and sketches, together with handwritten notes of stories, are reminiscent of journal entries and can be found on the menu, on coasters and ultimately also in the cuisine. A visit to this restaurant resembles a journey during which customers discover new animal and plant species.

client
Atelia Corporation Limited, Hong Kong

design
Substance, Hong Kong

creative direction
Maxime Dautresme

graphic design
Jeremy Huen

text
Lynette Chiu

illustration
Vincent Wong

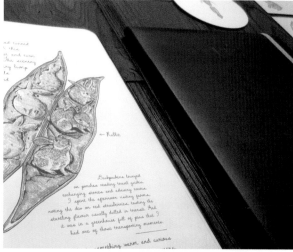

EST.1894
Comfort Food

[Brand Identity]

The identity of this South Korean fast food chain tells the story of the hamburger in an unconventional way. Based on the idea that this popular snack was born in 1895, the design concept goes back one year to 1894 so it may rewrite the cultural history of the hamburger. With a corporate design focused on typography, positive memories of joyful indulgence and a healthy diet are triggered. The logo "1894" was integrated into the facade design in a high-contrast, eye-catching way.

client
EST.1894 Comfort Food,
Seoul

design
S/O PROJECT,
Seoul

creative direction
Hyun Cho

brand & concept direction
Soyoung Lee

art direction
Jihye Lee

head of marketing
Jongkuk Yi

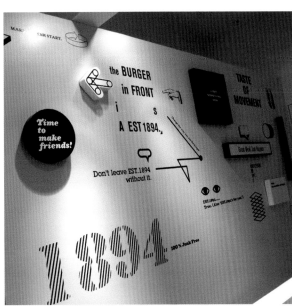

BraufactuM

[Brand Building, Corporate Design]

The corporate design of BraufactuM springs from a manufactory idea. An elaborately detailed logo shows, among other elements, two brewers stirring a mash barrel. Enhanced by choice lettering, a graphically balanced composition takes form, one that aims to set itself apart from the crest aesthetics of other beer brands. A label in elegant black was created to unify the collection, which is comprised of different products. The small booklet accompanying each bottle is designed to appeal to cultivated gourmets aged 30 and above.

client
Die Internationale
Brau-Manufacturen GmbH,
Frankfurt/Main

design
Flaechenbrand, Wiesbaden

creative direction
Kai Geweniger,
Friedrich Wilhelm Detering

art direction
Peter Kohl, Marvin Zimmer,
Johannes Schiebe,
Holger Blockhaus

concept
Kai Geweniger, Julia Detering,
Friedrich Wilhelm Detering

strategic planning
Kai Geweniger,
Friedrich Wilhelm Detering

project management
Friedrich Wilhelm Detering

text
Ron Böttcher, Eva Bender,
Julia Detering

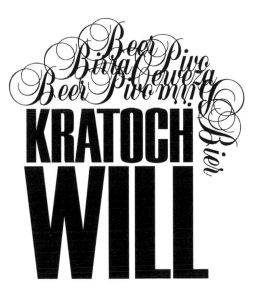

Kratochwill

[Logo]

With a note of intensity and surprise, this logotype highlights beer
as the most important product of
the company. While the company
name Kratochwill in compact majuscules visualises a beer glass,
curved typography forms a crown
of beer foam. Upon closer examination, the beholder recognises
the word "Beer" in the foam –
written in seven different languages. The illustrative design of
the company logo was developed
in two variants: complementing
the black-and-white version is a
colour logo in a yellow font.

client
Pivovarna in pivnica Kratochwill
d.o.o., Ljubljana

design
Futura DDB d.o.o., Ljubljana

creative direction/art direction
Žare Kerin

concept
Žare Kerin

graphic design
Žare Kerin

project management
Ana Por

1772
Count Coreth
Prachensky

[Branding]

The identity of this spirituous liquor manufacturer has a dynamic and fresh appeal yet also conveys the centuries-old family tradition of the company. To communicate high-quality standards, the corporate design uses a detailed image vocabulary: artistic illustrations against a blue background speak of the tropical fruits from Thailand used for distillation. The silver-grey, navy blue and orange of the corporate colour scheme correspond harmoniously to the distinctive drop shape of the 1772 bottle.

client
MC International, Maximilian Coreth, Salzburg

design
Spirit Design – Innovation and Branding, Vienna

customer advisory service
Daniel Huber (Managing Partner), Maria Hell

creative direction
Maria Hell

design direction
Alexander Pohl

2d/3d design
Yuhsuke Akamatsu, Rainer Flassak, Tomas Maly

illustration
Heri Irawan

text
Mathias Miller-Aichholz

Sovilj Joaillerie
[Visual Identity]

The visual identity of the jewellery manufacturer Sovilj Joaillerie is inspired by the timeless style of Art Deco. The graphic pattern of filigree lines and rich black-and-white contrasts appears elegant and mysterious. Particularly convincing is its successful integration into a glossy fabric. Textile jewellery bags as well as advertising materials form a unified, eye-catching and recognisable system. The elegant logotype and the reduced typography harmoniously counterbalance the distinctive graphic pattern.

client
Nenad Sovilj, Zagreb

design
koržinekdizajn, Zagreb

art direction
Marko Koržinek

design team
Marko Koržinek, Ana Petak

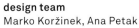

I AM

[Campaign]

The Auckland Museum holds a large collection of Maori art along with art by other indigenous peoples of the Pacific region. The challenge in the development of the museum's corporate design involved creating a campaign identity that communicates both internally and externally. The solution was secured through a fundamental questioning of the role of a museum. In describing this institutional function, the museum's initials "AM" were developed into a striking campaign logo.

client
Auckland Museum, Auckland

design
Alt Group, Auckland

creative direction
Dean Poole

graphic design
Dean Poole,
Toby Curnow,
Shabnam Shiwan,
Tony Proffit,
Jinki Cambronero,
Aaron Edwards,
Sam Fieulaine

photography
Toaki Okano

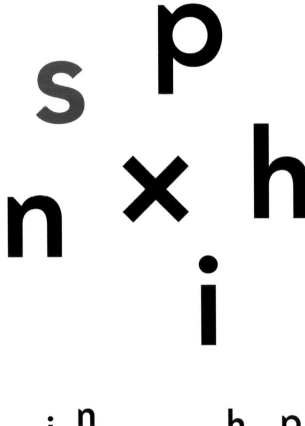

Sphinx

[Logo Series]

Sphinx is a new community hub for debates and visions in Maastricht. So as to illustrate that at Sphinx the word takes centre stage, an astonishingly changeable logo was developed. Each manifestation of the logo appears new, as the five letters of the word Sphinx dance around the virtual central "x", taking ever-new positions. For better orientation, a red "s" always marks the beginning of the name. The unpredictability of this logo symbolises the diversity of the community centre in a stunningly simple way.

client
Sphinx, Maastricht

design
Zuiderlicht, Maastricht

creative direction
Bert van der Veur

graphic design
Tom van Enckevort

strategic planning
Martijn Kagenaar

designer portrait
→ Vol.1: p.511

olleh signal
[Visual Identity]

client
kt, Korea Telecom, Seoul

design
Lippincott, Hong Kong

creative direction
Jaehee Lim, Soo Hyun Kim

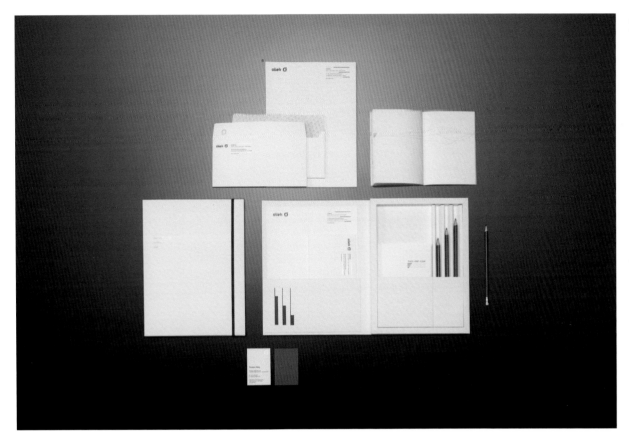

As a flexible key design motif, the dynamic olleh signal raises interest in IT services provided by telecommunications provider kt (Korea Telecom). The design of this icon reflects a new interpretation of generally known communication signals. The reduction to a high-contrast colour scheme achieves high brand recognition. The visual identity flexibly adapts to diverse corporate applications thanks to a target-group-specific approach. As such, the branding varies when applied to various publications or different media, reflecting the company's creative and innovative brand management as well as its qualified IT service.

CITINIC

[Corporate Design]

client
CITINIC, Frankfurt/Main

design
CITINIC, Frankfurt/Main

creative direction/art direction
Nicole Franke, Nico Wallfarth

concept
Nicole Franke, Nico Wallfarth

graphic design/photography
Nicole Franke, Nico Wallfarth

printing
Druckerei Gebhard,
Heusenstamm

Experiencing cities, metropolises and regions from unusual and hitherto unknown perspectives, and being amazed by new facets – this is the claim staked by CITINIC. The company produces editions of city postcards and print media which evince an ambitious visual language, with an eye to adding new points of view to the existing market. Focusing on black-and-white photography, the design concept defines itself in contrast to the colourful images of an era in which digital pictures are increasingly favoured, aiming to preserve old traditions and the convention of writing postcards. The collection also features folding cards as well as limited-edition art prints. Editions of further cities and regions are in development.

EIGA

[Corporate Design]

The nature and brand imaging of design company EIGA is determined by a diverse range of colourful and elaborate projects. Thus the concern of the designers has been to keep their own corporate design as simple as possible in order to provide plenty of scope for showcasing their work. This design approach is particularly apparent on their website, which presents a list of large-scale case studies for quick and easy browsing. The elegant layout is marked by a mix of fonts and the use of fine lines.

client
EIGA Design, Hamburg

design
EIGA Design, Hamburg

creative direction
Elisabeth Plass

art direction
Henning Otto

graphic design
Josefine Freund

designer portrait
→ Vol.1: p.473

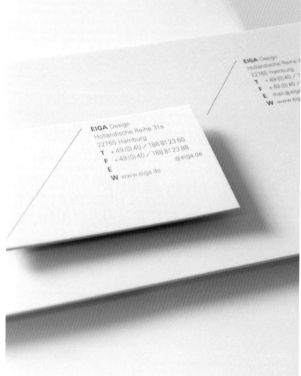

Gas-Union:
Energie in neuer Form /
Gas-Union:
Supply, Sale and Services
[Brochure]

Complementing its international role, Gas-Union has strong local roots connected with the Frankfurt/Main location of its head office. The company's new corporate image brochure is thus marked by a series of distinctive views of the city and images from the company's different divisions. The page layout features a light and clear design, skilfully accentuated by a confident typeface. The overall harmonious colour scheme makes the bright orange colour of the square logo stick out in an eye-catching manner.

client
Gas-Union GmbH, Frankfurt/Main

design
josephine prokop
identity design, Wuppertal

photography
Jörg Baumann,
Norbert Miguletz et al.

printing
Druckstudio GmbH

BUNTESAMT

[Corporate Design]

Berlin-based BUNTESAMT, a one-man graphic design office, consists of no more than a desk 1 sqm in size and some utensils. It appeals to small- and medium-size companies and brushes aside its small size with high spirits and a measure of self-mockery through distinctive office stationery. The typographic simplicity of the typewriter font and government-agency-like codes is eased by humorous prose and partially handwritten communication elements. The "clerk in charge", Herr Schmidt, holds all of the agency's relevant positions and is responsible for all clients from A to Z.

client
BUNTESAMT, Berlin

design
BUNTESAMT, Berlin

concept
Jan-Hendrik Schmidt

graphic design
Jan-Hendrik Schmidt

text
Jan-Hendrik Schmidt

printing
Anja Moritz, Moritzdruck, Berlin

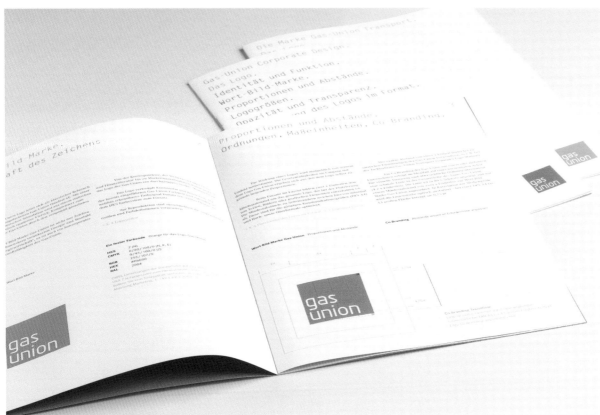

Gas-Union
Corporate Design

[Corporate Design Manual]

This corporate design manual presents the pivotal corporate identity element: the logo of Gas-Union and its affiliated company Gas-Union Transport. It defines the colouring and usage of all related logos as well as principles for their placement and layout. Topic areas build upon one another and are easy to understand, linking underlying principles with concrete details, the large with the small. This printed manual highlights corporate values and complements the digital version of all instructions and templates.

client
Gas-Union GmbH, Frankfurt/Main

design
josephine prokop
identity design, Wuppertal

photography
Jörg Baumann

printing
Druckstudio GmbH

Jackson and Sandra's Wedding

[Wedding Invitation]

This distinctive visual identity was developed as part of a design project that conveys traditional Chinese wedding culture through contemporary communication media. The use of traditional Chinese wordplay aims to express harmony and unity. As a fundamental graphic design element, the circle emphasises – with diversified ornamentation – a harmoniously balanced overall presentation. This comprehensive project involves a diverse range of communication media, all of which feature a traditional colour palette of red, white and gold.

client
Jackson Chun Wei Ko,
Singapore

design
Nanyang Technological
University, Singapore

art direction/concept
I-Hsuan Cindy Wang

graphic design
I-Hsuan Cindy Wang

text
I-Hsuan Cindy Wang

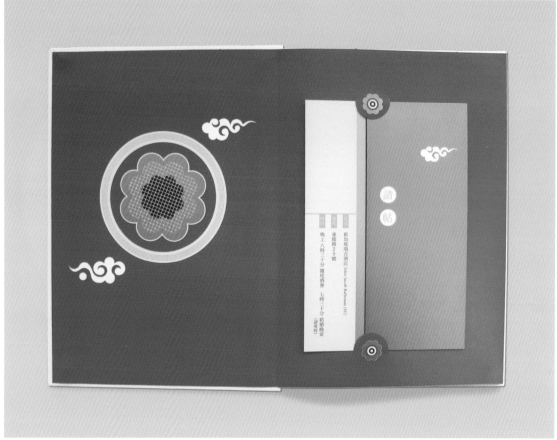

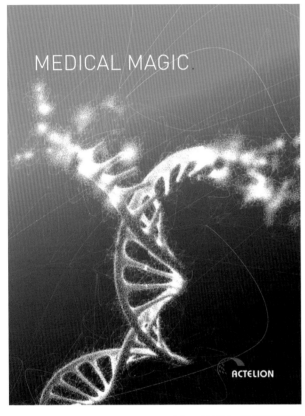

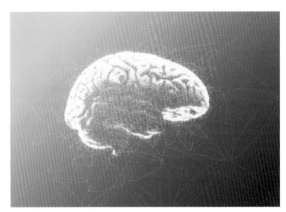

MEDICAL MAGIC
[Corporate Design]

Actelion is a biopharmaceutical company. Its visual identity is based on the idea "From medical industry to medical magic". The imagery is generated using an innovative image processing technique, especially developed for Actelion, that displays the smallest possible entity – digital molecules. The images capture the invisible, magical moment when an idea is transformed into a solution and a molecule becomes a medicine – Medical Magic. The result is a corporate identity that visualises scientific precision in a striking and multicoloured design.

client
Actelion Ltd, Allschwil

design
Interbrand, Zürich

creative direction
Andreas Rotzler

customer advisory service
Gernot Honsel,
Dr. Ulrike Grein

graphic design
Damien Julien,
Claudia Roethlisberger,
Julia Gleichauf,
Janina Derger

3d design
Helga Capitaine,
Michaela Burger,
Janina Lamers

software development imagery tool
Onformative, Berlin

The 46th Golden Camera Award

[Event Kit]

For the awarding of the 46th Golden Camera of HÖRZU an extensive design concept was developed, with the motto "stay golden" permeating every single element: from large-scale hot foil stamping in gold on the invitation to a gilded postage stamp. All icons used were hand-drawn and printed in letterpress on GMUND Cotton. A highlight is the invitation itself, which works as a pop-up – presenting the Golden Camera to the recipient when the card is opened up.

client
Axel Springer AG, Hamburg

design
Paperlux GmbH, Hamburg

creative direction
Marco Kuehne

art direction
Hassan Haider

customer advisory service
Soraya Kuehne

project management
Sebastian Heberle

illustration
Marco Kuehne

printing
Bölling GmbH &
Eurodruck Hamburg

Walser Privatbank

[Brand Identity,
Brand Communication]

The new brand appearance of
the Walser Privatbank sets out
to perform a balancing act between traditional values and the
onset of a new era. The design
concept provides an alternative
to the typography, image style,
colours and layout of its previous
visuals. Even the bank's former
name longer catered to the new
demands and was replaced. The
redesign of the brand – from the
established black-yellow appearance of the Raiffeisen bank group
to a new corporate guise – uses a
broad colour palette contrasting
with black-and-white photography.

client
Walser Privatbank, Riezlern

head of marketing
Markus Kalab

design
MetaDesign AG, Zürich

creative direction
André Stauffer

art direction
Monica Bühlmann,
Uta Zidorn

graphic design
Salomon Gut,
Fabian Bertschinger

project management
Christoph Knecht

Tango Mania

[Corporate Design]

Tango Mania is a non-profit association centred on promoting and cultivating Argentinean tango. The design focus lies with the logotype: its Antiqua typeface is inspired by the floral ornamentation of Art Nouveau, the word arrangement points out the dichotomy united within tango, while the colour purple alludes to the sensual red of this dance. The corporate presentation, with its appealing visual language, encompasses various flyers and posters for events, event calendars, banners, stationery, stickers, and a website.

client
Tango Mania Argentino Landshut e.V., Landshut

design
Grafik Design Sandra Tröger, Pfaffenberg

VAUD VALAIS FRIBOURG

HEMU

[Branding, Corporate Communication]

The brand strategy for this music academy comprises corporate design as well as a brand name conceived to be easily understood internationally, with a logo that reflects the high standards of teaching. The design evinces strong lines which reference the rigour and thoroughness of the institute; an emphasis on the last two letters "MU" highlights the full importance of the musical domain. An extreme schematisation of sound waves is used as a further design element that may be flexibly applied to various advertising materials.

client
HEMU, Haute École de Musique de Lausanne

design
Moser Design SA, Lausanne

head of marketing
Nicolas Peter

creative direction
Caroline Mesple-Moser, Alexandre Henriques

graphic design
Emilie Mattille, Andreas Richter

text
Alain Perusset

project management
Géraldine Nicole

web development
Fabien Kupferschmid

OCOCO
new fashion brand
identity

client
CJ O Shopping Co., Ltd.

design
Firefly Branding

creative direction
Jiwon Shin

strategic planning
Rudy Lee

art direction
Elisabetta Minischetti

graphic design
Marie Vesela

photography
Jaroslav Kviz

designer portrait
→ Vol.1: p.475

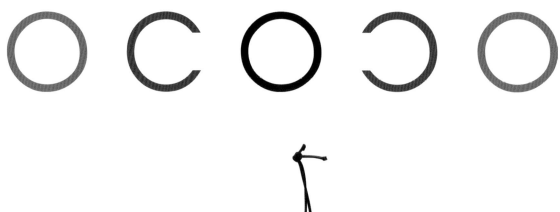

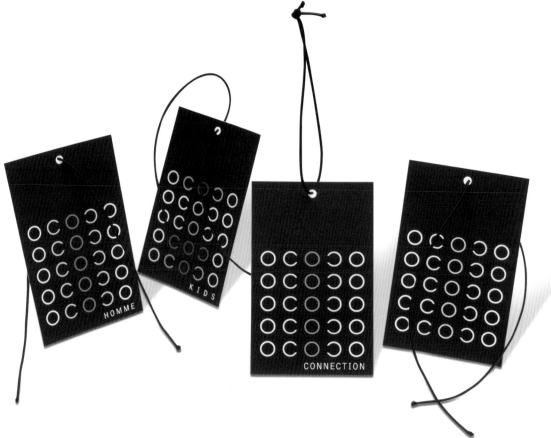

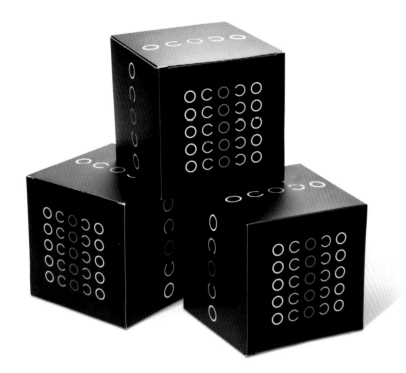

To break through into Korea's online market, the OCOCO brand needed to go beyond the design of clothing. Accordingly, a design approach that communicated a distinctive, contemporary brand identity was mandated and a seamless visual and verbal powerhouse brand identity developed. Using the tagline, "Updated Basic", the simple design concept imbued classic items of clothing with an invigorated, contemporary flair. The brand name is presented in an eye-catching, black-and-white typographic design style. The impact of the symmetrical layout of the brand's five-letter name was enhanced by a quintuple repetition. The result was a square-d logo which could be positioned with utmost flexibility across all advertising materials, and a visual identity that consistently reflected OCOCO's brand positioning.

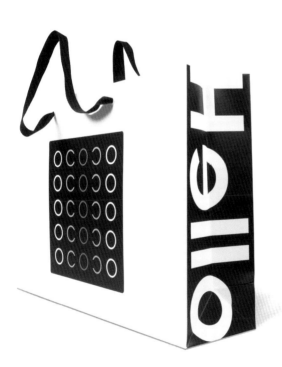

Stadt Viersen

[Corporate Design]

This logo – as an element of the new corporate design approach of the German city of Viersen – illustrates the connection between urbanity and nature. Accordingly, the newly designed logotype consists of two squares in blue and green standing side by side. Uniting to form a stylised letter "V" are 15 dots that can be viewed as a check-sign pointing upwards, while the dots are also indicative of Viersen's status as county seat. In their reference to this new corporate identity, the dots thus also elucidate and illustrate the network concept and the idea of centrality.

client
Stadt Viersen, Stadtmarketing, Viersen

design
28 LIMITED BRAND, Bochum

graphic
Mirco Kurth

text
Bernhard Koppenhöfer

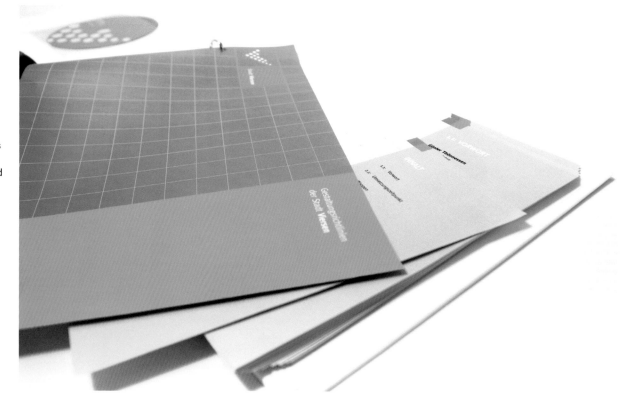

Conservatoire de Lausanne

[Branding, Corporate Communication]

C: conservatoire de lausanne

The Conservatoire de Lausanne aims to initiate children and young adults into the pleasures of music. As part of defining a brand strategy, a new corporate design was developed that playfully combines the bass clef with the first letter "C". Score-like illustrations of sound vibrations on advertising materials playfully allude to the institute's area of expertise. The pictorial language features a series of photos from everyday life, showing students who enjoy making music at home.

client
Conservatoire de Lausanne

design
Moser Design SA, Lausanne

head of marketing
Nicolas Peter

creative direction
Caroline Mesple-Moser,
Alexandre Henriques

graphic design
Pierre Terrier,
Andreas Richter

text
Alain Perusset

project management
Géraldine Nicole

web development
Fabien Kupferschmid

Bardehle Pagenberg

[Corporate Design]

A new visual identity was developed for Bardehle Pagenberg, an industrial property law firm, with the aim of positioning the firm as a leading expert in intellectual property. The logo, which is unusually minimalist for the industry, combines this content with the initials of the company name: "IP" is translated into a "P" crowned by the dot from the letter "i" and then inverted to form a lower-case "b". The distinctive corporate colours, which combine a shade of the precious metal iridium with a brilliant yellow, create a strong and unmistakable brand identity.

client
Bardehle Pagenberg, Munich

design
KMS TEAM, Munich

creative direction
Knut Maierhofer
(Managing Partner, Design)

art direction
Helena Frühauf

graphic design
Susanne Elhardt, Heidi Kral,
Michael Reinhardt,
Lars Breitenfeldt

project management
Eva-Maria Schleip,
Manuela Liebertz

production
Anja Wilczek

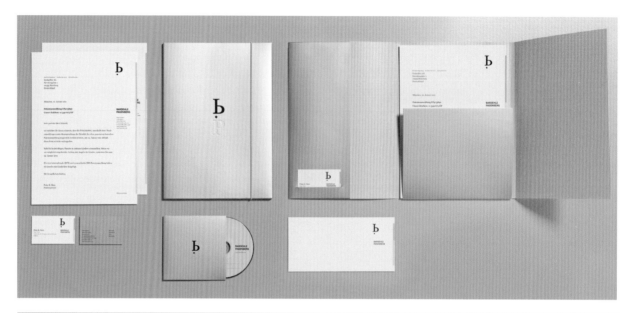

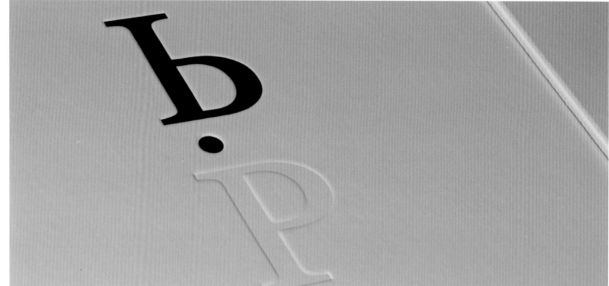

Museum Kunst der Westküste

[Corporate Design]

The newly established Museum Kunst der Westküste on the German island of Föhr sets out to address a broad public. Its corporate design is based on a clear and comprehensive creative frame with flexible typography and a variable colour spectrum. This allows the design to unfold as a consistent and distinctive representation of more than 500 individual items in the areas of advertisement, public relations, guidance systems, exhibition labelling, museum sales, museum education, museum gastronomy, Internet, publications, management, lobbying and trade-fair presence.

client
Det Paulsen Legaat gGmbH, Alkersum/Föhr

design
Aalhai, Strategie Konzeption Gestaltung, Wyk auf Föhr

creative direction/concept
Jörg Stauvermann

graphic design
Jörg Stauvermann, Artur Gawron

customer advisory service
Jörg Stauvermann, Hilke Theis

illustration
Tobi Dahmen

programming
Jörg Zabel

RuhrKunstMuseen

[Corporate Design]

client
RuhrKunstMuseen,
RUHR.2010 GmbH, Essen

design
ENORM, Agentur für Visuelle
Kommunikation, Cologne

art direction
Stefan Kaulbersch,
Mark Michael Maier

graphic design
Sarah Berndes,
Sabine Schweckhorst,
Eva Pauli

Since 2010, twenty art museums of the Ruhr area have bundled their activities under the new RuhrKunstMuseen brand. The dynamism of possible interaction between the individual museums inspired the design of the distinctive logo, which is the key graphical element of the new museum group's corporate design. Involved museums include the Museum Folkwang in Essen, the Lehmbruck Museum in Duisburg and the Museum Ostwall in Dortmund. A unique typeface was developed for the lettering and is also used consistently as a font for headlines. In combination with the robust typography and bold colours, angular shapes derived from the logo with their transparent overlays define this striking corporate image.

Glückspilz

[Corporate Design]

client
Glückspilz Mode und Accessoires
GmbH & Co. KG, Grevenbroich

design
VOON Werbeagentur GmbH,
Grevenbroich

The Glückspilz children's fashion store presents itself as charming, familiar and colourful – both off- and online. Marked by playful colour contrasts, the logo is directed at the target group of 2- to 14-year-olds, aiming to make those who enter the virtual "mushroom" feel at home immediately. Design details integrated into price labels and mats create an entertaining personal articulation and natural warmth. Furthermore, one euro from each purchase goes to a children's project in the German city of Grevenbroich. Glückspilz also spreads joy with many other ideas, including a welcoming rhyme and a newsletter. And interested customers are informed about new promotions, special offers and the latest product range on social network websites.

zgoll: Konferenzraum GmbH

[Corporate Design]

First-class, innovative and passionate – these are the standards defining this conference room specialist's work. This self-understanding is reflected not only in the up-to-date furniture and high-end media technology by company zgoll, but also in its corporate design. A stylised letter "Z" is the main design element for its office stationery and print media, as well as for its web presence. A clearly defined colour palette and print media with triangularly notched edging complement this appealing corporate design.

client
zgoll: Konferenzraum GmbH, Neuss

design
labor b designbüro, Dortmund

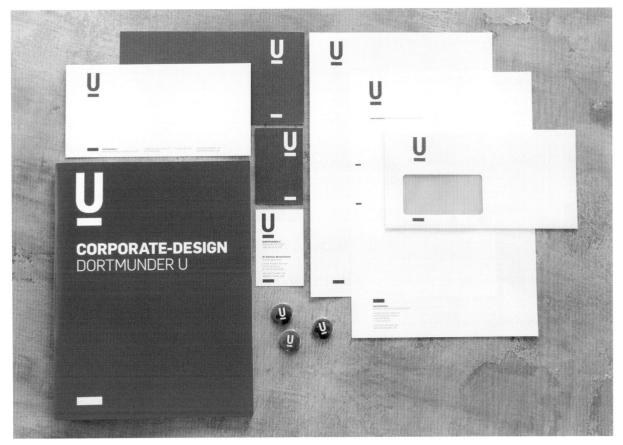

Dortmunder U – Zentrum für Kunst und Kreativität

[Corporate Design]

The Dortmunder U stands for great industrial history like no other building in the German town of Dortmund. After prolonged and elaborate remodelling, the former high-rise brewery structure reopened in 2010 as a centre for art and creativity. A pivotal facet of its corporate design is the logo: a distinctively shaped letter "U", which refers to the U-shaped neon lights that have been towering over the city for more than 40 years. Together with the subjacent bar, it forms an umbrella brand in the truest sense for all institutions entering into cooperation with the Dortmunder U.

client
Dortmunder U – Zentrum für Kunst und Kreativität, Dortmund; Regionalverband Ruhr, Essen

design
labor b designbüro, Dortmund

blomus
[Brand Relaunch]

In 2010, the corporate design of manufacturer blomus experienced a relaunch – with the aim of defining a consistently sophisticated design statement. The motto "pure life" encapsulates the company's commitment to creating lifestyle products of timeless beauty. The graphically reduced and clear layout of this new corporate design uses modern icons in subtle pastel colours to present the company's four product universes: garden, home, taste and spa. The product catalogue serves as a design guideline for all future communication channels.

client
blomus GmbH, Sundern

design
cyclos design GmbH, Münster

designer portrait
→ Vol.1: p.469

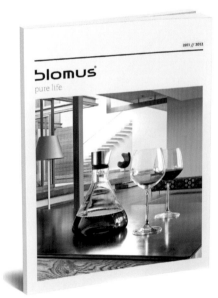

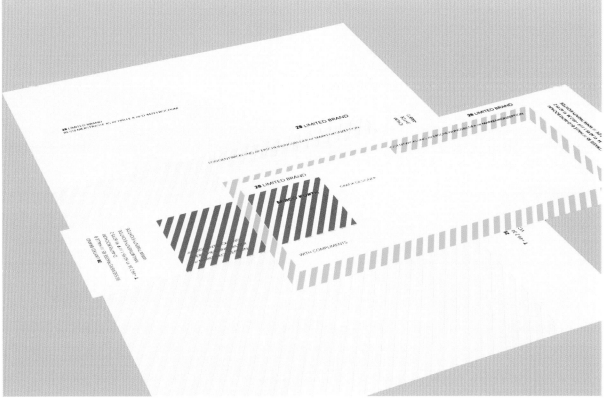

28 LIMITED BRAND
[Stationery]

28 LIMITED BRAND is a design agency with an emphasis on logo development and corporate design. The unconventional features of the agency's corporate stationery are marked by the distinct use of differently coloured areas, representing flexibility and creativity. Neon colours were deliberately chosen to generate heightened attention. The design concept of tilted bars facilitates the signalling effect of the corporate image while simultaneously referencing the specialisation of the design agency.

client
28 LIMITED BRAND, Bochum

design
28 LIMITED BRAND, Bochum

graphic design
Mirco Kurth

Parador

[Corporate Design]

The company Parador elevates itself with a new corporate design conveying the high demands of a premium producer of exclusive flooring and wall designs. The multifaceted brand concept is established through a classically reduced logotype, sophisticated colouring in a warm brown tone against a black background, and pictures of upmarket living worlds. The expressive claim "living performance" was developed with the aim of addressing a target group of performance-oriented customers possessing a sense for quality and style. The integration of a slacker as a key visual serves to highlight the significance of the product "flooring" by its very absence.

client
Parador GmbH & Co. KG, Coesfeld

design
Martin et Karczinski GmbH, Munich

creative direction
Peter Martin

art direction
Marcus-Florian Kruse, Patrick Wachner

graphic design
Christina Bee, Martin Buck, Holger Königsdörfer

text
Wolfgang Wirsching

photography
Thomas Popinger

designer portrait
→ Vol.2: p.495

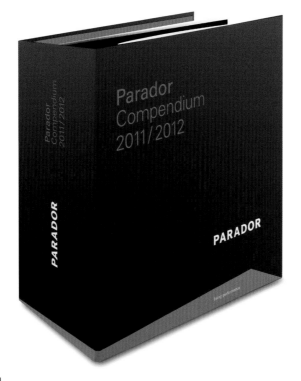

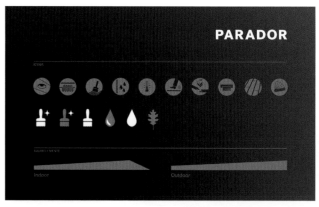

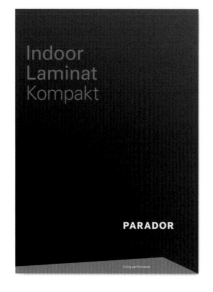

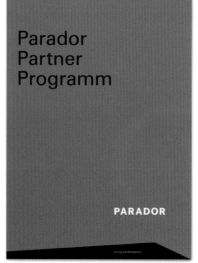

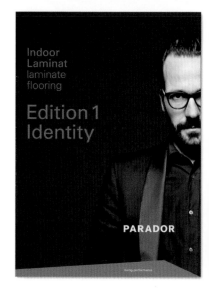

Desertec Foundation

[Corporate Design]

A new corporate design was developed for Desertec, an initiative that aims to harness solar energy on a large scale by building solar power plants in the Sahara Desert. The distinctive logo is a stylised representation of the earth with the sun shining on it, the half-circle on the right also forming the letter "D". The symbolic colours are derived from the company's activities and are globally understandable: green stands for environmentally friendly energy, yellow-orange for the sun, and beige for the desert sand.

client
Desertec Foundation, Hamburg

design
KMS TEAM, Munich

creative direction
Knut Maierhofer
(Managing Partner, Design),
Michael Keller
(Managing Partner, Creation)

art direction
Helena Frühauf, Atli Hilmarsson

graphic design
Jessica Krier

project management
Sandra Ehm

production
Matthias Karpf

pre-press
Bernd Müller

designer portrait
→ Vol.2: p.486

Qatar 2022
FIFA World Cup™ Bid
[Brand Identity]

Qatar's bid to host the 2022 FIFA World Cup™ faced the challenge of being credible as the so-called "dark horse" in the bidding race. Based on an existing logo, a multifaceted brand identity was designed which successfully stood out from the competition. Combining a high degree of flexibility with a clear message, this dynamic identity is adaptable to a wide range of communication channels. Harnessing the energy of this youthful nation, the design system includes a series of illustrations, action photography as well as a unique calligraphic font.

client
Qatar 2022 Bid Committee

design
Lambie-Nairn

photography
Rick Guest

typography
Dalton Maag

calligraphy
Ali Hassan Ali Al-Jaber

EXPECT AMAZING

Marken bauen /
Building brands

[Christmas Mailing]

KMS TEAM, a company specialised in brand strategy, brand
design and brand communication,
set out to design a unique Christmas gift for its customers and
partners with reference to the
individual recipients. The result
was a personalised set of Legos
arrayed as a conference room –
with the logo of each recipient
integrated as a projected image.
With the German headline "Mar-
ken bauen" (Building brands), the
enclosed greeting card highlights the sender's core competence, thus reinterpreting and
transforming a classic gift into a
friendly communication medium.

client
KMS TEAM, Munich

design
KMS TEAM, Munich

concept
Knut Maierhofer
(Managing Partner, Design),
Michael Keller
(Managing Partner, Creation),
Christoph Rohrer
(Managing Partner, Strategy),
Armin Schlamp
(Managing Director, Consulting)

art direction
Bruno Marek

graphic design
Gabriel Weiss

motion design
Cecil V. Rustemeyer

project management
Angelika Kresiment

production
Christina Baur

designer portrait
→ Vol.2: p.486

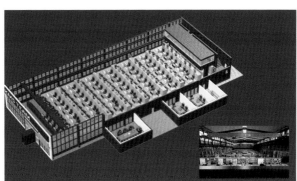

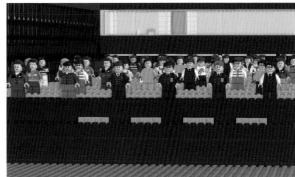

Porsche Intelligent Performance

[Logo]

The challenge in creating the corporate design for Porsche Intelligent Performance (PIP) involved expressing the company's philosophy in the development of modern vehicle concepts. Consisting of three gradients, the logo symbolises the drive and speed of the brand, thus serving to illustrate modern vehicle concepts that unite efficiency and top performance. Designed for flexible use, this logotype can be aligned either to the left or to the right, making it easy to adapt for all possible applications.

client
Dr. Ing. h.c. F. Porsche AG, Ludwigsburg

design
KMS TEAM, Munich

creative direction
Knut Maierhofer
(Managing Partner, Design)

art direction
Patrick Märki

graphic design
Bettina Otto, Daniel Perraudin

motion design
Gabriel Weiss

project management
Sandra Ehm

production
Christina Baur

pre-press
Bernd Müller

designer portrait
→ Vol.2: p.486

Klavierfieber / *Piano Fever*

[Corporate Design, Communication Concept]

For the piano and arts festival Klavierfieber (Piano Fever) in Berlin a multifaceted, attention-grabbing communication campaign was developed: posters, flyers, invitation cards, a website, a programme catalogue and a film trailer. The key visual is inspired by a stylised piano keyboard and communicates, in an eye-catching manner, both the dynamic aspect of the festival and the passion of the young pianists performing there. Abstract brushstrokes and colour spots further serve to highlight the artistic flair of the festival.

client
Dr. Gabriele Minz GmbH
Internationale Kulturprojekte,
Berlin

design
MetaDesign AG, Berlin

head of advertising
Prof. Uli Mayer-Johanssen

art direction
Marcus Wacker

graphic design
Marcela Grupp, Elke Haß

text
Marcel Linden, Regine Jung

account management
Ulli Mayrock

DROOM /
DESIGN YOUR ROOM

[Corporate Design]

A modular corporate design, including a typographic logo, was developed for this manufacturer of individually printable furniture and interior design. The lettering selected for the logo is founded on the basic geometric shapes of the circle, square and triangle, which are also elements of the product design. Variable positioning of the individual letters allows for six different versions, which may be freely used to mask or stamp surfaces, while sections of the logo can also serve as design elements. The playfulness of the logo forms a contrast to its strict typography.

client
DROOM GmbH & Co. KG, Cologne

design
Zum Kuckuck / Büro für digitale Medien, Würzburg

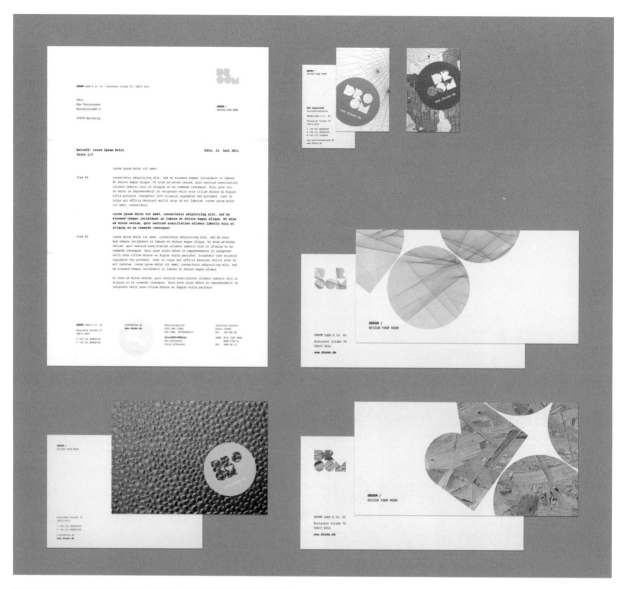

Blueprint 2011
[Event Brand Identity]

Blueprint 2011 stands for an international fashion event in Singapore, presenting emerging fashion designers under the heading "Brave New World". The key visual of the campaign shows a fashion model, dressed in avant-garde clothing, delicately emerging from a sculptural forest made of paper elements. The image thus evokes a sense of timeless beauty, yet also manages to convey a bold character of progressiveness. Itself an experimental exploration of the topic of fashion photography, the campaign merges aspects of art, design and fashion.

client
Blueprint Group Pte Ltd, Singapore

design
Trine Design Associates Pte Ltd, Singapore

head of marketing
Khoh Wan Chin

creative direction
Victor Lim

graphic design
Hao

project management
Ryan Hoe

photography
Joel Lim, Calibre Pictures

design team
Justin Yeo, Ling Goh & MC

NTR

[Corporate Design, Idents,
Introduction Movie]

NTR is a Dutch public service broadcaster specialising in the fields of information, education and culture. The central element of its visual identity is an adaptable logo consisting of the company acronym succeeded by a colon. The contours of the rounded typography form small windows displaying a variety of different backgrounds. A set of manuals, with an enclosed DVD, elucidates this entirely new brand identity, including its application to various design areas, such as graphics, motion, audio and Internet.

client
NTR – Dutch Public Service Broadcaster for Information, Education and Culture

design
Jan Paul de Vries,
Volta_ontwerpers + René Gast,
Gastproducties

music / sound design
Joosten Kuitenbrouwer

motion design
Thijs Dikshoorn

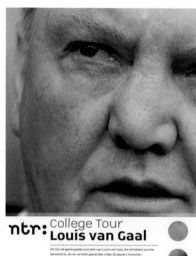

Balea Trend it up
[Packaging Design]

Borrowing inspiration from night-life, the new Trend it up brand identity stands out with its trendy pictorial language. As such, it is optimally geared to the young, fashion-conscious target group of the Balea hairstyling brand. The challenge was to communicate the product features in an easy-to-understand and recognisable way. Abstract motifs with a surrealistic appeal illustrate each product's benefits and are complemented by creative product names.

client
Balea, dm-drogerie markt GmbH + Co. KG, Karlsruhe

design
WINcommunication, Aachen

ceo
Cathrin Jo Ann Wind

creative direction
Marcus Lichte

art direction
Mareike Mohr, Jana Krüger, Sebastian Hampen

customer advisory service
Julia Bos

final artwork
Harald Strang

InnoCentre
Open House 2011
[Visual Identity]

The aim behind the exhibition
concept of the InnoCentre Open
House, which presents itself as
a meeting place for the creative
industry in Hong Kong, was to
establish a platform for the design industry. A colourful design
implements an appealing,
cartoon-like visual language, and
the corporate design has been
applied in an engaging way in the
exhibition spaces as well as in
all other communication areas.
Versatile media and merchandis-
ing products foster a creative
environment, combining aesthetic
colour gradients with a number
of different icons.

client
InnoCentre, Hong Kong

design
Circle Design Ltd., Hong Kong

creative direction/art direction
Clement Yick

graphic design
Nancy Chan, Cheung Man Kit

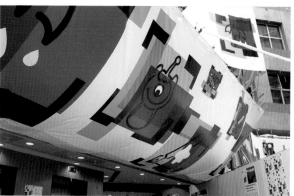

Gärtner von Eden

[Corporate Design]

The logo of Gärtner von Eden, a Germany-wide cooperative of landscape gardeners, is inspired by the apple as the symbol of paradise and reinterprets it into a symbol of longing. This highly abstract and pared-down key visual serves as the nucleus of the corporate design relaunch. The portfolio includes business stationery, adverts, greeting cards, notepads, doorknob hangers, labels, stickers, stamps and mailings. It is accessible to all 60 landscape gardeners via a secure web portal, allowing them to customise and order all ready-to-print artwork at a reasonable price.

client
Gärtner von Eden, Gütersloh

design
cyclos design GmbH, Münster

designer portrait
→ Vol.1: p.469

Gärtner
von Eden®

Deichmann
[Corporate Design]

client
Deichmann SE, Essen

head of international marketing
Christian Hackel

head of marketing
Andreas Conze

design
KW43 BRANDDESIGN,
Düsseldorf

creative direction
Prof. Rüdiger Goetz,
Jürgen Adolph

graphic design
Meike Hartmann,
Marc Schäde,
Tobias Wienholt

account management
Michael Rewald,
Alexandra Sobota

The challenge in designing the brand relaunch of the Deichmann shoe company was to communicate the quality standards and fashion expertise of this multinational enterprise through a new and comprehensive corporate design concept without confusing its existing customer base. The scrupulous redesign of the trademark and the development of a corporate typeface form the basis for a clear and modern design principle. The large, transparent logo thus becomes an integral structural design component: an elegantly curved recess at the bottom of the letter "D" features in all media involved in this new brand presence. The familiar colour coding of the brand was maintained in order to ensure brand recognition within the target group.

Christmas greeting

[Mailing]

With a large measure of humour, a holiday mailing conceptualised by the Fuenfwerken design agency for their clients highlights the recorder as "weapon of harmony" for Christmas. The design combines folklore festivity with contemporary chic: a mix of historic prints, etchings and engravings – in black, gold and neon orange – illustrates the contents with some minor macabre details. A rustic box made of grey chipboard serves as packaging, decorated like the recorder with a neon orange band. On the website, a recorder concert played by the agency team merrily invites clients to join in.

client
Fuenfwerken Design AG,
Wiesbaden/Berlin

design
Fuenfwerken Design AG,
Wiesbaden/Berlin

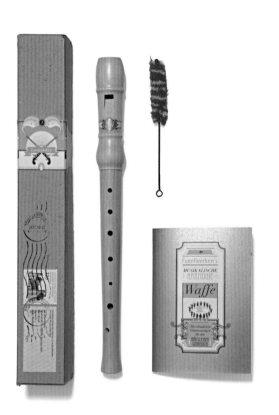

Family Business
[Corporate Design]

The reduced figurative mark of symmetrical lines visualises the fact that the Sandscheper office unites under one roof ten family businesses with three managing directors. The symmetrical layout of the lines is extendable, thus communicating growth and development, while a harmoniously balanced colour scheme helps to distinguish the individual companies. For company group communications, the logo is presented in a warm grey. Furthermore, high-grade materials and print finishing convey an elegant overall appearance.

client
Büro Sandscheper,
Bocholt

design
Lockstoff Design,
Grevenbroich

creative direction
Susanne Coenen,
Nicole Slink

graphic design
Susanne Coenen,
Nicole Slink

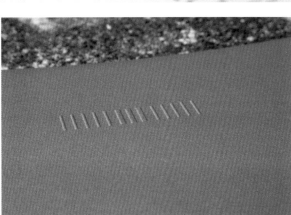

HOCH III –
café.bar.club
[Corporate Design]

Hoch III represents an exceptional café-bar-club concept, spread across three storeys, within Hamburg's trendy St. Pauli district. A concise and distinctive logo highlights the venue's name. The clear corporate design, which is reduced to black and white, has a strong impact in print, on the Internet, and as an element of three-dimensional ambience within the venue's architecture. The interior design features a mystic visual language, which has been appealingly integrated into the branding.

client
HCBCzwei Verwaltung UG & Co. KG, Hamburg

design
weissraum.de(sign)°, Hamburg

creative direction
Bernd Brink, Lucas Buchholz

art direction
Nils Zimmermann

graphic design
Aggi Berg

photography
Hannes Cunze

production
Susann Buchholz, Christoph Schmidt, alvons design; Karlo Mertens, Firma Mertens

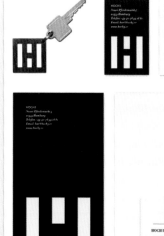

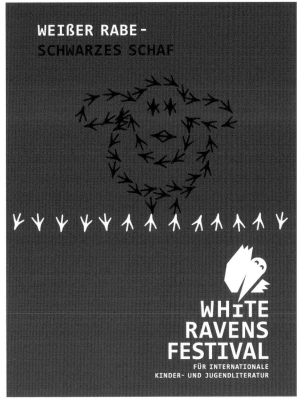

White Ravens Festival

[Corporate Design]

The White Ravens Festival is dedicated to international literature for children and young adults and is hosted by the International Youth Library (IJB) in Munich. The name refers to the annually published list of recommended, high-quality children's and youth literature by the IJB. The logo of the festival – a combination of book and raven – illustrates the ambitious objectives of the festival. With a range of different motifs composed of white claws, this visual identity communicates the festival's diverse topics.

client
Internationale Jugendbibliothek /
International Youth Library,
Munich

design
Büro Alba GbR, Munich

creative direction
Christian Rother,
Tina Strobel-Rother

art direction
Andreas Pischetsrieder

graphic design
Marie-Christine v. Locquenghien

Act Research

[Logo]

Act Research is a company that works with large amounts of different data from all over the world. The logo illustrates these data as one entity in a concise combination of word and image: in a multifaceted illustration, a variety of letters and symbols form the contours of a sphere. As a synonym for the earth, the logo thus refers to the company's international orientation; and its monochrome design is highly distinctive, against both black and white backgrounds.

client
Act Research, SIM, Tbilisi

design
George Bokhua, SIM, Tbilisi

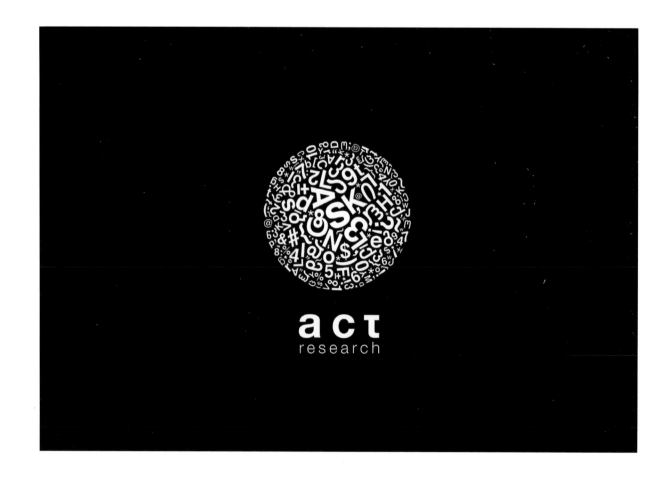

Febrü
[Corporate Design]

At the heart of the timeless, elegant presentation of this international manufacturer is a reduced logotype combined with the skill statement "office furniture" in four different languages. The flexible positioning of the Febrü logo is suitable for various media and achieves a high degree of recognition. The company's design standards are reflected in its photographic product presentation – purist in style and harmonious in colour spectrum. The design concept of brand and product identity focuses on the parameters of information and emotion.

client
Febrü Büromöbel Produktions-und Vertriebs-GmbH, Herford

head of marketing
Brunhild Redeker

design
beierarbeit GmbH, Bielefeld

creative direction
Christoph Beier

photography
Christian R. Schulz

web design
André Nickels

programming
Thomas Fiedler

50 Jahre Mobilität /
50 years of mobility
[Visual Identity]

This visual identity was developed for the anniversary of a large VW dealer in Germany. The objective was to portray a local company as an institution for mobility. A stylised series of photos creatively narrates the history of 50 years of mobility with images of steering wheels. This approach successfully conveys an aesthetic depiction of technical development without resorting to a retro look. The corporate design interprets the half-century period in a congenial manner, facilitating customer identification.

client
Volkswagen Zentrum Freiburg

design
identis GmbH, design-gruppe joseph pölzelbauer, Freiburg

creative direction
Joseph Pölzelbauer

art direction
Jean Mierecke

graphic design
Joseph Pölzelbauer,
Jean Mierecke, Reinhard Groh

text
Burghard Müller-Dannhausen

project management
Ursel Linder, Svenja Schneppe

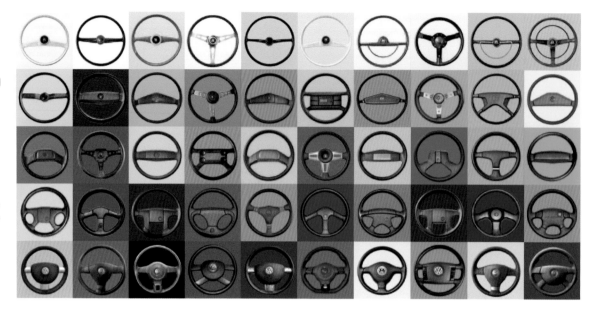

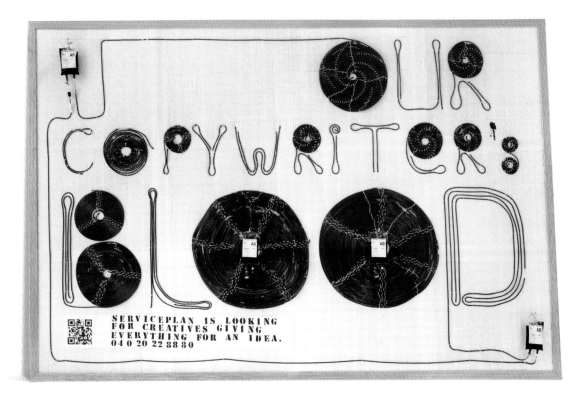

Posters of Passion:
Blood, Sweat & Tears

The serviceplan creative group thrives on creative people who will give everything for a good idea, meaning blood, sweat and tears. To communicate this message, a poster series was created from precisely these materials: the first poster consists of a tube system filled with a copywriter's real blood; the typography of the second poster is made of the designers' artfully applied salty sweat deposits; and the third poster features the tears of the artistic directors in a collage of paper tissues.

client
serviceplan, Hamburg

design
serviceplan, Hamburg

chief creative officer
Alexander Schill

creative direction
Maik Kaehler, Christoph Nann

art direction
Savina Mokreva, Manuel Wolff

graphic design
Christoph Kueckner,
Maren Wandersleben,
Christoff Strukamp

programming
Steffen Knoblich, plan.net

designer portrait
→ Vol.1: p.503

MAINFELD –
Raum für Kultur /
MAINFELD –
space for culture
[Flexible Logo]

MAINFELD is a culture and community centre in Frankfurt/Main. Its flexible and variable logo is composed of countless grey dots on a white background, or vice versa, which together shape the name of Frankfurt's Mainfeld district. It metaphorically illustrates the activity of local citizens – both those engaged in the cultural sector as well as the audience – whose ideas are in constant flow. The logo is applied in various forms: as pins and dots of light on architectural structures, as animation on the Internet, or printed on items of clothing and print media. In addition, colourful photographs vibrantly contrast with the monochrome logo design.

client
kombinat gmbh,
Frankfurt/Main

design
Impulslabor,
Frankfurt/Main

art direction
Ulrike Gauder, Uwe Tischer

graphic design
Ulrike Gauder

text
Cora Walker

photography
Andreas Reeg

animation
Mathias Baske

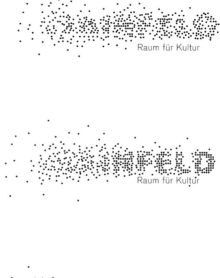

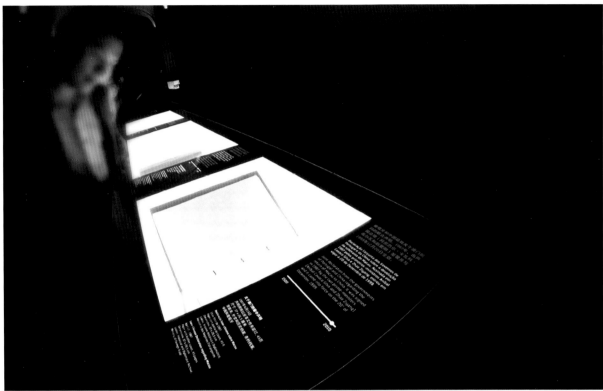

Portugal Pavilion Expo 2010 Shanghai China

[Communication Design, Exhibition Design]

The communication and exhibition design of the Portugal Pavilion at the Expo 2010 in Shanghai creates a visual identity that is based on country-specific themes. The cork facade of this pavilion was inspired by bearings on ancient nautical charts, which were now translated into a triangular morphing grid representing the country's 500-year-old relationship with China. This design element can be found in all related communication media and conveys a dynamic effect. Cork is furthermore an ecological product that remains widely unknown in China.

client
Parque EXPO 98, S.A.,
Lisbon

commissioner general
Rolando Borges Martins

design
FPGB · Consultoria e Design,
Lda., Estoril

creative direction
Francisco Pestana,
Gabriela Borralho

design team
Francisco Pestana,
Gabriela Borralho,
Ana Bica,
António Salsinha

project management
Francisco Pestana

SÜDWESTBANK
[Brand Relaunch]

client
SÜDWESTBANK AG,
Stuttgart

head of marketing
Jochen Sautter

marketing management
Petra Brehm, Stephanie Feger

design
Keim Identity GmbH,
Zürich

creative direction
Matthias Keim

strategic planning
Christine Keim

photography
Sebastian Mölleken,
Mölleken Fotografie

A brand identity was developed for SÜDWESTBANK that individually addresses different target groups, focusing especially on upmarket clientele. The claim "Werte verbinden" (Values connect people), in positioning the medium-size private bank, highlights an ambiguity of material and immaterial values. A unique element of the brand design are so-called dialogue boxes – comprised of dialogues of text or image/text that foster communication – which can be applied flexibly to render a vivid experience of identity. In addition, distinctive and authentic imagery connects all communication media. A classic depth-of-field blur symbolises the bank's proximity to its customers.

Maria Stahl Architekten

[Corporate Design, Stationery]

In developing this corporate stationery, the objective was to manifest a simple yet high-grade corporate design for the Maria Stahl architecture firm. The duality of discipline and variability, which characterises this architecture office, inspired the basic concept of a straight-forward corporate design. The result was a logo module that can be applied consistently yet also flexibly to different formats and media. The decision to do without diverse colours and forms focuses heightened attention on the company name.

client
Maria Stahl, Düsseldorf

design
KW43 BRANDDESIGN, Düsseldorf

graphic design
Jürgen Adolph

printing
Letterpress 77

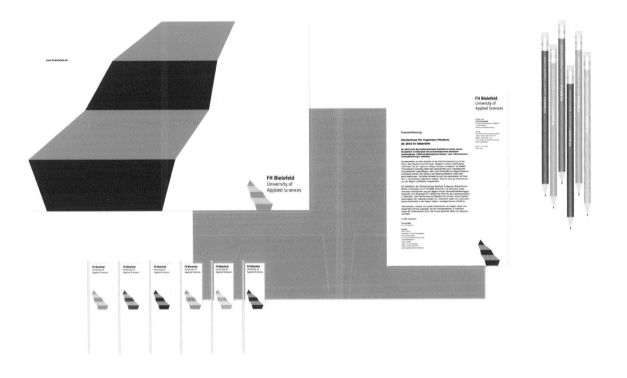

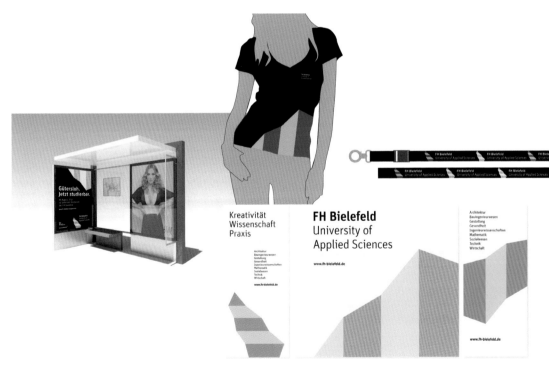

FH Bielefeld – University of Applied Sciences

[Corporate Design]

The word mark of the FH Bielefeld – University of Applied Sciences, illustrated as an abstract staircase, plays with the visual charm of two- and three-dimensionality. Its orientation is deliberately contrary to design conventions and appears unusually bulky. This aims to express how – in the process of study and research – a straight path is not necessary for attaining success. Here, both logo and colour scheme are easy to recognise. When applied to different media, the flexible basic form of the logo assumes various magnifications, orientations and turns.

client
FH Bielefeld –
University of Applied Sciences

design
beierarbeit GmbH, Bielefeld

creative direction
Prof. Dirk Fütterer,
Prof. Uwe Göbel

graphic design
Mareike Knocks,
Michael Erdmann,
Robert Fischer

Bricmate
Design Programme
[Graphic Design]

Bricmate is a Swedish company which specialises in selling ceramic and porcelain tiles. Here the objective was to design a new corporate identity based on existing elements, with a modernisation and enhancement of brand awareness. An analysis of the old logo showed that the height of the capital letters was six times the width. Accordingly, the new logo is divided into six identical squares to symbolise ceramic tiles. The playful application of this idea allows for highly flexible implementation.

client
Bricmate AB, Stockholm

design
Kazakoff Design, Stockholm

head of marketing
Hans Croon

creative direction/concept
Igor Kazakov

graphic design
Igor Kazakov

text
Christer Alm

designer portrait
→ Vol.1: p.484

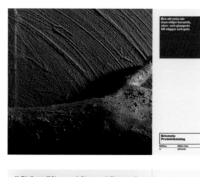

Swop Book

[Idea Book]

The Swop Book was conceived as frontal attack against the fear of the blank page. With more than one hundred pictures from all possible areas of life, it offers multifarious inspiration. The pictures narrate short tales which help readers to spin their own stories or endings; they entice readers to start scribbling, drawing or writing. The black cover features an eye-catching title design and a ribbon. This book of ideas is complemented by a website that invites "swoppers" to upload and virtually leaf through their own drafts.

client
brandbook.de,
Frankfurt/Main

design
brandbook.de,
Frankfurt/Main

creative direction
Bernd Griese

text
Christoph Herold

project management
Sandra Elm

photography
Shutterstock

production
Sabine Kochendörfer

Van Gogh Museum

[Visual Identity]

The Van Gogh Museum tells the story of this artist's eventful life in both pictures and words. The challenge was to focus this ambitious idea into one consistent visual identity. The starting points for the new corporate design are the characteristic brush strokes of Van Gogh's painting "The Mower". Inspired by the colouring of his key works, the colour palette features as a vibrant background for select quotes by the artist. The black-and-white logo provides an eye-catching contrast and is reminiscent of a stamp inspired by the angular shape of the museum building.

client
Van Gogh Museum,
Amsterdam

design
Koeweiden Postma,
Amsterdam

concept
Jacques Koeweiden,
Eddy Wegman

graphic design
Mark Holtman,
Tessa van der Eem,
Rogier Bisschop

customer advisory service
Sander Tóth

strategic planning
Hugo van den Bos

project management
Cathy Noordhuizen

dtp
Ingmar Evers

Tony Petersen Film

[Corporate Design]

This corporate design demonstrates the versatility of Tony Petersen Film and the directors that work there, featuring a company logo which comes in a selection of different versions. So as to mark the various film categories – such as food, beauty or cars – a unique "TPF" logo was handcrafted and photographed for each genre. With the materials used in the logos inspired by the individual categories, the eight different logo versions are applied to business cards, letterhead and the company's Internet presence.

client
Tony Petersen Film GmbH,
Hamburg

design
Kolle Rebbe / KOREFE,
Hamburg

creative direction
Katrin Oeding

art direction
Ana Magalhaes

image editing/final artwork
PX Group GmbH,
Hamburg

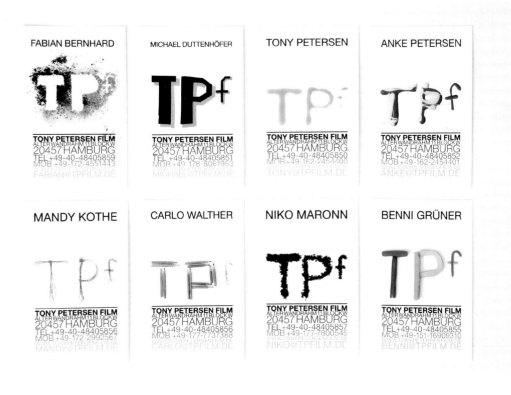

MAO

[Corporate Identity]

The comprehensive visual identity of the Slovenian Museum of Architecture and Design (MAO) was conceived as a frame within which the plethora of divergent fields covered by the museum can be highlighted. Architecture, graphic and industrial design as well as photography are integrated into the logo, featuring unique colouring and symbolism for each field. This design principle guarantees a high degree of recognition while at the same time allowing events, artists or works to be flexibly emphasised.

client
MAO, Muzej za arhitekturo in oblikovanje / Museum of Architecture and Design, Ljubljana

project management
Matevž Čelik, Anja Zorko

design
IlovarStritar, Ljubljana

creative direction
Jernej Stritar, Robert Ilovar

graphic design
Jernej Stritar, Robert Ilovar, Miha Kosmač, Kaja Kopitar

programming
Neolab

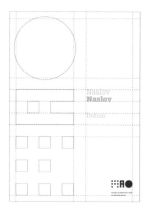

MUZEJ ZA ARHITEKTURO
IN OBLIKOVANJE

Griffin
Theatre Company
[Corporate Identity]

The Griffin Theatre Company is a new writing theatre who have been at the forefront of Australian playwriting for the past 30 years. Since writing is at the heart of Griffin, the new corporate identity situates words at centre stage. Keywords, such as titles of the individual productions, are showcased in a design reminiscent of crossword puzzles. Attuned to each theatre production, the mood can be shifted by exploring different combinations of words, colours and imagery, while the theatre company logo always remains constant.

client
Griffin Theatre Company,
Sydney

design
Interbrand, Ultimo/Sydney

creative direction
Chris Maclean

design director
Andrew Droog

graphic design
Malin Holmstrom,
Elliott Scott

Tapwell Design
Programme
[Graphic Design]

client
Tapwell AB, Stockholm

design
Kazakoff Design, Stockholm

head of marketing
Niklas Nordblom

head of advertising
Carl Reuterswärd

creative direction/concept
Igor Kazakov

graphic design
Igor Kazakov

designer portrait
→ Vol.1: p.484

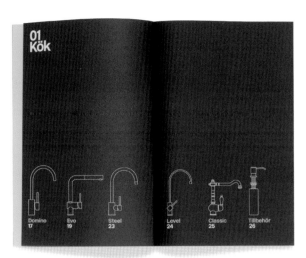

Tapwell AB is a Swedish company which sells faucets for kitchens and bathrooms, with a sub-brand specialising in mixer taps for new buildings. The objective was to develop a new identity for this sub-brand and also to redesign the corporate identity of the umbrella brand. The initial of the company name thus became a point of origin for the design concept. The logo consists of the letter "T" as symbol for a hot/cold water mixer tap and the subjacent letter "I" as a symbol for water running from the tap. The catalogues exemplarily present a harmoniously balanced colour concept that is complemented by flexible pictorial language. Emotionally appealing photographs are combined with product illustrations and technical drawings.

The Great Blandini

[Corporate Identity]

The objective was to create an identity for the highly skilled retoucher Stephen Bland. Looking for an innovative solution that would stand out and appeal to the creative industry, the idea was born to showcase the Photoshop magician as "The Great Blandini". A typographical concept inspired by the Victorian era is reminiscent of a time when magic was still truly magical. The unique mix of contemporary, technical terminology and Victorian English lends this design identity a humorous and amusing flair.

client
Steve Bland

design
Interbrand, Ultimo/Sydney

creative direction
Mike Rigby

design director
Andrew Droog

graphic design
Malin Holmstrom

text
Mike Rigby, Mike Reed

production
Oliver Kendal

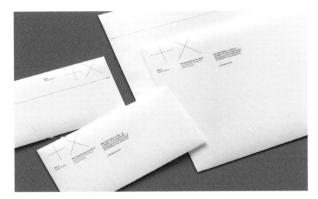

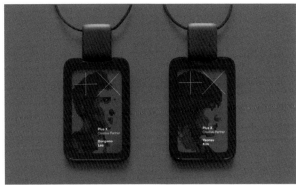

Plus X
[Corporate Identity]

The design philosophy of Plus X follows an experience-oriented approach that makes use of various media channels for strategic marketing. The company's logo was designed with the signs "+" and "x", both of which are considered to be fundamental signs. Black hues and neutral colours direct attention to a self-contained visual language made up of specifically developed pictograms and typefaces. As part of the extended corporate design project, portraits of all employees were illustrated and printed on business cards and employee ID cards.

client
Plus X, Seoul

design
Plus X, Seoul

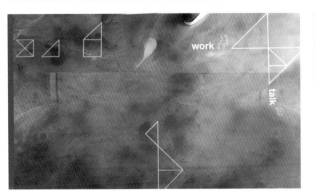

Nezu Private

[Corporate Design]

The private logo and stationery for the director of the Nezu Museum and his wife have been conceptualised independently from the museum's corporate design while also providing a subtle connection. Inspired by the initials of these two individuals, the design is marked by personalised colour coding: platinum for him and jade green for her. For joint correspondence, both colours are combined into a Möbius strip, a symbol of eternal bonding that represents the couple's relationship. The logo maintains a traditional formal language, transferred into a modern and Western context.

client
Nezu Institute of Fine Arts, Tokyo

design
Peter Schmidt Group, Hamburg

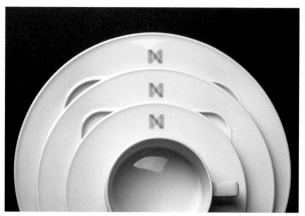

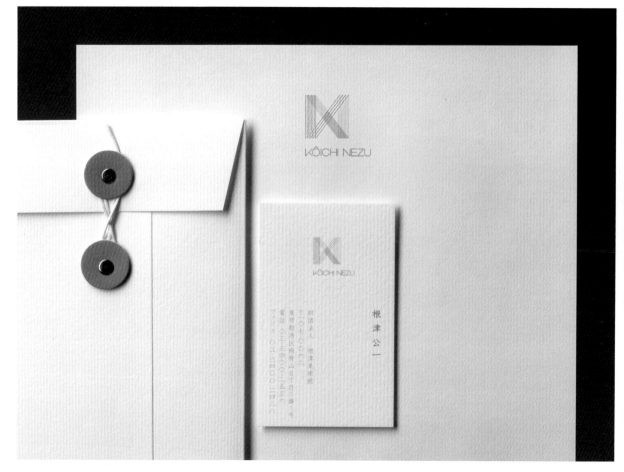

Study programmes
[Information Leaflets]

The information leaflets for the Faculty of Economics study programmes at the University of Ljubljana were designed to highlight the diversity and fascination of these programmes. At the same time, the easily recognisable layout is consistent with the overall visual appearance of the faculty. The cover illustrations feature various styles and themes which communicate the multifariousness of the faculty. Each topic contains a quotation by a famous person, complementing the message of the image.

client
University of Ljubljana,
Faculty of Economics,
Ljubljana

head of marketing
Monika Lapanja

text
Jana Pucelj, Barbara Leskovec,
Ajda Lah, Tina Vujaškovič

design
IlovarStritar, Ljubljana

creative direction
Robert Ilovar

graphic design/illustration
Robert Ilovar

137

SONAE –
Expanding circles to
reach the world
[Boards]

client
SONAE, Maia

design
Ivity Brand Corp, Lisbon

creative direction
Paulo Rocha

graphic design
José Carlos Mendes,
Cesária Martins

strategic planning
Pedro Pires

project management
Nuno Rainho, Vera Rhodes

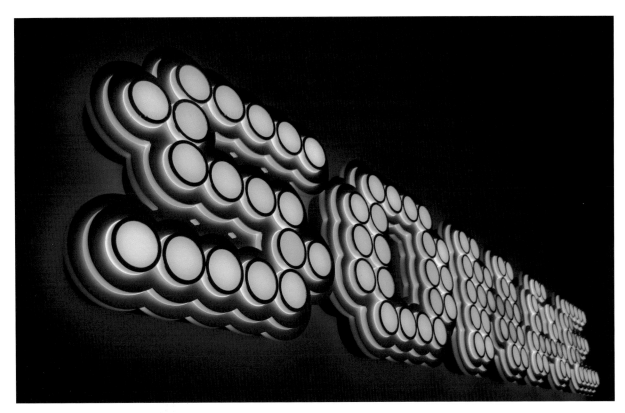

For the 50th anniversary of the international retail group SONAE a new visual identity was sought – one that would also incorporate the recent structural changes within the company. A three-dimensional system of layers was developed to reflect the diversity within the trade group. The result is a flexible, multicoloured brand identity inspired by the idea of metamorphosis. Special graphics software was used to generate different versions of the logo, all of which stand out due to their futuristic appeal and high technical standards. The surprising visual language features three-dimensional circles in various colour spectrums. As a symbol for constant change, this flexible identity represents the group's ambitious orientation towards the future.

Schmitt + Sohn Aufzüge

[Corporate Brochure]

This 100-page corporate brochure was produced as part of the new visual identity for Schmitt + Sohn Elevators, a company with a working base throughout Europe. In this brochure, which illustrates the company's values, products and references, it is the staff that gives the enterprise a face – each subject is represented by one employee who introduces it with a personal quote. The design concept surprises through a variable use of typography and distinguishes itself through consistent portrait and documentary photography.

client
Aufzugswerke M. Schmitt + Sohn GmbH, Nuremberg

design
Projekttriangle Design Studio, Stuttgart

creative direction
Martin Grothmaak,
Prof. Jürgen Späth

graphic design
Franz-Georg Stämmele,
Theresa Brandau

text
Myriam Guedey

image photography
Martin Grothmaak,
Tom Ziora

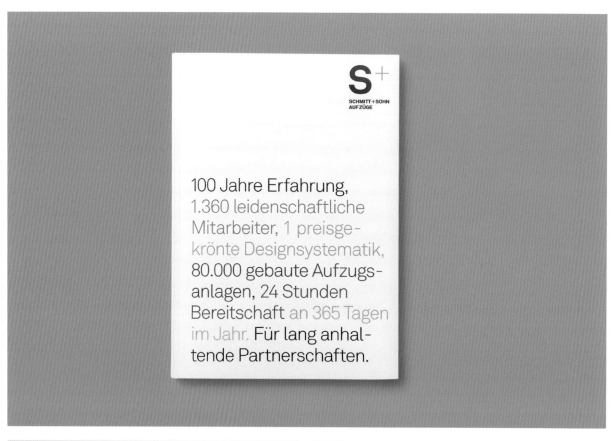

S+

SCHMITT + SOHN AUFZÜGE

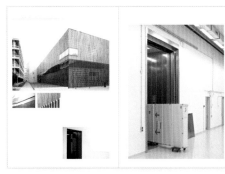

100 Jahre Erfahrung, 1.360 leidenschaftliche Mitarbeiter, 1 preisgekrönte Designsystematik, 80.000 gebaute Aufzugsanlagen, 24 Stunden Bereitschaft
Für lang anhaltende Partnerschaften.

Schmitt + Sohn Aufzüge

100 Jahre Erfahrung, 1.360 leidenschaftliche Mitarbeiter, 1 preisge-krönte Designsystematik, 80.000 gebaute Aufzugs-anlagen, 24 Stunden Bereitschaft
Für lang anhal-tende Partnerschaften.

Schmitt + Sohn Aufzüge
[Corporate Design]

The visual corporate identity of Schmitt + Sohn Elevators is marked by the clear lines of its new logo, a reference to the tradition of this family-run company. The formal precision of the lettered logo and a corporate identity font by the name of Akkurat underline technological competence. In combination with this new, multicoloured corporate design, an open and distinctive visual presentation is fostered. Also redesigned were, among other things, office equipment, vehicle graphics, product branding, and style guidelines for portrait and documentary photography.

client
Aufzugswerke M. Schmitt + Sohn GmbH, Nuremberg

design
Projekttriangle Design Studio, Stuttgart

creative direction
Martin Grothmaak,
Prof. Jürgen Späth

graphic design
Franz-Georg Stämmele,
Daisuke Nitta

image photography
Martin Grothmaak,
Tom Ziora

Fedrigoni
Hotel Book

client
Fedrigoni S.p.A., Verona

head of marketing
Chiara Medioli

design
Thomas Manss & Company

team
Thomas Manss, Enrica Corzani,
Annika Beste, Adele Bacci

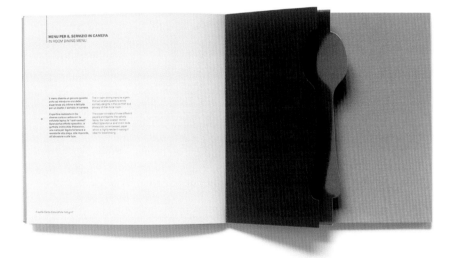

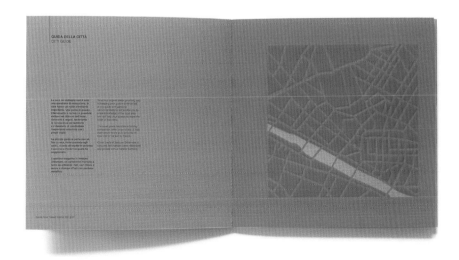

The aim of this lavishly designed, bilingual image brochure was to convey an elusive home-away-from-home feeling to hotel guests. The design concept is inspired by the visual and haptic properties of paper, complemented by artistic punch-outs that enhance the harmonious colour combinations – with the cover featuring a letter "H" for hotel, unveiling the colour surfaces of the pages underneath. Inside this hotel book guests will find, among other things, a personal note upon arrival, restaurant menus, and information on the city. An appealing page layout underlines the upmarket character of this limited edition book, which realises an array of different themes on an assortment of 50 paper variants.

Ein Blick / *In sight*

[Book, Film]

This book and film, titled "In sight", presents with humour, charm and light-heartedness the corporate design of Messe Frankfurt – its characteristics and those who have been instrumental in its creation. Leaving objective guidelines aside, both media stimulate interest and take a playful, emotional and humorous approach to what is so often a dry topic. The film features candid and authentic statements by staff members (from lift attendants to executive managers) as well as external designers and was shot at trade fair sites that play a role in the visual corporate identity.

client
Messe Frankfurt GmbH,
Frankfurt/Main

project management
Gerrit Schade

design
Lion & Bee, Berlin

concept
Prof. Alessio Leonardi, Lion & Bee

text
Prof. Alessio Leonardi, Lion & Bee

photography
Marc Jacquemin (Book),
Knut Adass (Camera)

film production
Frank Schneider,
Filmstyler Pictures GmbH

cutter
Dirk Farin

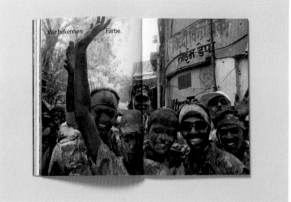

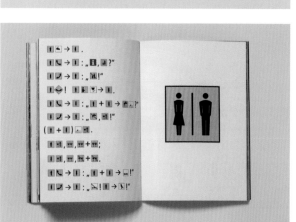

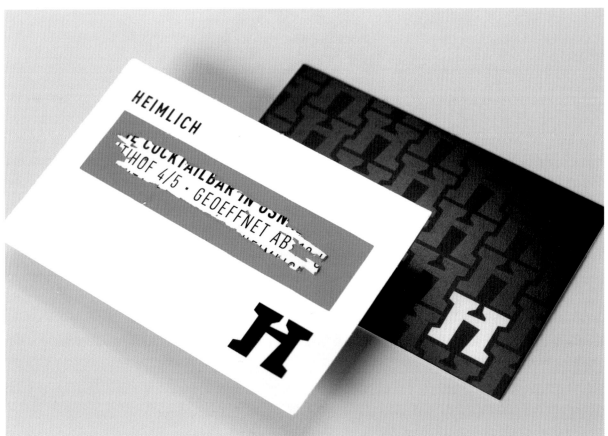

Heimlich Cocktailbar

[Visual Identity]

Heimlich is a cocktail bar located in the German town of Osnabrück. The aim in creating its visual identity was to mediate exclusivity, comfort, intimacy and tradition as well as to communicate the bar's unusual name, which means "secret" and "homey". Relying on a small visual vocabulary – including a simple monogram, handwritten typography, and a strong black/white contrast – has resulted in a remarkable visual language. The central theme of this new visual identity is the concealment of content by using a seal, rub-off ink, a stamp, and unobtrusive external lettering.

client
Schlukat, Remmert, Möllmann GbR, Osnabrück

design
DURST, Büro für konzeptionelles Design, Osnabrück

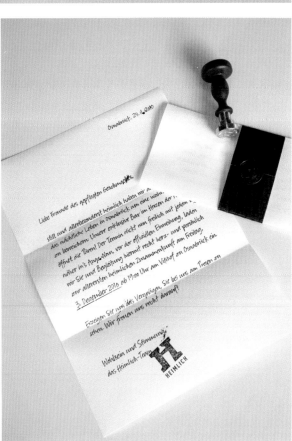

Katholische Kirche in Wuppertal

Katholisches Stadt-dekanat Wuppertal /
Catholic Deanery of the City of Wuppertal
[Corporate Design]

The logo for the Catholic Deanery of the City of Wuppertal is centred on Saint Lawrence and the Catholic community. Saint Lawrence distributed the property of the church to the poor, thus revealing community to be the real treasure. This tradition forms the basis for the design concept, which aims to convey a modern image of pastoral care. In Catholic tradition, the colour blue represents Heaven as well as intellectual transparency and clarity. The logo can also be flexibly adapted to other application areas within Wuppertal's Catholic parish.

client
Stadtdekanat Wuppertal

design
roemer und höhmann, strategisches design, Wuppertal

art direction/concept
Marion Roemer, Daniela Höhmann

graphic design
Daniela Höhmann

text
Marion Roemer

printing
Druckerei Huth

designer portrait
→ Vol.1: p.499

a b c d e f g h **i** j k l m n o p r s t u v z

Institut Ruđer Bošković

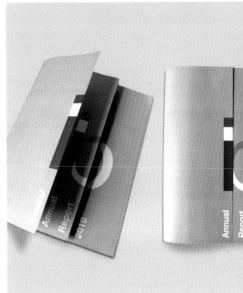

IRB
[Corporate Identity]

The visual identity of this Croatian research institute plays with the initials of its name, Institut Ruđer Bošković. The contours of the "i", "r" and "b" have been artfully merged into one single letter, with the overlapping areas marked by different colours to help the viewer differentiate and recognise each letter upon closer examination. Inspired by science and research, this corporate design provokes an analytical point of view. It also visually reflects the combination of several disciplines into one project.

client
IRB, Institut Ruđer Bošković, Zagreb

design
STUDIO INTERNATIONAL, Zagreb

creative direction/art direction
Boris Ljubičić

concept
Boris Ljubičić

graphic design
Boris Ljubičić

3d graphic
Igor Ljubičić

designer portrait
→ Vol.1: p.506

147

SCHÖNWALD

[Corporate Branding,
Brand Relaunch]

client
SCHÖNWALD,
Eine Marke der BHS tabletop AG

head of marketing
Birgit Dubberke
(BHS tabletop AG),
Sonja Schiebelhut
(SCHÖNWALD)

design
Schließke Werbeagentur,
Munich

head of advertising
Thomas Schließke

creative direction
Annette Hobday

art direction
Lars Breitenfeldt

concept
Dr. Ingrid Schließke

account management
Sabrina Scheicher

The new corporate branding of porcelain manufacturer SCHÖNWALD is inspired by the working atmosphere of a professional kitchen. The dynamic visual language shows hotel and catering scenes where porcelain plays a significant role. Aesthetics are, after all, essential in preparing, serving and enjoying food. The corporate brochure presents motifs suffused with light and set against a maritime blue background, creating a pleasant contrast to the white lettering. Additional product brochures stage noble porcelain as a flexible presentation means for imaginative dishes. The new brand image offers a glimpse behind the scenes while simultaneously communicating the full service range provided by a professional porcelain manufacturer.

IGH
[Corporate Identity]

client
Institut IGH d.d., Zagreb

design
STUDIO INTERNATIONAL,
Zagreb

creative direction/art direction
Boris Ljubičić

concept
Boris Ljubičić

graphic design
Boris Ljubičić

3d graphic
Igor Ljubičić

designer portrait
→ Vol.1: p.506

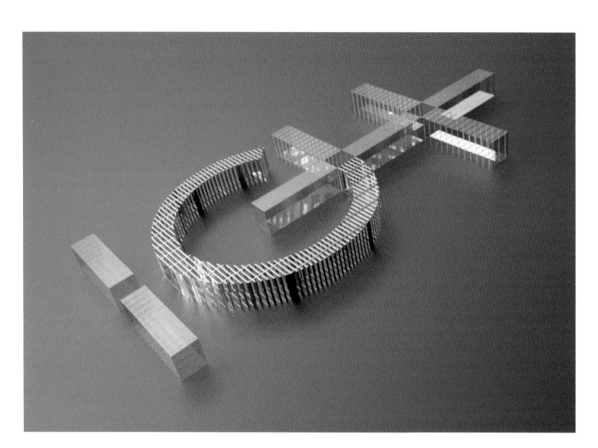

The Institut IGH d.d. has developed into a leading civil engineering consultancy in Central and Eastern Europe. The institute's services include planning, supervision and the construction of roads, bridges and other large structural and civil engineering projects. Based on a design language that is inspired by visual elements specific to the field of construction, the company logo features the letter "H" on a square grid. A colour scheme centred on red enhances the impact of the company's visual identity, which involves of a variety of advertising materials. The logo can be applied in 2D and 3D, with the 3D version realised in two versions of cross sections: either as a square or as a circle.

W'Law

[Visual Identity]

This puristic corporate design was developed for a Swiss law firm. Its partners, Weber and Wicki, present themselves with the unconventional name W'Law. The telling logo embodies a stunningly simple solution: the name has been reduced to a catchy typographic sign. It stands for integrating tailor-made solutions into traditional juristic work within a young company. Realised in monochrome dark blue, the logo possesses an appeal that is equally elegant and unobtrusive.

client
W'Law Weber Wicki Partners Ltd., Zürich

design
Gottschalk+Ash Int'l, Zürich

creative direction
Fritz Gottschalk

art direction
Sascha Lötscher

graphic design
Irmi Wachendorff

Constellium

[Corporate Identity]

The visual identity for the Constellium company takes up the versatile properties of aluminium as a metaphor for the brand's flexibility and versatility. The imagery is inspired by the basic elements of an atom in order to illustrate that in principle anything is possible. The corporate design conveys a distinct and differentiated corporate identity with a new orientation, as is illustrated by the brand statement "Ideas Materialized". In addition to the website, detailed stationery and an array of colourful advertising ensure that this company stands out from the competition.

client
Constellium

design
Interbrand, Paris/New York

team
Bertrand Chovet, Hugh Tallents, Odile Samson, Jason Brown, Carole de Faucamberge

Expodium

[Visual Identity]

Expodium is a production house that organises events in the public domain as a reaction to urban development in cities. The starting point for designing this visual identity was a honeycombed cube built from an isometric grid, featuring a letter "E" that appears to be cut from the left side of the cube. This logo serves as a typographic grid on all communication media and is complemented by tape used for highlighting, labelling and marking. Based on the idea of highlighter markers, flyers and posters are printed in fluorescent colours.

client
Expodium, Utrecht

design
CLEVER°FRANKE, Utrecht

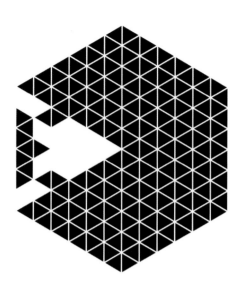

Ospelt.
Wo ma mi kennt. /
Ospelt.
Where they know me.

[Corporate Design]

Ospelt has grown from a village butcher's shop into a medium-size enterprise with branches specialised in butchery, event catering and corporate catering. The umbrella brand strategy integrates all three business fields, with the company name taking centre stage. The result is a purist identity with a striking "O" as the key visual element. The claim "Wo ma mi kennt" (Where they know me), spelled out in local dialect, underlines the regional character of the company. This corporate design is consistently applied to packaging, corporate clothing, the website, and to all advertising material.

client
Ospelt AG, Nendeln

design
Leone Ming, Visible Marketing, Schaan

creative direction
Leone Ming

art direction
Christine Böhmwalder

graphic design
Andreas Schenkel

text
Leone Ming

project management
Kathrin Konzett

Kö-Bogen Düsseldorf

[Corporate Design,
Communication Concept]

client
Landeshauptstadt Düsseldorf,
Dezernat Planen und Bauen,
Düsseldorf

design
Lutz Menze Design, Wuppertal

creative direction
Lutz Menze

graphic design
Janina Maisler, Astrid Grahl

text
ag-text

photography
Dirk Krüll, Düsseldorf

illustration
FSWLA Landschaftsarchitektur,
Düsseldorf

exhibition stand construction
Ueberholz GmbH, Wuppertal

The corporate design and communication concept for the Kö-Bogen construction project was developed with the objective of making sure citizens remain thoroughly informed. The well-known term "Kö", short for the street name Königsallee, was reinterpreted and implemented as a logo. This innovative composition fosters space and – together with the slogan "Zukunft für Düsseldorf" (Future for Düsseldorf) – communicates a vision. The central motto "Leben Gefühl Stadt" (Life Feeling City) complements this communication. A harmonic colour scheme of blue and green symbolises a lifestyle connected to nature. The transparent exhibition pavilion was conceived as a synthesis of communication, design and architecture; its modular construction is flexible, allowing the pavilion to be set up in various locations.

Schule für
Gestaltung Basel

[Corporate Design]

client
Schule für Gestaltung Basel /
School of Design Basel

design
Neeser & Müller, Basel

graphic design
Thomas Neeser, Thomas Müller

assistance
Ramon Classen, Daniela Rota,
Elisa Huber

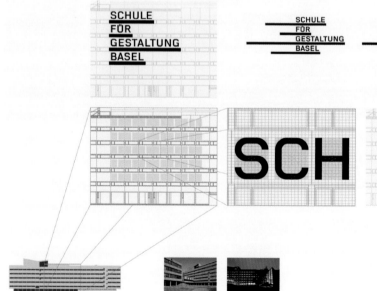

A modular structure lends this visual identity a maximum of flexibility. The School of Design Basel logo and corporate font are based on a grid derived from the school's facade architecture in Basel. This approach allows for significant variety in corporate appearance, with both logo and font highly flexible in application. Depending on the specific communication media, the word mark is aligned to the left, right or centre; and in addition to heavy typography, a distinctive underscore creates a high degree of recognition. The logo, asserting a strong black appearance, is complemented by colourful visual language. Moreover, the modular system allows for constant alterations in corporate design without losing the visual identity.

Beyond British-style Card

[Credit Card Design]

The Beyond British-style credit card features an outstanding visual language that is rather unusual for this industry. This expressive corporate design was developed in close collaboration with the British illustrator Si Scott. Artistic hand drawings decorate the set of cards with classic motifs, each contrasting with a different base colour on a white background. This future-oriented design approach has also been applied to television ads and various promotion materials, creating an identity that is full of life.

client
BCcard Co., Ltd., Seoul

design
BCcard design team

creative direction
Hojae Lee

art direction
Sehoon Oh

graphic design
Si Scott

designer portrait
→ Vol.1: p.462

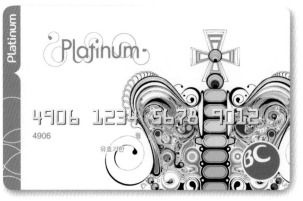

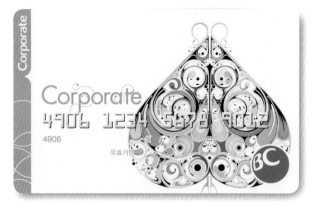

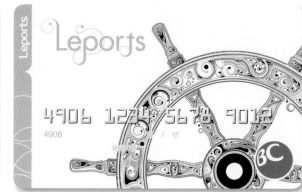

KEYREUS
[Image Brochure]

The challenge in staging the brand KEYREUS, a social network, involved toying with the idea of exclusiveness: sparking interest, personally inviting people to join, and yet not being open to just anyone. Manifesting surprising pictorial language, this high-quality image brochure offers a taste of the networking world and communicates its most important benefits. Refined production techniques such as thread stitching, hot foil stamping, and lamination – along with the key message "Superior networking happens behind closed doors" – convey a promising exclusiveness.

client
KEYREUS Holding AG, Zürich

design
grasundsterne Werbeagentur und Corporate Publishing GmbH, Munich

creative direction/art direction
Tim Grasmann

graphic design
Iris Fuchs

text
Mathias Dollinger

project management
Myriam Troester

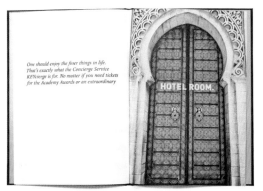

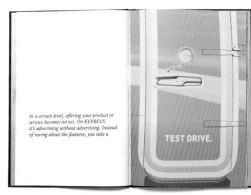

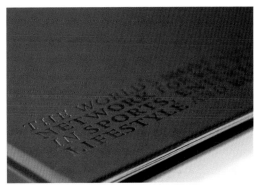

Timo Bader

[Corporate Design]

An artistic identity was created
for composer and arranger Timo
Bader: his corporate design
presents itself as serious and
valuable on the one hand, and as
creative and extraordinary on
the other. The logo is a combination of a light bulb and a clef,
symbolising musical ingenuity
and imagination. An unobtrusive
font and elegant colours underline the composer's artistic
character. All in all, the corporate
design comprises stationery,
business cards, envelopes,
invitation cards, a DVD/CD and
nameplates.

client
Timo Bader,
Düsseldorf

design
DIEGUTGESTALTEN,
Düsseldorf

creative direction
Andreas Ennemoser,
Goran Poznanovic

graphic design
Dirk Büchsenschütz

text
Alexander Arendt

designer portrait
→ Vol.1: p.471

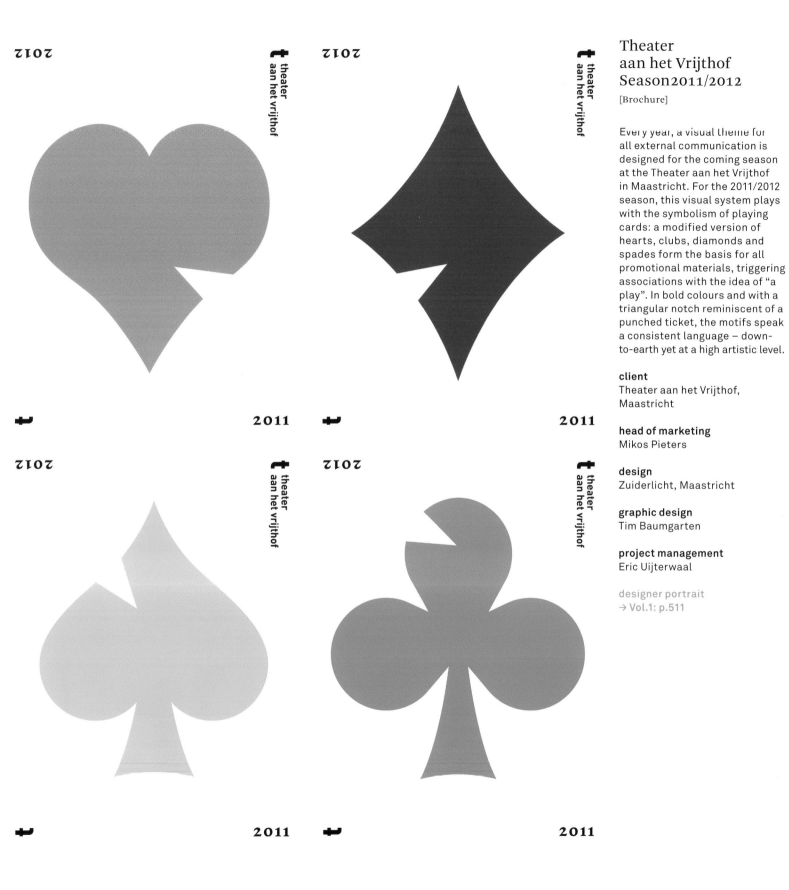

Theater aan het Vrijthof Season2011/2012

[Brochure]

Every year, a visual theme for all external communication is designed for the coming season at the Theater aan het Vrijthof in Maastricht. For the 2011/2012 season, this visual system plays with the symbolism of playing cards: a modified version of hearts, clubs, diamonds and spades form the basis for all promotional materials, triggering associations with the idea of "a play". In bold colours and with a triangular notch reminiscent of a punched ticket, the motifs speak a consistent language – down-to-earth yet at a high artistic level.

client
Theater aan het Vrijthof, Maastricht

head of marketing
Mikos Pieters

design
Zuiderlicht, Maastricht

graphic design
Tim Baumgarten

project management
Eric Uijterwaal

designer portrait
→ Vol.1: p.511

Seoul Zoo

[Corporate Identity]

The Seoul Zoo ranks among the ten largest zoos in the world and celebrated its 100th anniversary in 2009. According to its vision of being both an ecological zoo and a first-class theme park for the 21st century, the park's visual identity was optimised and an entire communication system created. In order to portray the zoo as a place where nature and humans grow together, the slogan "The Growing Planet" was developed. The zoo's logo shows the stylised face of a tiger, a familiar animal from ancient Korean fairy tales and traditional folk paintings.

client
Seoul Zoo, Gwacheon-si, Gyeonggi-do

design
CDR Associates, Seoul

team
Sung Chun Kim, Eunsil Yi, Hyuk Geun Yang

designer portrait
→ Vol.1: p.466

Greek Graphic Design & Illustration Awards

[Visual Identity]

The Greek Graphic Design & Illustration Awards is the leading event in Greece in the field of visual communication. Characterising its visual identity is a mergence of regional characteristics with contemporary design. To achieve this, a series of illustrations was developed which are inspired by ancient Cycladic figurines. These black, stylised interpretations lend the identity a dynamic and distinctive appeal. Further characteristic design elements are the unique typography and a colour palette that refers to ancient pottery.

client
Graphopress, Athens

design
Beetroot Design Group,
Thessaloniki

creative direction
Yiannis Charalambopoulos,
Alexis Nikou, Vangelis Liakos

art direction
Alexis Nikou

photography
Kostas Pappas

illustration
Alexis Nikou

music/sound design
Karolos Gakidis

animation
Giorgos Lemonidis

designer portrait
→ Vol.1: p.463

165

Shangri-La

[Hotel and Restaurants Branding]

On the occasion of their first European hotel opening in Paris, the Shangri-La Group had a new visual identity developed. The resulting design aesthetically associates the hotel group's Chinese origin with the original architecture of the Roland Bonaparte mansion. A harmoniously balanced colour concept with playful illustrations marks the different areas of the hotel, such as restaurants, bars and meeting rooms. The result is a self-contained identity inspired by the Belle Époque.

client
Shangri-La Hotel Paris

design
CB'a France, Brand Vision & Design Solutions, Paris

creative direction
Pierre Rhodes

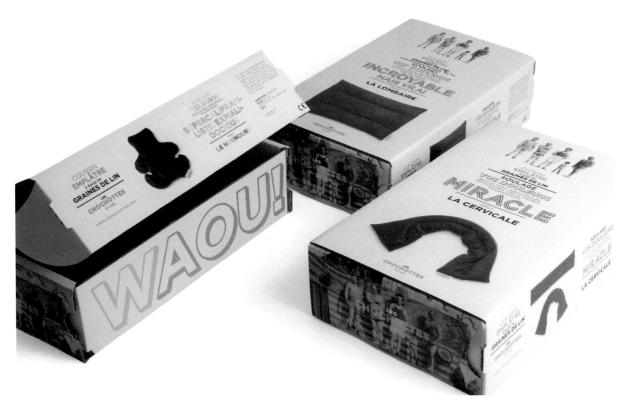

Les Chochottes

[Corporate Identity]

Les Chochottes is a family business that manufactures natural therapeutic products to assuage the intensity of illnesses such as tendonitis or stress. The company name means "the delicate" or "the refined" and fosters pride in those who look after themselves. The origins of this visual identity can be found in an old postcard depicting circus wrestlers standing next to a small boy, who is actually the great-grandfather of the company's founder. The apparent contradiction of muscle men and natural therapeutic products captures – with a touch of humour – the spirit of the brand.

client
Les Chochottes Laboratoire, Rodez

design
Run Design, Barcelona

creative direction
Xavier Roca Connétable, Eva Balart

graphic design
Thomas Rochon, Estefanía Aragüés, Xavier Roca Connétable

UUL –
National Art Museum,
Seoul
[Corporate Identity]

client
National Museum of
Contemporary Art,
Gwacheon-si, Gyeonggi-do

design
CDR Associates, Seoul

team
Sung Chun Kim, Eunsil Yi,
Hyung Seok Jung

designer portrait
→ Vol.1: p.466

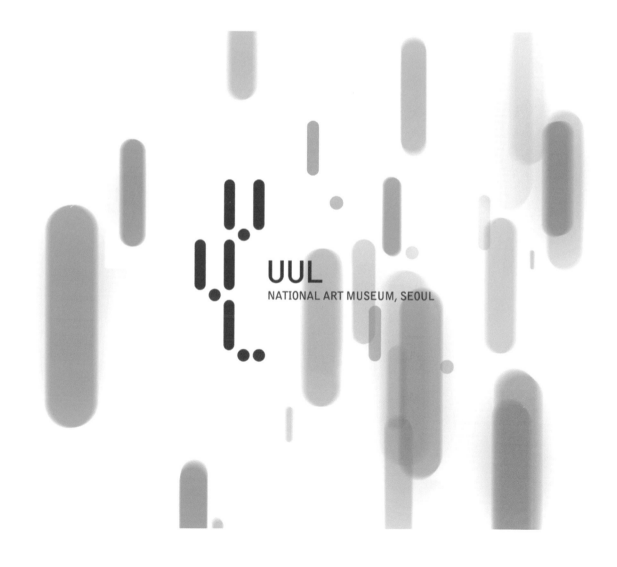

The logo of the National Museum of Contemporary Art in Seoul means "our museum next door" and emphasises the idea of a cultural institute that is attuned to the people. Not only the logo but also the entire corporate design is characterised by dots and lines smoothly blending into each other. This distinctive design feature, on the one hand, reflects the concept of the museum as a living organism. On the other hand, it expresses the connection of tradition and modernity through a binary system. Inspired by a digital world, the visual identity plays with the impact of two highly contrasting colours and the blending of their contours. The application of this design to various promotional materials achieves a multifaceted visual appearance.

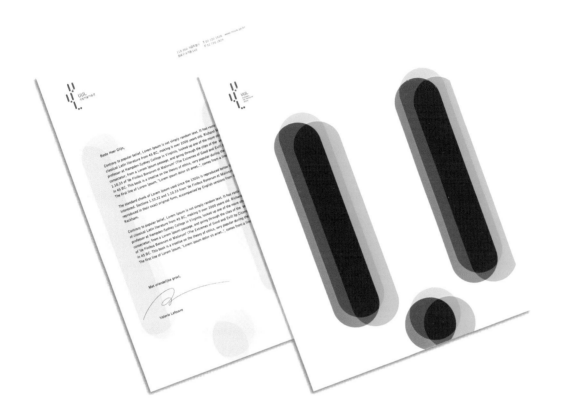

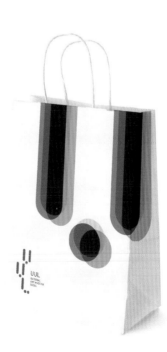

Netia

[Corporate Identity]

The adaptable design concept for Netia focuses on the importance of telecommunications as a rapidly developing industry. The result is a visual identity that reflects the cellular structure of the world by abandoning the idea of a fixed logo design. Instead, colourful dots in a variety of different positions create versatile motifs. Against a white background, this visual language has a highly distinctive and easy-going appeal. Complemented by the company's name, a consistent visual identity is created, which can be applied effectively to various media and advertising materials.

client
Netia S.A., Warsaw

design
White Cat Studio, Warsaw

creative direction/concept
Michał Łojewski

graphic design
Michał Łojewski,
Mariusz Lewczyk,
Marcin Kuczyński,
Tomasz Kuczma

project management
Ewa Ereńska-Szewczuk,
Paweł Łojewski

designer portrait
→ Vol.1: p.509

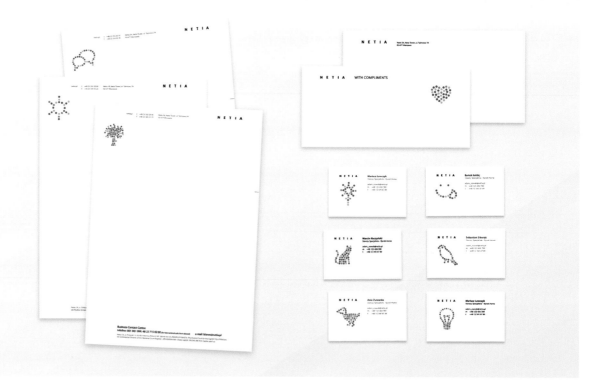

From grey mouse to blue frog – the NewRe brand story

[Corporate Design]

With the objective of building a progressive brand in the highly competitive financial industry, this extraordinary visual identity was developed for the New Re-insurance Company (NewRe). Integrated into the design concept are the relocation and expansion of the company, which boasts 50 new employees. The result is a surprising visual language to set NewRe apart from its competitors: photos of animals that are highly adaptable to their environments illustrate the flexibility of the company. And a comprehensive range of communication materials creates a consistent brand experience, both internally and externally.

client
NewRe, New Reinsurance Company, Zürich

design
Hotz Brand Consultants, Zug/Steinhausen

creative direction/art direction
Alexander Gächter

concept
Violetta Vitacca, Alexander Gächter

graphic design
Anna Fürer, Sidi Meier, Moreno Rossi

Erlebnis Charakter /
Experience with character

[Corporate Design]

client
Stiftung Berliner Philharmoniker,
Berlin

general manager
Martin Hoffmann

head of marketing
Natalie Schwarz

design
My Deer GmbH, Hamburg

creative direction
Tom Nagel

art direction
Hannes Drensler

graphic design
Andreas Teichmann

text
Jörg Bewersdorff

strategic planning
Robert Heim

project management
Christian Niemeyer

To enhance the recall factor of the brand identity, a new corporate design was developed for the Berliner Philharmoniker Foundation. With a sustainable communication concept geared to long-term use, it unifies the different orchestra institutions under one umbrella brand. The striking design element is a graphic mosaic inspired by the logo design. An extension of the logo's layout axes creates a flexible platform for presenting and highlighting various topics and events. The yellow segment of the mosaic is reserved as a brand stage for the logo on all communication materials. The characteristic formal vocabulary in the orchestration of surfaces and lines communicates the multifaceted experience of attending a concert.

Stiftung Sammlung Ziegler

[Corporate Design]

For a German art foundation with a top-class collection, a new and distinct visual identity was created. The objective was, in addition to designing a logo and corporate stationery, to develop consistent branding for the relaunch exhibition, including exhibition design, banners, posters and a website. An unobtrusive typographical approach – the negative intersection of two colour planes forming the "Ziegler-Z" – was intentionally selected so as to pay tribute to the foundation's tradition and history, and also to direct focus towards the artwork itself.

client
Dr. Michael Kuhlemann,
Stiftung Sammlung Ziegler,
Mülheim an der Ruhr

design
Jan Kromarek, zwobakk,
Mülheim an der Ruhr

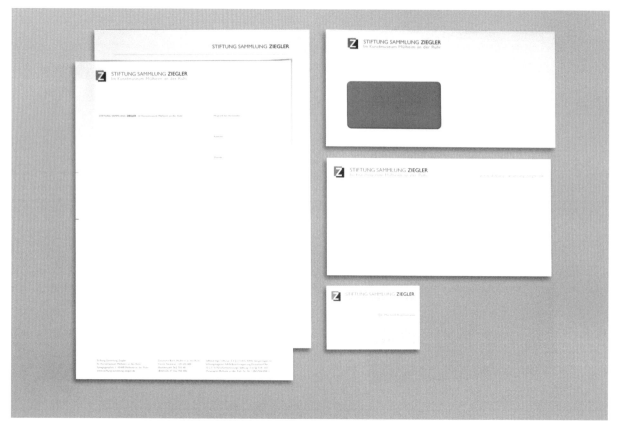

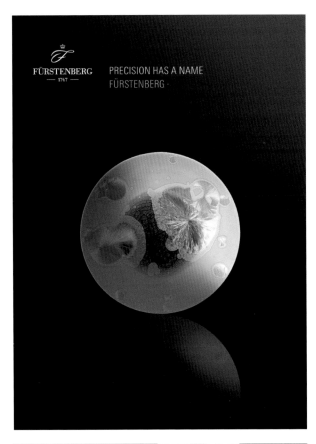

DER Porzellan
[Corporate Design]

In the repositioning of this long-standing porcelain manufacturer, the design objective was to develop a distinguishing corporate design as well as an attention-grabbing communication strategy – thereby appealing not only to established target groups but also to younger consumers. Using the masculine article "der" instead of the correct neuter article "das", the claim "FÜRSTENBERG – DER Porzellan" is initially perplexing and focuses on the masculine facets of the product: detailed precision, technical finesse and an uncompromising commitment to porcelain. The new visual identity sets the brand apart from competitors through its consistency, clarity and the distinctive use of black.

client
Porzellanmanufaktur FÜRSTENBERG GmbH, Fürstenberg

design
Interbrand, Cologne/Zürich

creative direction
Jens Grefen

graphic design
Jana Haserodt, Harald Mönch

customer advisory service
Anne Rehwinkel

3d design
Jens-Ole Kracht, Barbara Umann

FOR A STRONG IMAGE. An annual report can be a story about a company that is exciting to read. It do not have to be dull or boring. Even key company figures can be integrated easily into a layout that is original and award-winning.

The result is convincing when a well-balanced imagery, a clearly integrated CI and a consistent design concept are merged into an appealing and informative whole

red dot: grand prix

Zumtobel Annual Report 2009/10

The annual report by Zumtobel AG is subdivided into chapters on the main enterprise and its three daughter companies. The latter are each defined through different neon colours, a systematic design element that extends from the rubber bands strapped around the cover to the bookmarks and the design details of the book. The alternating colour scheme is complemented by a reduced approach in layout and typography: the distinctive font is used in one single type only, yet is allowed to vary in size. Full-page photographs and portraits of artists such as Olafur Eliasson, Zaha Hadid and James Turrell underline the expressive persuasiveness of this distinctively designed annual report and communicate the company as one of the leading manufacturers of lighting, as well as a science and technology leader and partner of international architects, light planners and artists.

Statement by the jury

»This annual report is marked by an outstanding combination of text and images. At first sight, its imposing cloth-bound format seems a bit too grand for an annual report and seems to make little sense in our digital age. However, the excellent quality shown in the images, typography, printing technique and the entire processing illustrates that this report delivers something that goes way beyond what digital communication can offer and communicate – it embodies an ideal merging of format, beauty and tactile pleasure.«

client
Zumtobel AG, Dornbirn

design
BOROS, Wuppertal / Berlin

art direction
Ingo Maak

project management
Ji-Yeun Youn

designer portrait
→ Vol.1: p.465

red dot: best of the best

Erfahrung / *Expertise*
Fresenius Medical Care
Annual Report 2010

"Erfahrung" (Expertise) – the topic of the Fresenius Medical Care annual report 2010 – is featured prominently in large-sized majuscules on the cover and is closer examined on the chapter separators through terms such as integration, motivation and competence, which serve as headlines that are visually highlighted by a clear, red typeface, partly overlapping images and text. Focusing on the topic of expertise, the report magazine reflects upon the company's philosophy towards attributes such as ability, observation and experience, thus clearly demonstrating what expertise means for the company and its position on the world market. The layout conveys the content, complemented by photo series and illustrations in black and white, in a vivid and charming manner and creates additional highlights for the individual chapters through subtly coloured paper. Characteristic of the trilogy, which was introduced in 2009, is the unique blend of corporate and financial report and magazine into one entity.

Statement by the jury

»The annual report, especially the merging of the three parts to form a whole, proves that an excellent concept, outstanding design and engaging texts can easily convey even complicated contexts. This work, featuring a range of surprisingly versatile layouts, is a sign of high expertise and demonstrates the future of commercial printing.«

client
Fresenius Medical Care AG & Co.
KGaA, Bad Homburg

design
häfelinger + wagner design,
Munich

creative direction
Frank Wagner

art direction
Sandra Gieseler,
Christina Strenger

project management
Sandra Loebich, Pamela Koroll

text
Dirk Böttcher, ag-text;
Charlotte Baumann,
Katharina Born,
Fresenius Medical Care

photography
Matthias Ziegler, David Maupilé

printing
Winfried Baldauf, Markus Maurer,
Eberl Print

designer portrait
→ Vol.1: p.478

red dot: best of the best

Kuoni Annual Report 2010

The annual report 2010 by Kuoni was issued in the form of a newspaper with three clearly defined sections, held together by an elegant-looking linen wrapper. The financial and market report sections feature a clear and straightforward layout that focuses on facts to inform readers about the company's financial and business development, as well as important news. The brand report section provides insights into Kuoni's intellectual exploration of the culture of travel through large photographs from around the world and text contributions from authors such as Orhan Pamuk, Hans Magnus Enzensberger and Roger Willemsen. The newspaper feuilleton-style was chosen for this multifaceted exploration because traditionally feuilletons feature lighter and more diverse content.

Statement by the jury

»This annual report is published in a form that is both a newspaper and a business report brochure at the same time, an unusual form of presentation that triggers curiosity and attention. What is special about it is the classic and meticulous design on the one hand, and the innovative approach to convey the message in the almost casual format of a newspaper on the other. A convincing concept that gets information across, separated clearly into business facts and an entertainment section.«

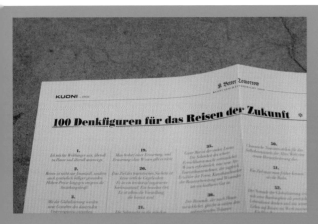

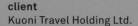

client
Kuoni Travel Holding Ltd.

design
Wolfgang Scheppe

**chief branding &
marketing officer**
Remo Masala, Kuoni

creative direction
Wolfgang Scheppe

art direction
Stephan Beisser, Büroecco;
Marie Letz

concept
Remo Masala, Kuoni;
Thomas Steinfeld,
Wolfgang Scheppe

project management
Simon Marquard,
Heidi Elsenhuber, Kuoni

red dot: best of the best

AICT Annual Report 2010

The design of the annual report for the AICT, the Advanced Institutes of Convergence Technology in Korea, combines the acronym of these institutes with the year of publication into a motif that is reminiscent of the shape of chemical compounds of various elements. This immediately visualises what the science institutes' research focuses on and illustrates the fact that AICT is an umbrella name for different institutes in various fields of research such as nanotechnology, IT and biology. The reduced and modern design with coloured circles, lines and diagonals visually marks the reference to natural sciences which is also on the inside of the report, and emphasises the high demands placed on environmental sustainability by the advanced research institutes through the selection of recycled paper. The content is thus presented in an unpretentious and clearly arranged layout.

Statement by the jury

»As mirror of a company, annual reports often reveal more through their appearance, style and focus on a special topic than through text. This work convinces by its reduction. Spaces and unobtrusive colours create an engaging and highly individual visual appearance without distracting from the content. Another astounding feature is the combination of two completely different fonts, a sans-serif linear Antiqua typeface of highly technical appeal with just as objective Asian characters.«

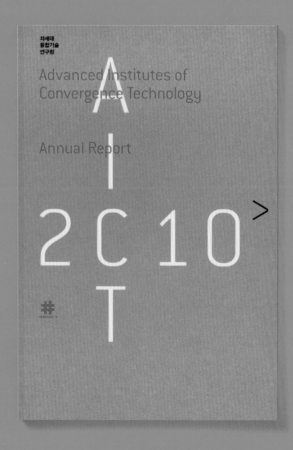

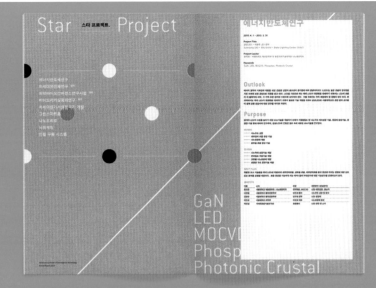

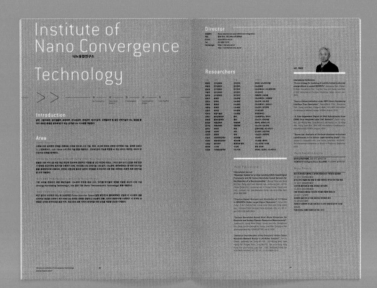

client
AICT, Advanced Institutes
of Convergence Technology,
Suwon-si, Gyeonggi-do

head of marketing
Yanghee Choi

concept
Mijun Kim, Joongseek Lee

design
Strike Communications,
Seoul

creative direction
Jangwoo Kim

art direction
Juhwan Kim

graphic design
Juhwan Kim

designer portrait
→ Vol.1: p.505

red dot: best of the best

GSK Annual Report 2010

GSK is one of the world's leading research-oriented pharmaceutical and healthcare companies – with an emphasis on the development of innovative pharmaceuticals to improve quality of life. The objective of this online annual report is to translate the strategy of the company, "Grow, Deliver, Simplify", into an appealing interactive format that communicates the company's business and social progress with a coherent and engaging approach. The result is the "The World of GSK" interface, a lively and colourful site explaining the individual company branches through objects and icons relating to specific business stories – and which, when clicked on, start moving. The health drinks, for example, stand for investment in healthcare, while a couple with an infant, presented in realistic graphics, highlights GSK's focus on the patient. The latter is substantiated in the next step with case studies, films, interviews, facts and slide shows. The website is backed up by a printed and online reporting suite and conveys the strategy of the company in a highly illustrative and convincing manner.

Statement by the jury

»This online annual report is one of the rare examples of a truly virtual application. The possibilities residing in the combination of multimedia elements, including films, animation, links and text, were realised with a professional, congenial approach as befits the topic. Only thus is it possible to ensure that content is read and understood – and it goes to show that, indeed, 'more is more'.«

client
GSK, GlaxoSmithKline,
Middlesex

design
SAS, London

creative direction
Al Baird

graphic design
Luke Helliwell,
Adam Holloway,
Enora Thépaut

project management
Laurélie Deardon

programming
Roger Domenech

designer portrait
→ Vol.1: p.500

red dot: best of the best

Woonpunt Annual Report 2010

The annual report of the Woonpunt housing corporation aims to visually express that an organisation standing at the centre of society will take action if it is no longer able to do its work well, but yet, as in this case, wants to continue offering its tenants a pleasant living environment in the future. In order to emphasise that corporations came under pressure, due to a new legislation passed by the Dutch government and the European Union in 2010, Woonpunt is presented as an activist. However, this goes further than just "yelling boo"; rather, Woonpunt is shown as an organisation that tackles issues and finds solutions. The report consists of ten printed sheets that unfold and, on one side, feature action-based messages, such as "Excuse me. What are we actually doing?" and "Enough = Enough", so to speak, messages with the appeal of a demonstration poster. The other side of the page features the past year in vivid and personal photo series, while the business figures are presented in clearly arranged lists.

Statement by the jury

»The annual report manages to communicate its message – the opposition against the current legislation as well as the commitment to assist the tenants of this corporation – in a convincing and authentic manner. Realised in the form of loose printed sheets and featuring a distinctive design, the report turns into a decisive statement.«

client
Woonpunt, Maastricht

design
Zuiderlicht, Maastricht

art direction
Melianthe Wouters, Zuiderlicht

concept
Eline Dekker, Zuiderlicht

text
Eline Dekker, Zuiderlicht

photography
Philip Driessen

illustration
Melianthe Wouters, Zuiderlicht

printing
Pascal Walters, Drukkerij Walters

designer portrait
→ Vol.1: p.511

Antibodies for Life MorphoSys Annual Report 2010

MorphoSys, a specialist in human antibodies, has matured from a pure antibody platform enterprise into a biopharmaceutical company with a rich pipeline of future therapeutic antibody products. The annual report underlines this development, following for the first time a design approach that, instead of creating a technological look, puts the human body centre stage. The combination of scientific illustrations and a straight image language direct the attention to concrete case studies. The annual report is printed on a paper stock that feels pleasant and interesting to ouch, underlining the purist layout and human-based approach to design.

client
Dr. Claudia Gutjahr-Löser, MorphoSys AG, Martinsried/ Planegg

design
3st kommunikation, Mainz

creative direction
Marcel Teine

art direction
Astrid Baumann

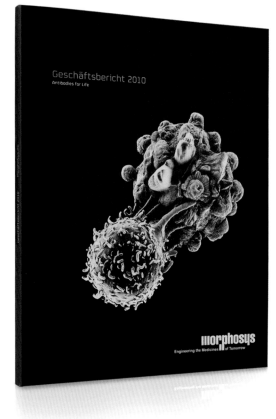

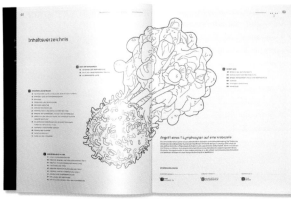

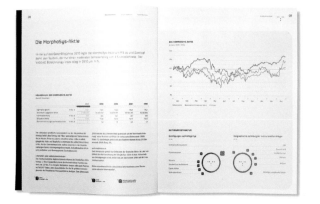

Vielfalt erfahren / *Experience D(r)iversity* Volkswagen Annual Report 2010

The car manufacturer Volkswagon offers mobility in any vehicle class and operates internationally. The 2010 annual report, published in both German and English, tells of people who are on the move and make a difference. In doing so, each story represents a facet of the company's diversity. Altogether 17 stories of the group and its brands provide interesting insights into Volkswagen's world of mobility. This concept is consistently applied, from the banderole on the cover to the printing on every page in each chapter.

client
Stefanie Lioe,
Volkswagen AG, Wolfsburg

design
3st kommunikation, Mainz

creative direction
Florian Heine

art direction
Caroline Klement

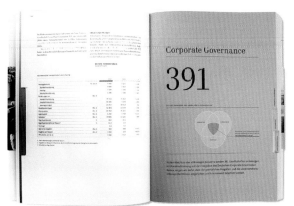

KFA
Annual Report 2009

The annual report of the Kölner
Freiwilligen Agentur (Cologne
Volunteer Centre) provides an
overview of voluntary work in the
city. It also serves to prove that
print finishing techniques do not
always require a large budget.
The defining design element is
the colour yellow, which is used
as a distinctive colour to create
high-impact highlights and a
clear structure. Two different
types of paper stock – uncoated
for the business figures and coated for all other pages – facilitate
visual and tactile orientation.

client
KFA, Kölner Freiwilligen Agentur,
Cologne

design
muehlhausmoers
corporate communications

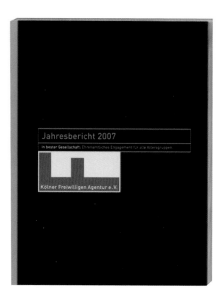

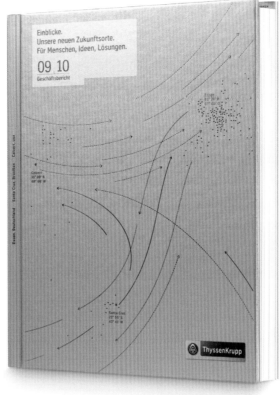

Einblicke. Unsere neuen Zukunftsorte. Für Menschen, Ideen, Lösungen. / *Insights. Our new locations. For people, ideas, solutions.* Thyssen-Krupp Annual Report 2009/10

As a blend of an informative atlas and a vivid travel diary, the annual report by Thyssen-Krupp invites readers to set out on a journey exploring new site locations. The report comes in magazine format and covers not only economic aspects but also values such as sustainability and corporate responsibility. Inspired by the typical look of climate maps, the creative idea of "streams" is implemented in the shape of streamlines. These illustrate in a vivid manner what impulses the new site locations imply for the company group, as well as the local economy, the region and its people.

client
ThyssenKrupp, Essen

design
häfelinger + wagner design, Munich

creative direction
Annette Häfelinger

art direction
Stefanie Kuttig

graphic design
Florian Doeffinger

project management
Stefan Schwarz

photography
Sorin Morar

printing
Ulrich J. Eberl, Eberl Print

designer portrait
→ Vol.1: p.478

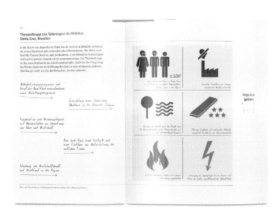

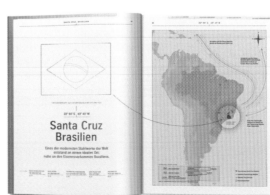

Vorwerk
Annual Report 2010

Putting centre stage Vorwerk's internationality as well as its close connection to the people, which characterises the company's direct sales, the 2010 annual report focuses on "living environments". Playful design elements, unusual illustrations and a dash of self-irony underline the individuality of a family-run enterprise and the permitted degrees of freedom within this company. The challenge for the designers was to modernise the existing design concept, yet remain true to its long tradition.

client
Vorwerk & Co. KG, Wuppertal

design
OrangeLab, Düsseldorf

creative direction
Wilfried Vollmary, Tina Peine, OrangeLab

project management
Martin Kraus, OrangeLab

text
Michael Weber, Alexandra Stolpe, Vorwerk; Thilo Redlinger, OrangeLab

photography
Ute Kaiser, Düsseldorf

illustration
Silja Götz, Madrid; Romy Blümel, Berlin

printing
Jan Vetter, Dirk Gottschalk, Druckhaus Ley + Wiegandt, Wuppertal

GESCHÄFTSBERICHT 2010

BMW GROUP

BMW Group Annual Report 2010

This Blue Angel certified annual report by BMW Group is the third part of a trilogy focusing on the topic of sustainability as a marketing strategy. The report is divided into four chapters, each designed to individually reflect on their topics. Held in a documentary style, the images place people at the heart of the subject matter. The repeated images on the covers serve to illustrate the link between people and cars. While the main cover shows a scene from the people's perspective, the cover of the image brochure shows it from an external perspective.

client
Christian Finkenzeller,
BMW AG, Munich

design
häfelinger + wagner design,
Munich

creative direction
Frank Wagner

art direction
Stefan Kaderka

graphic design
Christina Bee

project management
Frank Wagner

photography
Julian Baumann, Antonia Gern,
Marek Vogel, Andreas Reeg

printing
Michael Wachter, Mediahaus
Biering

designer portrait
→ Vol.1: p.478

2010's Fairest
Annual Report

client
LemonAid Beverages GmbH,
Hamburg

design
Jung von Matt AG, Hamburg

creative direction
Wolf Heumann,
Peter Kirchhoff

art direction
Annika Frey

graphic design
Katja Kirchner

text
Christina Drescher,
Peter Kirchhoff

project management
Antje Lindenberg

WE DON'T DISCRIMINATE – NOT BETWEEN HEADLINE AND COPY, AND NOT BETWEEN PLANTATION WORKER AND BOARD MEMBER.

TRADITIONAL BUSINESS MODELS ARE ALL ABOUT ONE THING – PRO-FIT. LEMONAID BEVERAGES IS DIFFERENT. IT IS NOT INTERESTED IN RUSHING TO PLUG GAPS IN THE MARKET, BUT IS MORE CON-CERNED WITH HELPING TO PLUG THE FAIRNESS GAP. IN SHORT, IT IS A SOCIAL BUSINESS. AS THE FOUNDERS OF THIS START-UP, WE

WANTED ABOVE ALL TO SUPPORT REGIONS THAT NORMALLY GET A RAW DEAL FROM INTERNATIO-NAL COMMERCE. OUR VERY FIRST MOVES ALREADY MADE IT CLEAR THAT WE WERE NOT BOUND BY CONVENTION, AS INSTEAD OF MIXING SYNTHETIC CHEMICALS IN HIGH-TECH LABS, WE EXPERI-MENTED WITH NATURAL PRO-DUCTS IN OUR KITCHENS AT HOME. ALL OUR EFFORTS WERE GUIDED BY ONE AIM: TO MAKE THE WORLD A SLIGHTLY FAIRER PLACE. THE RESULT WAS A RANGE OF SOFT DRINKS, SUSTAINABLY PRODUCED FROM FAIR TRADE RAW MATERIALS, THAT HAVE IN-STANTLY GAINED CULT STATUS.

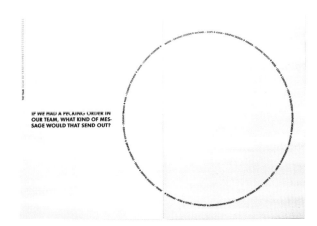

IF WE HAD A PECKING ORDER IN OUR TEAM, WHAT KIND OF MES-SAGE WOULD THAT SEND OUT?

To reflect the ambitious fair-trade philosophy of soft-drink manu-facturer LemonAid, an unconven-tional annual report was devel-oped at the end of 2010 which aspires to fill a unique position. With the motto "The world's fair-est annual report", the publication showcases a humorous page layout that is fully consistent with the social orientation of the fair-trade philosophy. Conscious-ly making no distinction between upper and lower case letters, every letter is treated fairly.
In addition, colour values, bar graphs and page numbers also follow this "fair" approach.

WE TREAT EVERYONE THE SAME – EVEN THE BARS IN OUR BAR CHARTS.

ALL THE INGREDIENTS FOR OUR PRO DUCTS ARE 100%* *except for water SOURCED THROUGH FAIR TRADE CHAN NELS – AND TO SHOW OUR TOTAL COM-MITMENT TO EQUALITY, WE'VE EVEN LE T THE FOOTNOTE INTO THE HEADLINE.

LEMONAID+

Neubau /
New Building

[Company Magazine]

The in-house magazine published by E.ON Ruhrgas (ERG) aims at motivating employees, especially in turbulent times. This special New Building issue, with information about the new company building at the Brüsseler Platz in Essen, was developed on the occasion of the upcoming relocation. The design concept makes use of versatile design elements in a magazine style: a large-sized, spacious typography is complemented by appealing illustrations, while the content conveys information on the strategy of the company as well as on the colleagues.

client
E.ON Ruhrgas, Essen

design
Lesmo, Düsseldorf

Two decades energy saving
Vlehan Annual Report 2010

The annual report of Dutch Vlehan association documents to what degree the energy consumption of household appliances was reduced over the past two decades. The design concept illustrates and compares the consumption of household appliances in 1990 with the consumption in 2010, both in text and image, and in an impressive way. A fold-out poster shows both, illustrations of a modern kitchen and illustrations of a kitchen of the 1990s. In addition, the annual report features two different sorts of paper, is staple bound and, together with the poster, comes in a firm folder.

client
Vlehan, Zoetermeer

design
52 graden noorderbreedte, Amsterdam

concept
Edith Lorentz,
Piet Jan van Bohemen

graphic design
Edith Lorentz

project management
Femke Roeleveld

printing
Druno en Dekker

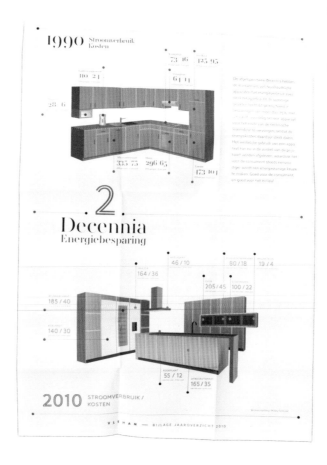

Verbundbericht 2009 / *Annual Report 2009*

Collage graphics are the key illustrative element in the 2009 annual report by public transport company Verkehrsverbund Bremen/Niedersachsen. Analogous to a group made up of several member companies, a collage creates a new entity by using different elements. The graphic elements consist partially of local public transport motifs and partially of elements that visually emphasise certain text statements. The collages invite the reader to take a closer look at the themes and realise the connections between graphics and text.

client
Verkehrsverbund Bremen/
Niedersachsen GmbH (VBN),
Bremen

design
construktiv GmbH,
Bremen

head of marketing
Kai Tietjen

creative direction
Christoph Reiprich

text
Hermann Priklenk

project management
Sarah Drücker

illustration
Christoph Reiprich

365 Tage Geschichten – Jahresbericht 2010 / *365 days of history – Annual Report 2010*

For the second time in a row, the annual report for Germany's Aktion Mensch lottery combines transparent reporting with exceptional image communication, in order to show the impact of the generated funds. Open to unconventional ideas, the design solution comes as a tear-off calendar that begins on the day of the general meeting and provides in-depth information in a visually enticing manner. The calendar is supplemented by a magazine, a consolidated figures brochure, as well as easily accessible media for people with disabilities.

client
Aktion Mensch,
Bonn

design
Strichpunkt Design,
Stuttgart

creative direction
Kirsten Dietz,
Jochen Theurer

graphic design
Jan Hartwig

project management
Alexandra Storr

project management client
Ulrike Jansen

photography
Eva Häberle

illustration
Frauke Berg

text
Anette Frisch, Anne Stolle

akf bank
Annual Report 2010

To set out and achieve new objectives – the annual report of akf bank impressively illustrates the dynamics of this process. Throughout the whole work a three-dimensional computer graphic visualises this windy road to the destination. Artful light reflections mark turnarounds and deviations. Inside the annual report, the combination and juxtaposition of strictly linearly arranged information and animated illustrations create an exciting yet also harmoniously balanced and appealing visual space.

client
akf bank, Wuppertal;
corviscom gmbh, Essen

design
herzogenrathsaxler design,
Düsseldorf

Welt-Zeit / *World-Time* TÜV SÜD Annual Report 2010

To express the idea that safety is a "product" that is always highly important, no matter where you are, the designers of this annual report use an aesthetically appealing image language. With the appeal of a travel magazine, readers experience the world of TÜV SÜD, its customers and partners. A journey into four different time zones communicates that the company is not only available at any time of day, but also anywhere on the globe, committing itself to being able to guarantee safety at all times.

client
TÜV SÜD,
Munich

design
Strichpunkt Design,
Stuttgart

creative direction
Kirsten Dietz,
Jochen Rädeker

art direction
Agnetha Wohlert

concept
Jochen Rädeker

project management client
Jörg Riedle

customer advisory service
Beate Flamm

project management
Anja Mittelstädt

photography
Tillmann Franzen,
Liu Bowen,
Andreas Hofweber,
Andreas Pohlmann

Uhde
Book of Ideas 2010

[Company Profile]

client
ThyssenKrupp Uhde GmbH,
Dortmund

design
act&react Werbeagentur GmbH,
Dortmund

head of marketing
Dr. Detlef Markmann

creative direction
Thomas Szabo

art direction
Dominik Jacky

text
Petra Weber-Lenz

project management
Emily Benecke

designer portrait
→ Vol.1: p.459

The 2010 Uhde company profile, created as a book of ideas, provides a very personal insight into the world of the engineering branch of ThyssenKrupp AG. The annual report represents past year's facts and figures, the range of services and products, news of all worldwide operating subsidiaries and associated companies, as well as ideas by employees. A customised font, vivid sketches and photos, consistently positioned spread notes, surprising elements of tactile quality and many stories reflect on the company's claim "Engineering with ideas" and bring it to life in an easy-to-understand manner. The book of ideas can be individualised and is available in German and English.

We Deliver the Future
OCI Annual Report
2010

The annual report by OCI, an international supply company for polysilicon, was created as a joint project between an Asian and a German design agency. The title, in particular, serves as a reminiscence of the seminal material that this company is providing. The landscape format of the report is inspired by roadshow presentations and supports the clear imagery. In an analogy to polysilicon and carbon, all other graphic elements were designed to follow rough black-and-white aesthetics. The content points out emerging markets and potentials.

client
OCI Company Ltd., Seoul

design
The Third Age, Seoul;
Strichpunkt Design, Stuttgart

creative direction
Jochen Theurer, Strichpunkt

art direction
Gi-Hwan Kim, The Third Age;
Jan Hartwig, Christopher Biel,
Strichpunkt

strategic planning
Jin-Wook Park, The Third Age;
Jochen Rädeker, Beate Flamm,
Strichpunkt

graphic design
So-Dam Park, Jung Nam,
The Third Age;
Jan Hartwig, Strichpunkt

text
Beate Flamm, Strichpunkt;
Kyung-Wha Park, The Third Age

project management
Daehong Communications
Design Center

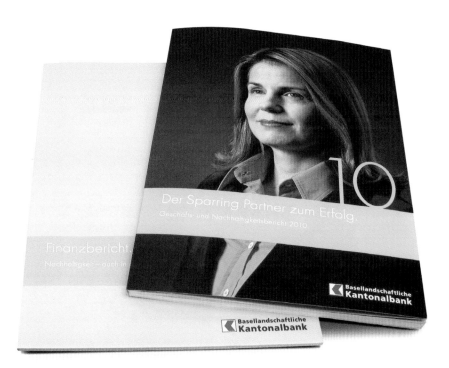

Der Sparring Partner zum Erfolg – Geschäfts- und Nachhaltigkeitsbericht 2010 / *The sparring partner for success – Annual and Sustainability Report 2010*

The Basellandschaftliche Kantonalbank positions itself as a sparring partner for its customers. The 2010 annual report takes up this idea by portraying its customer consultants who may not be well known to its customers, if at all. Profiles and brief interviews explain each individual's role. QR codes bridge the gap between the printed medium of the annual report and the online world, where videos, web pages and daily updated information can be found. For ecological reasons, the report's image and financial sections were split into two brochures.

client
Basellandschaftliche
Kantonalbank, Liestal

design
BSSM Werbeagentur AG, Basel

head of marketing
Christoph Loeb

creative direction
Urs Schneider

art direction
Pascal Rehmann

concept
Hannes Müller

customer advisory service
Claudia Paganini

photography
Maurice Haas

Hier bewegt Shape 2012 / *Shape 2012 is driving change* Metro Annual Report 2010

The annual report by Metro Group conveys the efficiency and value-adding programme Shape 2012 to shareholders, investors, analysts and employees. As a combination of transparent reporting with brand-building image communication, it highlights design details such as original proof sheets of own-label packagings and is complemented by an online report with functional and entertaining features as well as links and videos. The enclosed, lavishly illustrated report magazine takes the reader on a journey into the booming metropolis of Shanghai.

client
Metro AG,
Düsseldorf

design
Strichpunkt Design,
Stuttgart

creative direction
Jochen Rädeker,
Jochen Theurer

graphic design
Annabel Humel

text
Ketchum Pleon

project management
Beate Flamm

project management client
Katharina Meisel

photography
Olaf Unverzart

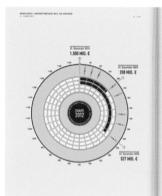

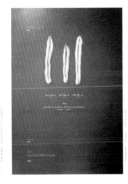

Facing Markets Beiersdorf Annual Report 2010

With the new business strategy "Focus on Skin Care. Closer to Markets", the 2010 annual report aims to raise Beiersdorf's profile. The title refers to the 100th anniversary of the Nivea brand. Inside the report an inventive visual language vividly illustrates the presentation of the annual results. In addition, six eye-catching portraits convey different consumer expectations of ideal skin care. Short text passages point to the regional characteristics of the respective market. This is complemented by employees who give an insight into their particular field of work.

client
Beiersdorf AG,
Hamburg

design
Strichpunkt Design,
Stuttgart

creative direction
Jochen Rädeker

art direction
Kirsten Dietz, Tobias Nusser

project management
Anja Mittelstädt

project management client
Linja Natalie Osann

photography
Götz Wrage,
Bernd Opitz

Spielzeitheft
2011/12 /
Season Programme
2011/12

Featuring a high-quality binding, the season programme of Theater Dortmund informs the public about the versatile spectrum in the fields of opera, ballet, child and youth theatre, concerts and plays. The design concept solved the challenge of unifying the five independent branches through an interplay of layers, so that readers can easily browse into the single branches. On the inside the purist layout of the season programme convinces through elegant black-and-white portraits and a clear typography printed on uncoated paper.

client
Theater Dortmund

organisation
Stefan Kriegl

design
xhoch4 | design plus kultur /
xhoch4 | design plus culture

design team
Boris Schmelter,
René Arbeithuber

photography
Tanja Kernweiss

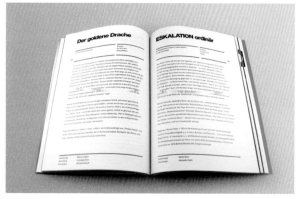

Unicer
Management Report

The design concept of Unicer's 2011 management report is based on the most important priorities of the company for a sustainable future. The six major objectives of the company are illustrated in numerical pictograms on the cover and throughout the report, which aims at a "handmade" look, reflecting the company's concern for the environment, recycling and sustainability. The collage of paper cut-outs with texts and images appears like a sketchbook of the company's activities during the last year.

client
Unicer Bebidas, S.A.,
São Mamede de Infesta/Portugal

design
LMS Brand Expression & Design,
Porto

creative direction
Luís Miguel Soares

art direction
João Oliveira

graphic design
João Oliveira, Luís Miguel Soares

printing supervisor
Graça Bahia

END THE LIES

[Annual Report]

With the motto "Ending the Lies", the annual report of the American Human Rights Campaign uses the words of those speaking out for or against human rights. The oversized self-mailer format and the thin, eco-friendly paper emphasise the campaign's easy-to-remember and cost-conscious design concept. The versatile use of typography illustrates the significance and the scope of the report, while an atypical colour scheme lends the rather text-heavy annual report a unique character and a certain sense of lightness.

client
Human Rights Campaign,
Washington DC

design
DESIGN ARMY, Washington DC

creative direction
Jake Lefebure, Pum Lefebure

art direction
Pum Lefebure

graphic design
Sucha Becky

printing
Mosaic Inc

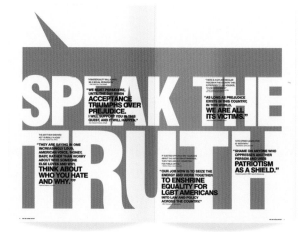

MEHR ERREICHEN / *RUN BETTER*

[Online Annual Report]

Inspired by the design of a printed report, the online annual report of SAP AG presents stories of success. Large cross-faded images, which at the same time convey transparency, attract readers' attention. Making extensive use of JavaScript, the online report provides features for mobile reading devices, including an interactive chart of key figures and a media centre where information and documents can be compiled and compared to individual needs. A main menu in the form of a banderole allows direct access to specific topics.

client
SAP AG, Walldorf

design
Kuhn, Kammann & Kuhn GmbH, Cologne

creative direction
Jan-Piet van Endert

art direction
Claudia Mislin

customer advisory service
Christiane von Bonin, Wendelin Auer

strategic planning
Viola Kammann

BLS Annual Report
2010

client
BLS AG, Bern
Stephan Appenzeller,
Hugo Wyler

design
hilda ltd., Zürich

creative direction
Jiri Chmelik

concept
Jiri Chmelik, Eric Hasler

graphic design
Jiri Chmelik

strategic planning
Eric Hasler

photography
Jiri Chmelik, Tobias Madörin,
Daniel Rihs

Was ist
besser
als gut?

Finanzbericht

Die operativ erfreulichen Leistungs-
zahlen führten zu einem höheren
Betriebsertrag. Gleichzeitig stie-
gen aber auch die Betriebsaufwen-
dungen, sodass das operative
Ergebnis dem Vorjahr entspricht.
Das Finanzergebnis wird durch
den schwachen Euro geprägt. Das
Konzernergebnis zeigt nach wei-
teren Sanierungsmassnahmen für
die Pensionskasse einen Gewinn
von CHF 4,0 Mio.

With the objective of expressing the vision of the traditional
Swiss mobility company BLS, an
innovative design was chosen for
the annual report. The publication consists of two parts: the
2010 annual report and the BLS
Gazette. This consumer-oriented
magazine, which is also available
in all BLS trains, popularises and
adds an emotional perspective
to topics of the business report
in an unconventional form. The
business figures are visualised
by futuristic illustrations within a
closely defined range of colours.
An attention-grabbing inlay en-
titled "The Joy of Travelling" was
created by the Swiss poet and
rapper Kutti MC.

Vielfalt
als Stärke

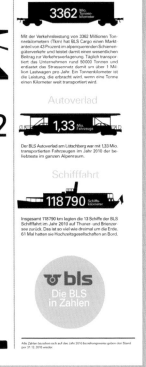

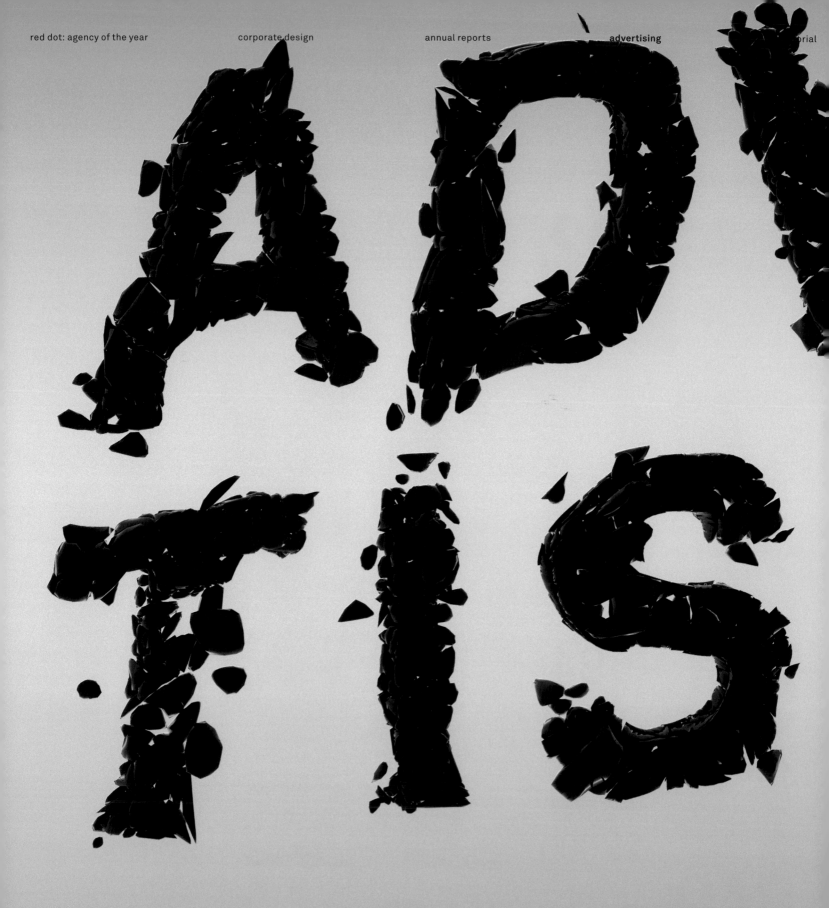

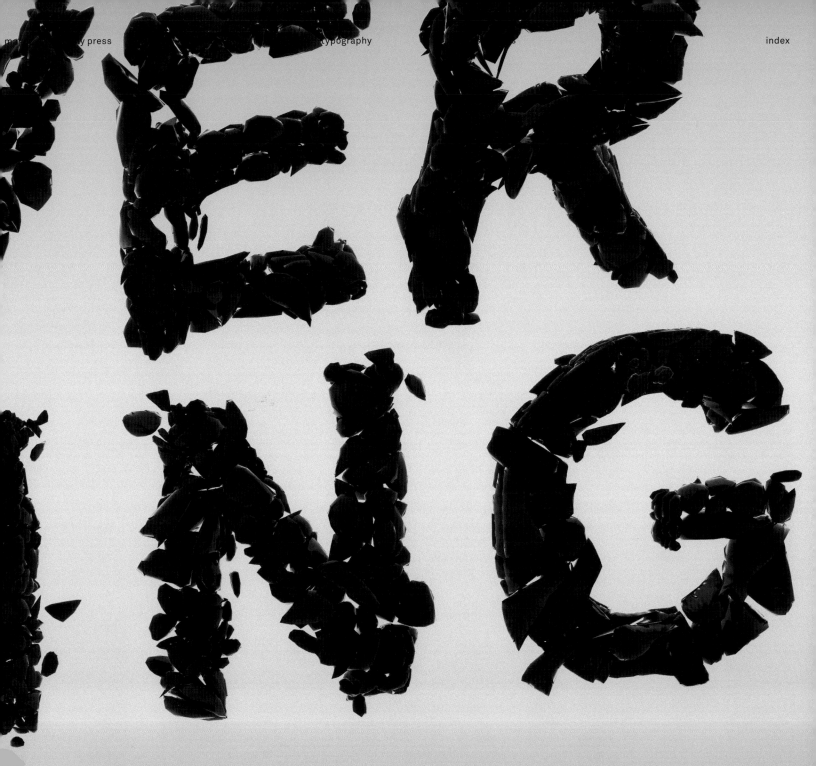

IMPRESSING CUSTOMERS OVER ALL CHANNELS. New customers don't grow on trees. They have to be won over, and this is achieved with a surprising design that places products at their best.

Interdisciplinary advertising measures thereby lead to creative campaigns that are striking, revolutionary and outstandingly distinctive. Whether through traditional or "new" media channels: the concept always has to provide the customer with decisive advantage.

Kopiert ruhig weiter / *Copy On Campaign*

[Print Campaign]

For every legal music download today there are six illegal downloads. Internet piracy and acquiring illegal copies of music via the Internet destroy not only the livelihood of musicians, but also that of a whole industry. The print campaign "Kopiert ruhig weiter" (Copy On) raises this issue by showing covers of legendary music albums, such as by the Beatles, the Rolling Stones and Pink Floyd, which have been copied over and over again on a standard black-and-white photocopy machine – until they were barely recognisable as the pieces of music history they represent. The campaign thus impressively demonstrates the effect of copying. The more you copy, the more you lose.

Statement by the jury

»The idea for this work is a very strong one: take the covers of world-famous music albums and repeatedly photocopy them until they become blurred and hardly identifiable. An impressive solution for communicating the message, which will surely leave an impact on the young target group and raise their awareness of the effects that their actions have.«

client
Axel Springer Mediahouse
Berlin GmbH, Berlin

design
Ogilvy Frankfurt,
Frankfurt/Main

creative direction
Dr. Stephan Vogel,
Helmut Meyer

art direction
Eva Stetefeld

text
Taner Ercan,
Dr. Stephan Vogel

consultant
Peter Heinlein

project consultant
Georg Fechner

art buying
Christina Hufgard

designer portrait
→ Vol.1: p.494

red dot: best of the best

wall-of-fame.com

[Advertisements]

These print advertisements for the celebration of edding's 50th anniversary aim to convey that edding pens for the past 50 years have sparked the creativity of the people who use them. The campaign is based on the idea of rendering a virtual experience of the fact that the quality of an edding pen is best shown when it is used for writing, painting or illustration. Thus, for the anniversary event, an interactive live-drawing-board was developed at wall-of-fame.com for all Internet users to participate in and add further details to a collaborative piece of art that thus changes and grows all the time – meanwhile it consists of over 150,000 drawings not just from illustrators but also other people from over 150 countries. Each advertisement shows one section of this enormous piece of art, a unique example that both demonstrates worldwide creativity and indicates how much space can be filled with writing or illustrations using the available ten markers.

Statement by the jury

»This ad campaign convinces through its self-evident content. Without the need for explanatory words, it shows what it is about and what edding pens can be used for. Furthermore, it impressively demonstrates the creation of something unique, an artwork to which people around the globe contribute by using the same 'tool' and which also reflects their individual style.«

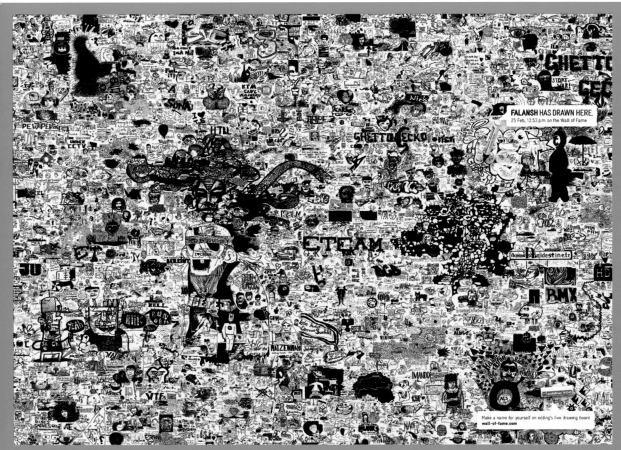

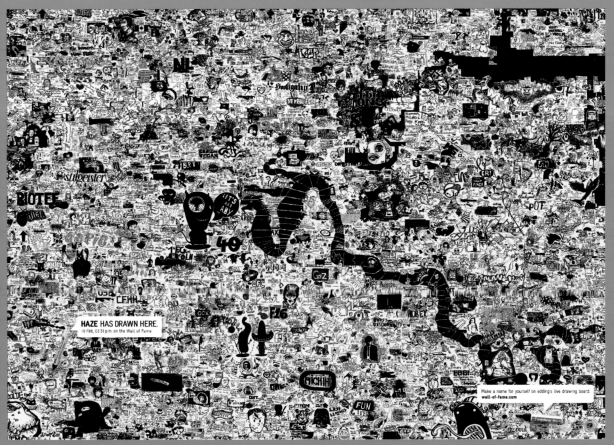

client
edding International GmbH,
Ahrensburg

design
kempertrautmann gmbh,
Hamburg

creative direction
Simon Jasper Philipp,
Christoph Gähwiler,
Stefan Walz,
Gerrit Zinke,
Christian Fritsche

art direction
Simon Jasper Philipp,
Stefan Walz,
Florian Schimmer

text
Christoph Gähwiler,
Samuel Weiß,
Michael Götz

customer advisory service
Niklas Kruchten,
Elisabeth Einhaus,
Andrea Bison,
Dorothea Feurer (Freelancer)

DREAM: HOME

[Poster]

Every year the Child Welfare League Foundation accompanies 200 children on their search for a new home. The biggest dream of orphans and abandoned children is not only that one about basic provision for life but also about a real home. Accordingly, the main motif of this image campaign shows a child that protects itself from rain. The aesthetically appealing mixture of traditional calligraphy and ink drawings was edited by contemporary computer techniques, creating an original and self-contained visual language.

client
Child Welfare League Foundation, Taipei

design
Hufax arts

creative direction/art direction
Fa-Hsiang Hu

text
Alain Hu, Janette Huang

illustration
Fa-Hsiang Hu

graphic design
Fei Hu, Di Hu

account management
Kai-I Lee

designer portrait
→ Vol.1: p.482

The New Year Card for the Year of the Rabbit

[Promotional Card]

This New Year card reinterprets the importance of the year of the rabbit in the Chinese calendar. As part of a promotional campaign these cards were sent to friends and clients of the design office, who are working in creative fields. The motifs communicate the duality of nature and city, tradition and modernity, digital and analogue as well as mind and matter. The content deals with overcoming these oppositions and harmonising them. For the mailing, the card sets were stamped with the symbol of the rabbit and the sign for happiness.

design
601bisang, Seoul

creative direction/art direction
Kum-Jun Park

graphic design
Kum-Jun Park

copywriter
Kum-Jun Park, Joon-Young Bae

photography
Kum-Jun Park

publishing
Jong-In Jung

coordination
Jung-Hye Lee, Sung-Kwon Joe,
Byung-Ha Ahn, Ji-Hye Lee

designer portrait
→ Vol.1: p.458

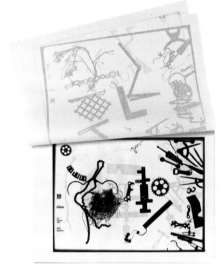

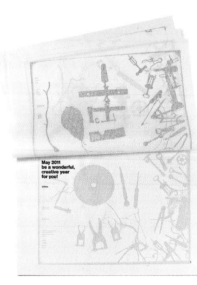

Palais 22

[Invitation]

The design of this aesthetically appealing invitation is based on the motif of the silk wallpaper in the new interior design show-room in Frankfurt/Main. The extension of the showroom is reflected in the design of the invitation card for the reopening. "Unfolding" is the theme for the invitation: it is sent as a post-card, but when opened it unfolds into a large-scale DIN A2 format. The peacock as the main motif of the design also illustrates the principle of unfolding.

client
Palais 22 - Interior Design, Julia Lee, Frankfurt/Main

design
mind the gap! design, Karl-Heinz Best, Frankfurt/Main

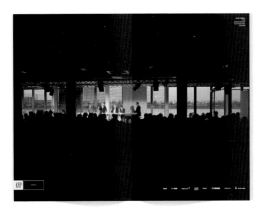

KAP Forum

[Image Brochure]

This large-sized image brochure introduces the responsibilities and activities of the KAP Forum for architecture, technology and design. The basis of the documentation is a selection of hosted events, lecturers, invitation cards, representative photos of theme nights and information on partner companies. The brochure features a single-colour black print on thin, pink newsprint paper; its design is generous and powerful, expressing the dynamics and diversity of the forum.

client
KAP Forum, Cologne
(Alape, Carpet Concept, Dornbracht, Gira, Silent Gliss, Wilkhahn, Zumtobel Licht)

design
großgestalten
kommunikationsdesign, Cologne

design team
Tobias Groß, Martin Schüngel

Wanderzeit –
Das ganze Jahr /
Hiking time –
the whole year
[Image Brochure,
Travel Companion]

The image brochure of Oy-Mittelberg goes beyond colourful image
worlds and focuses on a specific
characteristic of the region: all
year round hiking. As a convenient
companion, the brochure features
practical hiking tips, contact
information and special offers. A
dynamic visual language emphasises the experience of nature.
A strong love for nature is also
reflected in the environmentally
sound production of the thread-
stitched brochure, which is made
from FSC/PEFC-certified paper
and is printed with vegetable oil-
based inks.

client
Kur- und Tourismusbüro
Oy-Mittelberg

design
designgruppe koop, Nesselwang

creative direction
Andreas Koop

art direction
Alexia Waldschütz-Niestroj

photography
Alexander Kählig

designer portrait
→ Vol.1: p.486

Aktion Piepmätze / *Dicky-Bird Promotion*

[Advertising]

The colourful Görtz world of birds presents itself in all the Görtz sales areas set up for children's shoes. For this purpose, a lovingly designed birdhouse is of course indispensable: a big colourful book all about our feathered friends to play with and marvel at. Along with five different bird packagings for shoelaces, in the form of a sale special, it has served to increase customer frequency in the Görtz sales areas for children's shoes and to win over customers for the Görtz store card.

client
Görtz GmbH, Hamburg

head of marketing
Michael Jacobs

design
gürtlerbachmann Werbung GmbH, Hamburg

creative direction/concept
Uli Gürtler

art direction
Merle Schröder, Veronika Kieneke

project management
Anne Kukereit

illustration
Merle Schröder, Veronika Kieneke

text
Claudia Oltmann

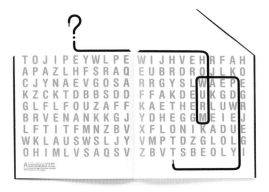

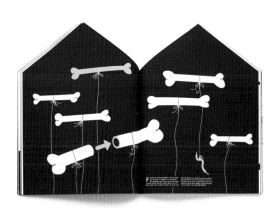

PowerTower

[3D Flyer]

With the motto "PowerTower", this set of three brochures playfully bridges the gap between the second and third dimension. By simply sticking the flyers together, an impressive 3D skyline arises on the desk. Each brochure presents one range of services offered by cadventure, an engineering office for 3D CAD services, whereas each cover features a different motif symbolising the provided service. A transparent banderole holds the flyers together and offers space for a personal, handwritten message.

client
cadventure, Gustavsburg

design
contrust [design], Riedstadt

creative direction
Stephan Ruh

art direction
Simone Stenger

designer portrait
→ Vol.1: p.468

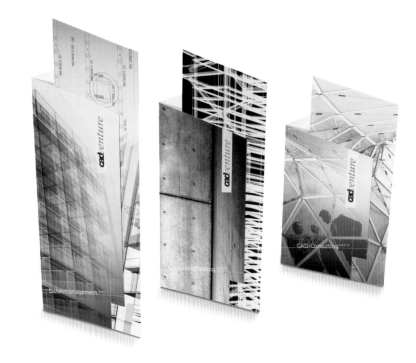

In Bewegung! –
50 Jahre Diakonische Jugendhilfe /
On the move! –
50th anniversary of the Diakonische Jugendhilfe
[Print Media]

The campaign "In Bewegung!" ("On the move!") for the Diakonische Jugendhilfe was developed for the youth welfare organisation's 50th anniversary. The objective of presenting a Christian institution in a modern, young and occasionally also provoking way, was realised with a strong colour and typography concept. The flexibility of the distinctive design elements was particularly well adapted in the book for the campaign, which unites findings from 50 eventful and moving years into one lively picture. The speech bubble as key design element represents the authentic voices of contemporary witnesses.

client
Diakonische Jugendhilfe Region Heilbronn e.V., Eppingen-Kleingartach

design
ARTelier Reiss KG, Volxheim

creative direction
Martin Reiss

art direction
Vasiliki Parashudi

concept
Silke Maurer, Martin Reiss

Jackson and Sandra's Wedding
[Invitation]

The intention of this wedding promotion was to foster appreciation for traditional Chinese culture and to emphasise its relevance for modern society. Conceptually speaking, the cultural heritage of societal traditions is utilised in the design strategy. The integration of popular blessings highlights the importance of harmony and unity as key principal features in family festivities. Altogether the design elements create a unique, emotional approach.

client
Jackson Chun Wei Ko, Singapore

design
Nanyang Technological University, Singapore

art direction/concept
I-Hsuan Cindy Wang

graphic design
I-Hsuan Cindy Wang

text
I-Hsuan Cindy Wang

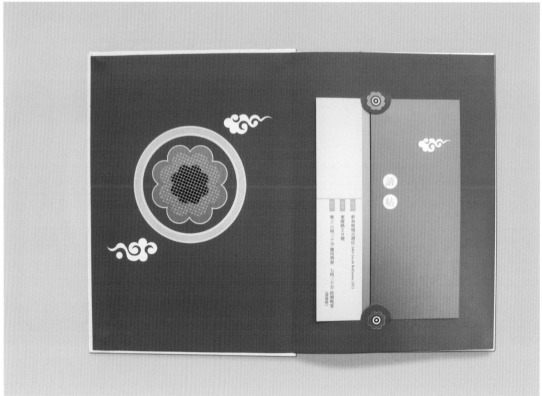

Macro Maison

[Notebook, Promotional
Printed Material]

Macro Maison is the retail chain
of a Taiwanese wood furniture
manufacturer. Globalisation has
exposed Taiwanese furniture to
Western trends, which is why
these furniture pieces are more
closely aligned to the traditional
Asian lifestyle. Advertising materials employ Taiwanese characters and phrase a claim that can
be translated as "Just love the
lines". The line – as an element
of Chinese aesthetics – represents
a formative design element in
the notebooks and tools of the
retail chain's direct marketing
campaigns.

client
Yeong Jin Furniture Factory Corp.,
Ltd.

design
Creative-E Design Studio.,
Taichung

creative direction/art direction
Wen Chun Fong

head of marketing
Steve Chaing

head of advertising
Tung Liang Chen

project management
Evonne Lin

photography
Chun Hsiung Chiu, J.P. Studio

copywriter
Hong Zhen Wang

Carlswerk – Werkstatt and Kupferhütte

[Property Brochure]

The dramaturgy, layout, photography, typography and graphics of the brochure convey the fascination of former industrial constructions. The cover shows all the buildings on the industrial site that are for sale. Inside the brochure, the typography of the cover is echoed in the form of structure due to dividing pages. The strict design grid with only few variations in the page layout emphasises all topics equally and presents the commercial real estate property in a strong and credible manner.

client
Beos AG, Berlin

design
großgestalten
kommunikationsdesign, Cologne

design team
Tobias Groß, Jazek Poralla

photography
Frederic Lezmi

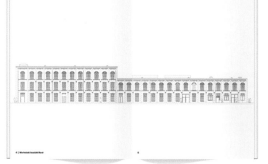

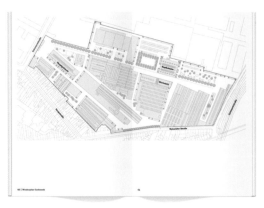

Die Geschichte der Versicherung /
The history of insurance
[Book]

The image brochure targeted at existing and potential new clients is based on an eye-catching, rather unusual design concept for the brand. It refers to the history of the ARAG insurance company as well as its diverse service portfolio that has grown throughout the years. Humorous texts, printed in ancient typography, connect historical information with contemporary insurance cases. The cover is inspired to the minutest detail by a richly ornamented leather binding which discreetly integrates the logo.

client
ARAG Allgemeine Rechtsschutz-Versicherungs-AG, Düsseldorf

design
BUTTER. GmbH, Düsseldorf

creative direction
Matthias Eickmeyer,
Reinhard Henke,
Nadine Schlichte

text
Reinhard Henke

illustration
Nicole Hoffeins

production
Lars Schlentzek

Parador Compendium

[Brochure Collection]

The Parador Compendium comprises various image publications about the company, its brands, innovations and partner programmes, as well as special issues and customer brochures about the range of products. Its sophisticated design conveys the brand's positioning in the premium segment. Elaborately composed image worlds use target-group-specific details to show living spaces that are full of life and that all tell their own story. Large-scale icons on the inside of the brochure refer to specific product features and surfaces.

client
Parador GmbH & Co. KG,
Coesfeld

design
Martin et Karczinski GmbH,
Munich

creative direction
Peter Martin

art direction
Marcus-Florian Kruse,
Patrick Wachner

graphic design
Christina Bee, Martin Buck,
Holger Königsdörfer

text
Wolfgang Wirsching

photography
Thomas Popinger

designer portrait
→ Vol.2: p.495

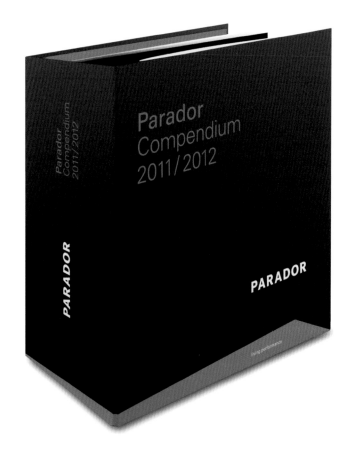

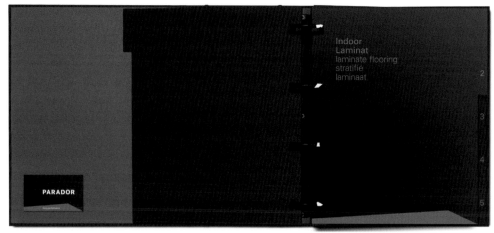

Kohler Numi
[Launch Campaign]

With the objective of creating a brand positioning that communicates the unique values of the Numi toilet for discerning customers, a comprehensive launch campaign for print, TV and web was developed. The communication strategy and all its individual elements were conceived as one entity to underline the sense of mystique, luxury and power that characterises this technically innovative product. An image language inspired fashion photography uses cinematic locations, where the promoted product is perceived only at second glance.

client
Kohler, Kohler

design
Ammunition, San Francisco

creative direction
Brett Wickens, Ammunition;
Tristan Butterfield, Kohler

art direction
Jeremy Matthews, Ammunition

text
Jenny Shears

photography
Paolo Zambaldi

film production
Logan

programming
Noble Studios

designer portrait
→ Vol.1: p.460

Comfort bis Care –
Produktbroschüre
*Comfort to Care –
Product brochure*

client
HEWI Heinrich Wilke GmbH,
Bad Arolsen

design
Markwald & Neusitzer
Kommunikationsdesign,
Frankfurt/Main

photography
Studio Casa, Münster

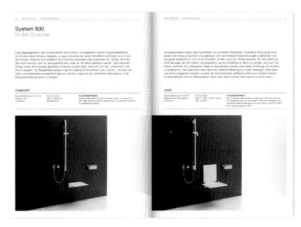

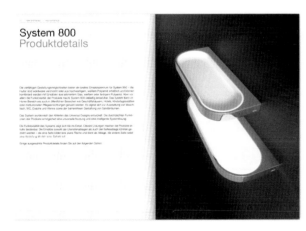

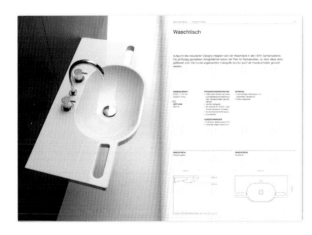

For many years now, the topic "barrier-free sanitary installation" has been the core competence of HEWI. Since this particular issue is still somewhat regarded as a limiting element in bathroom design and planning, it is essential to display the product range in a desirable way. The communication concept "Comfort to Care" was developed to target architects, planners and operation managers. The main idea is to demonstrate a scale of simple comfort solutions to complex care concepts. The planning stages are displayed and made easy to compare via clear and modern product photography. Additional articles by specialist writers on topics like "universal design" round out this specialty catalogue.

EDG/DOGA

[Service Brochures]

A distinctive design concept showcases DOGA as a waste disposal
company for industry, commerce
and the trades, which plans and
implements complete solutions
for disposing commercial and
industrial waste. The general brochure illustrates and explains
industry solutions, waste management and disposal units.
The special brochure Allesfresser
(Omnivore) describes the new
container services in a detailed,
humorous and visually appealing
way, presenting and cataloguing
the range of available containers.

client
EDG, Entsorgung Dortmund
GmbH, Dortmund

design
Paarpiloten, Düsseldorf

creative direction
Christopher Wiehl, Nanni Goebel

art direction/concept
Christopher Wiehl

graphic design
Anna Gemmeke,
Stefanie Marniok

designer portrait
→ Vol.1: p.496

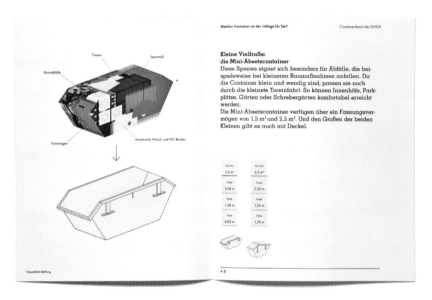

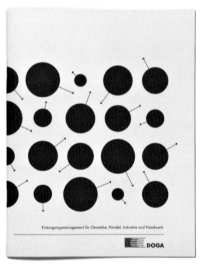

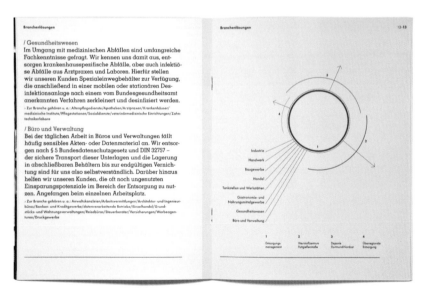

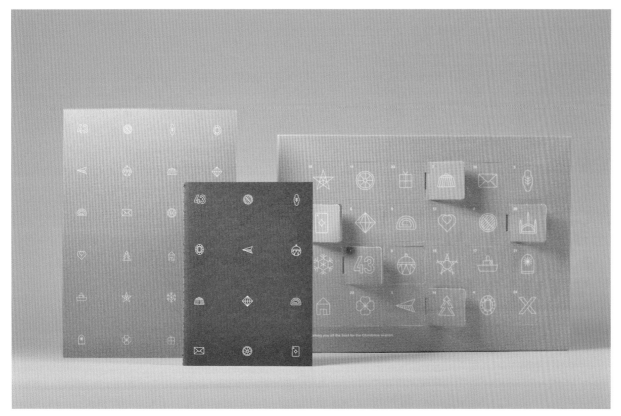

Stratley

[Christmas Mailing]

This 2010 Christmas mailing consists of a greeting card, an Advent calendar and a small book. The symbols used on all three media represent Christmas customs from different countries. Since Stratley is one of the top management consultancies for the chemical industry, countries that are significant chemical locations were chosen. The book juxtaposes these symbols with the corresponding regional customs. The concept creates a numerical connection: 24 chemical locations, 24 Christmas customs and 24 days until Christmas.

client
Stratley AG, Cologne

design
Paarpiloten, Düsseldorf

creative direction
Nanni Goebel, Christopher Wiehl

art direction/concept
Nanni Goebel

graphic design
Stefanie Marniok

designer portrait
→ Vol.1: p.496

MA*

[Property Brochure]

Starting with a property in an un-favoured area in Frankfurt/Main and with a negative history of the building, a marketing strategy that went beyond classic real estate marketing was developed. For the communication concept "MA – Wohnen anders" ("MA – living differently") a self-contained language was conceived that challenges existing patterns of thought, asking "Kann man Glück wohnen?" ("Can you live luck?"). The magazine-style layout of the brochure combines a cosmopoli-tan image language with short information in texts and eye-catching graphical elements.

client
Material Arts GmbH,
Frankfurt/Main

design
Nordisk Büro Plus GmbH,
Frankfurt/Main

creative direction/concept
Frank Lottermann, Lorenzo Bizzi,
Ulf Appel

art direction
Florian Dylus, Hanna Blumenrath,
Achim Römer

graphic design
Frank Lottermann, Florian Dylus,
Hanna Blumenrath

text
Hanna Blumenrath,
Frank Lottermann,
Susanne Müller-Schunck

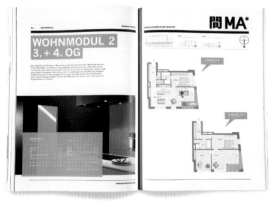

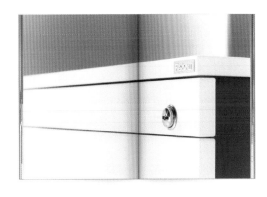

Febrü

[Product Catalogue]

The timeless, reduced layout of Febrü's product catalogue grants product photography, which it presents against a set of differently coloured backgrounds, a maximum amount of expression. This emotional visual language forms a strong contrast to the informative texts and factual product pictures that are set against a white background. The uncoated volume paper which was not varnished in the printing process feels pleasant to the touch and underlines the colour and lighting concept. The cover design features a partial relief painting, which increases the degree of attention and recognition value.

client
Febrü Büromöbel Produktions-und Vertriebs-GmbH, Herford

head of marketing
Brunhild Redeker

design
beierarbeit GmbH, Bielefeld

creative direction
Christoph Beier

photography
Christian R. Schulz

preprint
d&d digital data medien, Bad Oeynhausen

printing
Gieselmann Druck und Medien-haus, Bielefeld

Drehbuch /
Turn-Around Book

[Paper Journal]

The Drehbuch (Turn-Around Book), a paper journal for creative ideas, was developed for the Art Directors Club Germany. It follows a colour concept that is rich in contrast, and consists of a black and a white part. The book features a Z-shaped construction which allows users to flip through the white pages from one side and through the black pages from the other side. The Turn-Around Book comes together with a "turn-around pen" which writes in both black and white. In this way, positive people are allowed to think negative at times, while pessimists can discover their positive sides.

client
Art Directors Club für
Deutschland (ADC), Berlin

design
brandbook.de, Frankfurt/Main

creative direction
Bernd Griese

text
Christoph Herold

project management
Sabine Kochendörfer

production
Dirk Mahlke

CATALOG 25
[Brochure]

The catalogue for the 25th anniversary of designer Karla Colletto presents a retrospective of her swimsuit collections from the past quarter century. In order to meet the challenge of creating a particularly comprehensive catalogue with only half of the usual budget, the idea of a cost-effective photo shooting with mannequins was born. The result was a convincing, high-contrast production with professional lighting. Matching the design of each swimsuit, the futuristic appeal of the mannequin is broken up by playful design elements.

client
Karla Colletto, Washington DC

design
DESIGN ARMY, Washington DC

creative direction
Jake Lefebure, Pum Lefebure

art direction
Pum Lefebure

graphic design
Lucas Badger

text
Holly Sheldon

photography
Taran Z

printing
Mosaic Inc

RENOLIT DESIGN
[Product Brochure]

A bilingual product brochure was developed for the new positioning of RENOLIT DESIGN. The brochure shows the design possibilities of high-quality plastic films in interior decoration and store construction. Fine relief textures demonstrate the two- and three-dimensional mouldability of the films and translate this special feature of the material to the medium of paper. Thus surfaces are created that appear to be three-dimensional. A clear layout underlines the high-quality feel of the brochure, which is appealing to architects and interior designers.

client
RENOLIT SE, Worms
Business Unit RENOLIT DESIGN

design
Projekttriangle Design Studio, Stuttgart

creative direction
Prof. Jürgen Späth,
Martin Grothmaak

graphic design
Jan Maier, Franz-Georg Stämmele

text
Myriam Guedey

photography
Martin Grothmaak

architectural visualisation
DesignRaum GmbH

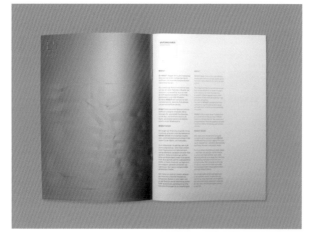

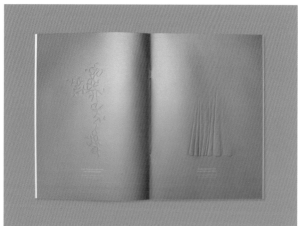

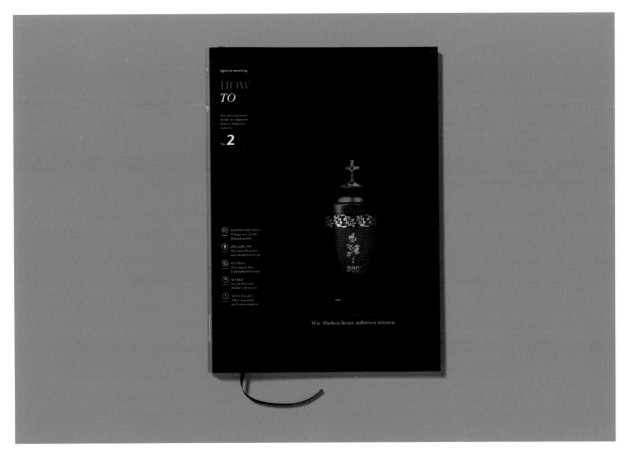

HowTo 2

[Magazine]

To raise its profile as a competent communications specialist, the advertising agency Ogilvy & Mather decided on a magazine as a marketing instrument. The second issue features target-group-specific guest authors from universities, the communication industry and trade. Interesting and diversified artworks by renowned illustrators characterise the high-quality design of the periodical. This high standard of design is complemented by production refinements such as Japanese binding, bound inserts and ribbon markers.

client
Ogilvy Deutschland,
Frankfurt/Main

design
Ogilvy Frankfurt, Frankfurt/Main

creative direction
Helmut Meyer, Delle Krause

art direction
Helmut Meyer, Catrin Farrenschon

project management
Delle Krause, Jonas Bailly

illustrations
Hampus Ericstam/peppercookies.com, Markus Färber, Nora Fehr, Aisha Franz, Andreas Gefe, Sarah Illenberger/Emeis Deubel, Aerosyn-Lex Mestrovic, Doc Robert/2 Agenten, Keiichi Tanaami, Mario Wagner/2 Agenten, Nick White/Heart

designer portrait
→ Vol.1: p.494

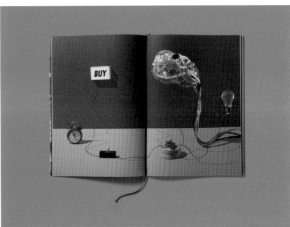

Nichts bewegt mehr als die Wirklichkeit – Rambo und Grüne Männchen / *Nothing moves you more than reality – Rambo and Little Green Men*

[Advertisements]

With the intention of attracting new audiences, beyond the actual core target audience, to watch the news, this series of advertisements for a news channel draws surprising parallels: photos of politicians are tagged with humorous headlines to create a provocative context inspired by scenes from famous Hollywood film productions. The brand claim "Nothing moves you more than reality" reflects and points to the channel's hourly news programme. The current selection of images illustrates this proposition in an authentic manner.

client
n-tv Nachrichtenfernsehen GmbH, Cologne

design
Euro RSCG Düsseldorf

creative direction
Felix Glauner, Martin Breuer, Martin Venn

art direction
Ingmar Krannich, Melanie Doms

text
Sigi Zwar, Christian Kroll

customer advisory service
Harald Jäger, Sandra Lopez-Real

agency producer
Detlef Stuhldreier

Willkommen bei den Buschs /
Welcome to the Buschs
[Marketing Brochure]

This unpretentious brochure is aimed at marketing condominiums in Wilhelm-Busch-Straße, Frankfurt/Main. Inspired by the address, the layout echoes the congenial visual language of the poet and painter and intentionally does so without any computer renderings. The protagonists reflect a representative profile of the current residents. People interested in an apartment in close proximity to Uncle Nolte or Master Lämpel are invited in verse to a personal meeting. The humorous design concept lends each piece of real estate its own character.

client
Claus Wisser Verwaltungs- und Beteiligungs GmbH & Co. KG, Frankfurt/Main

design
Standard Rad. GmbH, Frankfurt/Main

creative direction
Kerstin Amend, Standard Rad.

art direction
Katharina Manz, Standard Rad.

concept
Claus Wisser; Kerstin Amend, Katharina Manz, Standard Rad.; Thomas Heise

text
Wilhelm Busch, Thomas Heise

project management
Katharina Manz, Standard Rad.

illustration
Wilhelm Busch & Standard Rad.

designer portrait
→ Vol.1: p.504

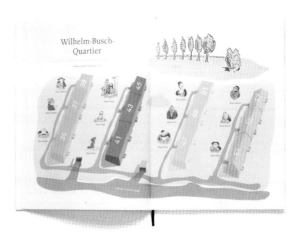

Die Raucherlunge /
The Smoker's Lung
[Installation]

This campaign for the Barmer
GEK health insurance points out
the risks of nicotine consumption.
The high-impact installation
showing how smoking harms the
lungs used a tree as a symbol for
the green lung of a city. It was
redesigned with a particularly
eye-catching effect: a wintry
sycamore tree was decorated
with 150 black balls, symbolising
the harmful tar in the pulmonary
alveoli. The arrangement of the
balls in form of a human lung
together with compelling signs
at the foot of the tree serves as
an appeal to stop smoking at the
turn of the year.

client
Barmer GEK, Wuppertal

design
serviceplan, Hamburg

chief creative officer
Alexander Schill

creative direction
Maik Kaehler, Christoph Nann

art direction
Savina Mokreva, Manuel Wolff

graphic design
Maren Wandersleben,
Maximilian Kempe,
Robert Haehle

text
Maik Kaehler, Christoph Nann

designer portrait
→ Vol.1: p.503

Situation
OWL is a manufacturer of stylish glasses, based in Berlin. The challenge was to find an easy and budget friendly way to make the brand visible to urban fashion conscious people.

Solution
Hit the people where fashion is made: on the streets of the city. By putting a big nose to windows all over the city – and made these windows an inspiration and demonstration for the variety of designs of the OWL brand.

Result
OWL is more than the name of a smart bird – the brand found a smart way of communicating to it's target group. After thae ambient action OWL got tons of requests via e-mail. Also the brands website, facebook and twitter traffic increased.

OWL Optics
[Outdoor Campaign]

OWL is a manufacturer of glasses based in Berlin. The challenge of this advertising campaign was to raise the awareness of the brand among a fashion-oriented target group using only a small budget. The design concept follows the idea that trends are made on the streets: in particular places around the city huge noses and the logo were placed between two windows, creating urban faces. This communicates that the city and its diversity inspires the manufacturer to its unusual designs.

client
OWL Optics, Berlin

design
Leo Burnett GmbH,
Frankfurt/Main

chief creative officer
Andreas Pauli

creative direction
Gen Sadakane, Axel Tischer

concept
Gen Sadakane

photography
Lina Gruen

printing
David Cuenca,
Gigant Bildproduktion

designer portrait
→ Vol.2: p.473

Berlusconi

[Advertisement, Poster]

Highlight of the Ruhrfestspiele festival 2011 is the play "The Giacomo Variations" starring John Malkovich as Casanova. However, on the advertisements and posters of festival sponsor Evonik, Malkovich has to share the spotlight – with Silvio Berlusconi. They both play the ageing seducer: one of them on the theatre stage, the other one at Bunga Bunga Parties. The photographic juxtaposition presents both in a similar colour setting, while the headlines provocatively reflect on the implied common characteristics of both figures.

client
Evonik Industries AG, Essen

head of advertising
Markus Langer

design
KNSK Werbeagentur GmbH, Hamburg

creative direction
Vera Hampe, Olaf Hörning

art direction
Caroline Labitzke

text
Olaf Hörning

customer advisory service
Verena Gillwald, Hanna Petersen

Boxherz /
Boxing Heart
[Poster]

Contrary to what many people think, boxing is not just about fighting – It Is also a good work-out for the cardiovascular system. This message is focused on image and text in this impressive poster for Everlast, an internationally successful supplier of boxing equipment. The eye-catching key motif consists of two red boxing gloves that are cleverly arranged in form of a human heart. The rough structure of the background appears to be the interior of a chest, underlining the deliberately bloody appeal of the design.

client
Pan World Brands Limited,
Manchester

design
Euro RSCG Düsseldorf

creative direction
Felix Glauner, Martin Venn

art direction
Alexandros Antoniadis

text
André Bastian

customer advisory service
Daniel Grube

photography
Alexandros Antoniadis,
Jochen Kirchhof

agency producer
Detlef Stuhldreier

251

BVB
[Advertisements]

client
Evonik Industries AG, Essen

head of advertising
Markus Langer

design
KNSK Werbeagentur GmbH,
Hamburg

creative direction
Vera Hampe, Olaf Hörning

art direction
Martin Augner, Caroline Labitzke,
Berta Meins

text
Dirk Junski

customer advisory service
Verena Gillwald, Hanna Petersen

Wir stehen hinter dem BVB.
Genau wie Schalke.

Wir gratulieren dem BVB zu Platz 1 in der Ruhrgebietsmeisterschaft.

Hier unsere Nominierung für
den Friedensnobelpreis 2009.

Wir freuen uns auf ein großartiges Revierderby.

With this emotionally appealing series of advertisements the Evonik industrial group emphasises that it is not only the main sponsor of the Borussia Dortmund (BVB) soccer team, but also one of its biggest fans. Large photographs reflect on authentic facets drawn from the everyday life of BVB fans. This expressive and bold image language is framed by individual, corporate-specific design elements. Humorous captions appear like speech balloons, harmoniously matching in colour with the logo. Depending on the occasion, the sponsor acts as spontaneously and moodily as a fan – commenting, tattling and cheering. The advertisements are published in the BVB stadium magazine Echt at every home match and, on special occasions, also in other newspapers and magazines.

Die Flagge /
The Flag
[Advertisement]

The number of executions in China exceeds the total number of executions in all other countries in the world. The objective of this strongly expressive newspaper advertisement for the Human Rights Day on December 10th is to raise the awareness that the execution of criminals and political dissidents is guarded like a state secret by the Chinese government. It subtly integrates the scene of an execution into the Chinese flag, so that, upon a closer look, this secret becomes terribly obvious.

client
IGFM, Internationale Gesellschaft für Menschenrechte, Frankfurt/Main

design
Euro RSCG Düsseldorf

creative direction
Felix Glauner, Martin Venn, Martin Breuer

art direction
Alexandros Antoniadis

text
André Bastian

customer advisory service
Felix Kropp

illustration
Alexandros Antoniadis

agency producer
Detlef Stuhldreier

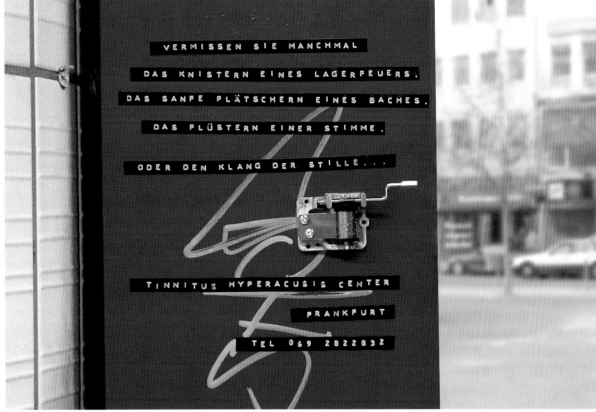

Tinnitus Center Frankfurt – *Sounds of Silence*
[Ambient Installation]

More and more people suffer from tinnitus – the high-frequency ringing in the ears which is a constant annoyance. Loud sounds intensify the symptoms, while pleasant sounds alleviate it. The design concept of this interactive and informative ambient installation was developed to inform those suffering from tinnitus about the assistance and services of the Tinnitus Center in Frankfurt/Main. Memorable messages with an almost lyrical appeal about the beauty of sound are complemented by small music boxes, thus creating emotional moments and islands of silence in the middle of the city's hustle and bustle.

client
Tinnitus-Hyperakusis-Zentrum, Frankfurt/Main

design
Leo Burnett GmbH, Frankfurt/Main

chief creative officer
Andreas Pauli

creative direction
Hans-Jürgen Kämmerer

art direction
Bjørnar Thorsen,
Jenny Solem Vikra

text
Bjørnar Thorsen,
Hans-Jürgen Kämmerer

customer advisory service
Xenia Arro

photography
Gerard Delmas

designer portrait
→ Vol.2: p.473

Nevermind

[Advertisement]

A surprising change of perspective lends this advertisement an exclusive and fascinating appeal. It presents the cover photo of Nirvana's album "Nevermind", but from a new perspective. Viewers get the impression that they are looking at a previously unpublished motif from the original photo series. With this photo, which was specifically created for this campaign and which reenacts the original scene down to the last detail, the image archive "spuk stock pictures" advertises its exclusive photo series. The brand claim of having unseen images is thus given proof.

client
SPUK Pictures

design
BBDO Proximity GmbH,
Düsseldorf

head of advertising
Liselotte Schwenkert

creative direction
Christian Mommertz,
Carsten Bolk,
Wolfgang Schneider

art direction
Jake Shaw

text
Florian Birkner

art buying
Birgit Paulat

photography
Matt Barnes

designer portrait
→ Vol.2: p.470

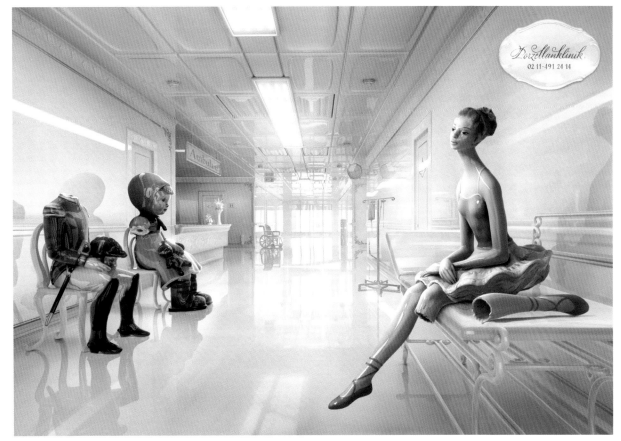

Porzellanklinik
[Advertisement]

The design concept in this advertisement takes the meaning of the company's name, "Porzellanklinik" (Porcelain Clinic), literally and has fairytale-like appeal. A typical hospital corridor is turned into an imaginative world of shiny, white porcelain. The aesthetically appealing computer graphics depict a hospital environment, true down to the very last detail, including waiting patients, an IV stand and appropriate signage. The message is immediately clear: the Porcelain Clinic is the place where broken off arms, legs and even heads are treated professionally.

client
Porzellanklinik, Düsseldorf

design
Ogilvy & Mather Advertising GmbH, Düsseldorf

creative direction
Rob Bruenig

art direction
Nina Wolke

text
Einar Armbruster

illustration
Blutsbrueder Design LLC

typography
Petra Beisse

designer portrait
→ Vol.1: p.493

The water shortage campaign

[Print Campaign]

This advertising campaign clearly illustrates that in the future water shortage will become a serious problem everywhere in the world. With a simple design detail, the striking image language calls for the economic consumption of the valuable resource: at first glance, the photographs appear to be realistic, but on closer look they perplex with a miniature water tap and fire hydrant. This makes water shortage become concretely visible and raises awareness of responsible behaviour.

client
SOLCOM, Seoul

design
SOLCOM, Seoul

head of advertising
Prof. Won Young Kug

creative direction
Kim Byung Jin

art direction
Kim Sung Sik

graphic design
Won Hyun Sik, Kim Min Jung

text
Ko In Kyong, An Eun Ju

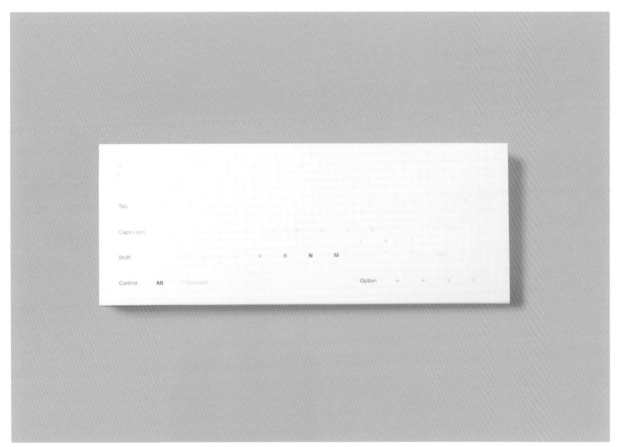

Alt XMAS 2010
[Christmas Gift]

This customer gift features a particularly tasty design idea. 150 full-size keyboards were made of Belgian chocolate to create an appealing and edible present for customers on Christmas 2010. The discreet packaging is predominantly white and hints at its content by marks and traces of single keyboard keys. The Alt key, highlighted in red, is the only element that implies the New Zealand agency Alt Group.

design
Alt Group, Auckland

creative direction
Dean Poole

graphic design
Clem Devine, Tony Proffit, Dean Poole

Staufen darf nicht zerbrechen! /
Don't let Staufen crumble!

[Print Media]

client
Stiftung zur Erhaltung der
historischen Altstadt Staufen

design
identis GmbH, design-gruppe
joseph pölzelbauer, Freiburg

creative direction
Joseph Pölzelbauer

art direction
Jean Mierecke

graphic design
Jean Mierecke, Reinhard Groh,
Simone Pölzelbauer,
Marcel Ermes

text
Burghard Müller-Dannhausen

project management
Ursel Linder, Svenja Schneppe

photography
Peter Adamik, Rolf Vennenbernd,
Judith Wagner, Wolfgang Wilde

**Staufen darf
nicht zerbrechen!**

Tomi Ungerer
Illustrator und
Schriftsteller

Staufen ist zerstört
und so mein Herz,
wie eine zerissene Mauer.
Nach Jahrhunderten,
unter dem Druck
von einem Schicksal,
das wir jetzt
zähmen müssen
um es zu überwältigen.
Eine Herausforderung
zur Rettungspflicht.
Nichts ist unmöglich.

Die Zeit wird es beweisen,
eine feste Burg ist unser Ort.

Senden Sie
eine Solidaritäts-SMS
an 81190
Kennwort: „Riss"
Sie helfen einmalig
mit **5 Euro!**

www.staufenstiftung.de

Stiftung zur
Erhaltung
der historischen
Altstadt
Staufen

Staufen darf nicht zerbrechen!

Cherno Jobatey
Journalist und Moderator

Ein Kulturdenkmal ist ein Dialogpartner, der uns viel zu sagen hat. Nehmen wir Staufen, ein ganzes Stadtbild, das mit uns spricht. Und was wir daraus erfahren, verliert nichts an Bedeutung. Auch über Jahrhunderte hinweg. Dass die Menschen, die nach uns kommen, diesen Dialog weiterführen können, legt heute an uns.

Senden Sie eine Solidaritäts-SMS an 81190
Kennwort „Riss"
Sie helfen einmalig mit 5 Euro!
www.staufenstiftung.de

Staufen darf nicht zerbrechen!

Ulrich Wickert
Journalist und Schriftsteller

In einer historischen Altstadt lesen wir wie in einem offenen Buch. Wir sehen, wie die Menschen sich früher entfaltet haben. Wie sie ihre persönliche Individualität zum Ausdruck gebracht und zugleich ein harmonisches, eng verbundenes Gemeinwesen gebildet haben. Solche Vorbilder dürfen uns nicht verloren gehen.

Senden Sie eine Solidaritäts-SMS an 81190
Kennwort „Riss"
Sie helfen einmalig mit 5 Euro!
www.staufenstiftung.de

Staufen darf nicht zerbrechen!

Gerhard Schröder
Bundeskanzler 2000 – 2005

Mit der historischen Altstadt Staufens droht etwas verloren zu gehen, was wir dringend brauchen. Denn nur wenn wir den Blick in die Vergangenheit richten, verstehen wir uns selbst. Wir sehen, was menschliches Maß bedeutet, wie eine Vielfalt in der Gemeinschaft entstehen kann, und warum unser Leben ohne diese Kultur unüberschaubar wäre.

Senden Sie eine Solidaritäts-SMS an 81190
Kennwort „Riss"
Sie helfen einmalig mit 5 Euro!
www.staufenstiftung.de

Staufen darf nicht zerbrechen!

Frank Elstner
Fernsehmoderator und Produzent

Unsere Vergangenheit hat uns etwas zu sagen. Wir sollten sie zu Wort kommen lassen. Darum geht es in Staufen. Dieses Kulturdenkmal ist eine Botschaft mit einer vielschichtigen Bedeutung. Wir brauchen solche Botschaften und sollten alles dafür tun sie zu erhalten.

Senden Sie eine Solidaritäts-SMS an 81190
Kennwort „Riss"
Sie helfen einmalig mit 5 Euro!
www.staufenstiftung.de

Staufen darf nicht zerbrechen!

**Sascha Zeus
Michael Wirbitzky**
SWR 3 - Moderatoren

Mit den Rissen kommen die Fotografen, die Fernsehkameras, das Radio. Bilder von geborstenen Wänden, klaffenden Lücken, besorgten Menschen bewegen das ganze Land. Und dann sind alle wieder weg. Nur die Risse nicht. Und die Lücken. Und die Menschen. Staufen „war" nicht, Staufen „ist". Und damit es bleibt, braucht Staufen unsere Hilfe.

Senden Sie eine Solidaritäts-SMS an 81190
Kennwort „Riss"
Sie helfen einmalig mit 5 Euro!
www.staufenstiftung.de

Staufen darf nicht zerbrechen!

**Prof. Dr. h.c. mult.
Meinhard von Gerkan**
Dipl. Ing. Architekt

Jeder Entwicklung liegt ein konstruktives Moment zugrunde. Das eine baut auf dem anderen auf. Das gilt auch für die Geschichte der Architektur. Die Bauformen früherer Jahrhunderte sind wie ein Fundament für heutiges Gestalten.

Baugeschichte muss erlebbar bleiben, kann nicht nur in Büchern stehen.

Senden Sie eine Solidaritäts-SMS an 81190
Kennwort „Riss"
Sie helfen einmalig mit 5 Euro!
www.staufenstiftung.de

In this national solidarity campaign prominent personalities explain why a medieval townscape is worthy of preservation. In the text, each person's message is conveyed in an individual and authentic speech. In the background of the images, the thread of damage to the city of Staufen is illustrated by massive uplift cracks which are the result of boreholes. Photos of cracks in the walls of buildings are stuck to an imaginary wall with red tape. This tape reoccurs as key design element throughout the whole communication and is consistent with the corporate design. The logo is also set against a red background. The key message "Staufen darf nicht zerbrechen!" ("Don't let Staufen crumble!") is a call for a solidarity text message.

Signature Theatre Posters

An elaborate imagery connects this series of posters for the Signature Theatre. The titles of the changing plays are showcased with an impressive inventiveness. The poster's main motifs feature a keyword for each play, visualising the theme with surprising image compositions. "See What I Wanna See", for example, is a musical about lust, greed, murder, faith and redemption and deals with the question "What is truth?". The poster for this play shows an abstract eye within a passionate variety of colours.

client
Signature Theatre, Washington DC

design
DESIGN ARMY, Washington DC

creative direction
Jake Lefebure, Pum Lefebure

art direction
Pum Lefebure

graphic design
Sucha Becky, Lucas Badger, Eric Rother

printing
Fannon Fine

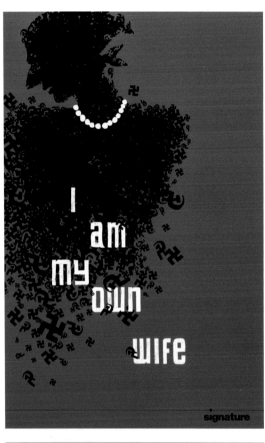

Buchstabenmailing /
Falling Letters Mailing

The earthquake tragedy in Haiti at the beginning of 2010 was covered by every media outlet. The Catholic relief organisation MISEREOR wanted to persuade the most influential journalists in Germany not only to report on the disaster, but also to help with a donation. This extraordinary mailing reduces the text to the provocative call "Taten statt Worte" (Deeds, not words). All other letters fall like confetti out of the envelope. The information on the donation account is simply introduced by the short message "Jede Spende hilft Haiti" (Every donation helps Haiti).

client
Bischöfliches Hilfswerk
MISEREOR e.V., Aachen

design
Kolle Rebbe GmbH, Hamburg

creative direction
Ales Polcar, Heiko Schmidt

art direction
Susanne Möbius, Reinhard Krug

text
Henning Flohr

customer advisory service
Jessica Gustafsson

production
Franziska Ziegler

Munken Cube

[Communicative Design Object]

The design object Munken Cube successfully increased the brand awareness of paper manufacturer Arctic Paper and the furniture brand e15. Its purist and radical workmanship of paper and wood is unconventional and offers the open-minded many ways to use it – as shapeable sculpture, work tool or concept furniture. The Munken Cube story was spread via microsite, film, events and postcard mailings as well as sent out by means of press releases to international off- and online media for highly effective publicity.

client
Arctic Paper Deutschland,
Hamburg

design
JUNO, Hamburg

creative direction/concept
Björn Lux, Wolfgang Greter

text
Frank Wache

film direction
Jan-Frederic Goltz

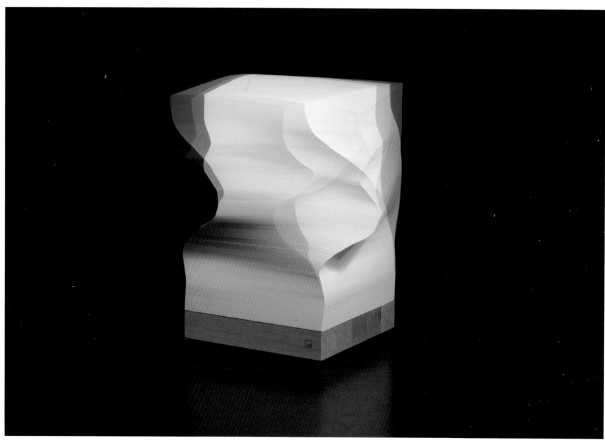

Individueller Musik-unterricht /
Individual music lessons

[Advertisement]

To emphasise the individualised character of music lessons for children, the advertisement illustrates the creative approach taken by the Allegro music school. Without compromising, it focuses on the individual skill levels of students. The motif humorously demonstrates how music is consistently brought to the student's level: following the claim, "Individuelle Musikförderung" (individual music education), they go so far as to saw the legs off of a grand piano to adjust it to the height of a given child.

client
Musikschule Allegro, Düsseldorf

design
Ogilvy & Mather Advertising GmbH, Düsseldorf

creative direction
Rob Bruenig

art direction
Nina Wolke

text
Einar Armbruster

photography
Michael Haegele

designer portrait
→ Vol.1: p.493

Standox International

[Image Campaign]

The objective of this innovative image campaign for Standox, a producer of automotive refinish technology, was the development of a concept that could be applied internationally. The appealing motifs look like coincidentally spilled paint and, among other things, take up the shape of a face. They are reminiscent of picture puzzles that reveal their full interpretation only upon a second closer look. The art of varnishing is reinterpreted according to Standox's corporate philosophy. Short texts explain the brand values and the advantages for customers.

client
Standox GmbH, Wuppertal

design
Lutz Menze Design, Wuppertal

creative direction/art direction
Lutz Menze

graphic design
Astrid Grahl

text
Bernhard Koppenhöfer, Essen

illustration
Ottenlinger GmbH,
Digital Imaging, Düsseldorf

IN LOVE WITH COLOR.

Professional vehicle refinishers know that identifying the right color is the be all and end all in this trade. Standox, the European leader in automotive repair technology, helps you find the perfect color match reliably and efficiently. Our advanced Color Tools include Color Search Software, an electronic Spectrophotometer as well as an Online Color Search. This way you always have access to the latest information, even when using a mobile. For the perfect color match, Standox delivers the best results. For more information visit www.standox.co.uk/colortool

STANDOX
The Art of Refinishing.

FORMACIÓN SOBRE EL COLOR.

A medida que van apareciendo nuevos materiales o técnicas innovadoras, es necesario actualizarse. Si quiere seguir siendo los mejores en el futuro, tiene que invertir en más formación ahora. Como líder europeo en tecnología de reparación de automoción, Standox goza de una excelente posición para ayudarle a mejorar su técnica y ampliar sus conocimientos. En nuestros cursos aprenderá todo lo que necesita saber para aplicar nuestros productos de la forma más eficiente y para identificar el color con absoluta precisión, así como cuestiones sobre salud y seguridad. Cuando se trata de ampliar conocimientos y mejorar la técnica, Standox le ofrece los mejores resultados. Más información en www.standox.es/formacion

STANDOX
El arte del pintado.

GLANZLEISTUNG IN FARBE.

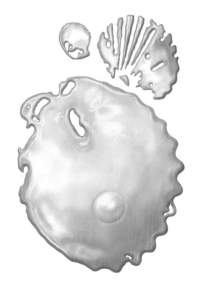

Mit uns lohnt sich das Lackieren: Denn Standox, der europaweit führende Anbieter von Autoreparaturlacken, bietet Ihnen das komplette Spektrum an innovativen Produkten: von anwenderfreundlichen Vormaterialien bis zur neuesten Basislack-Technologie. Ihre Erfolgsgrundlage – auch in wirtschaftlicher Hinsicht. Da unsere Produkte heute schon die Qualitäts- und Umweltstandards von morgen erfüllen, sind Sie optimal auf die Zukunft vorbereitet. Lust auf glänzende Geschäfte? Standox sorgt immer für beste Ergebnisse. Mehr Informationen unter www.standox.de/standoblue

STANDOX
Die Kunst des Lackierens.

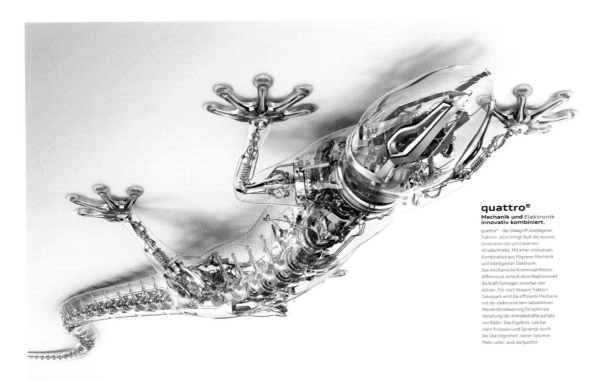

Audi quattro

[Advertisements]

How can customer value be demonstrated, along with the functionality of the latest quattro generation, in a simple and memorable way? An advertising campaign has solved this task using an analogy: a high-tech gecko, which combines mechanics and electronics in a sophisticated and intelligent way, was developed with different details and sizes shown. In addition, the advertisements also aim to convey Audi's technological leadership in the field of four-wheel drive systems, with the objective of thereby regaining its position as market leader.

client
AUDI AG, Ingolstadt

design
kempertrautmann gmbh, Hamburg;
Liga_01 Computerfilm GmbH, Munich

Die langlebigste Batterie /
The longest lasting battery
[Packaging Design]

Evoia batteries hold the Guinness World Record for being the alkaline batteries that provide the longest lasting power. The communication objective here was to highlight this unique selling feature to customers directly at the point of sale. The slogan "Hält doppelt so lang" (Lasts twice as long), an eye-catching message, has been printed on a half-empty package. Along with the simple concept of a surprising packaging idea, the cost efficiency of this product is demonstrated in an original way.

client
Panasonic Energy Europe N. V., Zellik/Belgium

design
Scholz & Friends

head of advertising
Martin Pross

creative direction
Matthias Spaetgens,
Wolf Schneider,
Michael Winterhagen

art direction
Walter Ziegler

text
Michael Schoepf

customer advisory service
Salvatore Amato

designer portrait
→ Vol.2: p.503

ars-vivendi.de

Ars Vivendi®
LOVETOYS

Sexplosion
[City Light Poster]

Inspired by fireworks, this vibrant city light poster illustrates with a stylish sense of exaggeration the benefits of Ars Vivendi love toys. Using a spectacular visual language, the poster illustrates how lovely it is to literally explode with pleasure – a striking message which becomes clear in context of the company logo and product name. The designers succeed in creating an advertisement which is humorous but not sexist.

client
Ars Vivendi AG,
Engen-Welschingen

design
Ogilvy & Mather Advertising GmbH,
Düsseldorf

creative direction
Rob Bruenig

art direction
Martin Nigl

text
Tobias Schelo

designer portrait
→ Vol.1: p.493

Equation

[Advertisement]

client
adidas Basketball

design
adidas Brand Image Design,
Portland

creative direction
Eric Vellozzi

art direction
Kathleen Grebe

type illustration
180 LA

Advertised in this adidas series is the Equation, a basketball shoe that can be worn flexibly as either a high- or low-top. The striking visual language utilises pictures of popular basketball players, together with their chosen shoe, as positive image transfer. The distinctive design concept enables athletes to express their own personal style. In emphasising this feature, the product images were designed using the contours and colouring of the respective team logos.

271

COMMUNICATION WITH ADDED VALUE. Convey the message to the customer. Holistic and effective editorial designs – paired with distinction and high recognition value – allow companies to stand out from the competition.

High-quality in-house publications, which do not lose relevance easily, have the potential to stand the test of time and genuinely fascinate readers by offering visual and tactile experiences.

red dot: grand prix

Typotron-Heft 28 – Lokremise St.Gallen

[Book]

The Typotron series of booklets is a cultural contribution that has been published since 1983 by Typotron AG, a printing factory based in St.Gallen. The booklets are created in cooperation with a variety of graphic designers, photographers and authors, with each issue dedicated to a particular cultural topic typical for the region. The topic of issue No. 28 is the old "Lokremise", an all-encompassing cultural centre located in a former locomotive round-house shed in St.Gallen. This also explains the booklet's shape, colour and the enormous weight of 1 kg: as a reminder of the history of the building, the book was given the look of a coal briquette. The reduced design of the cover, which is less sturdy than those of previous editions and sits flush with the pages instead of being slightly bigger, is taken up on the inside. A clear typography is used to produce a stringent appearance, which stands out due to text running across the centrefold.

Statement by the jury

»The book distinguishes itself through a tactile pleasant quality and a plain minimalist layout. The harmonious implementation of photography and typography make it both distinctive and a pleasure to read. Alongside the convincing idea of giving it the shape of a black coal briquette, it is the text running across the centrefold that is most refreshing, a technique that is normally taught to students as a no-go.«

client
Typotron AG, St.Gallen

design
TGG Hafen Senn Stieger,
St.Gallen

art direction
Dominik Hafen, Bernhard Senn,
Roland Stieger

text
Liana Ruckstuhl

photography
DDB Das Digitale Bild,
Speicher

designer portrait
→ Vol.1: p.507

Pfrontener Flurnamen /
Pfronten Field Names

[Scientific Book]

This work is a scientific book that compiles as many as 1,400 field and meadow land names in the municipality of Pfronten in Ostallgäu and their historic, linguistic, phonetic and etymological meaning. With 524 pages and 14 map supplements (in 50 x 70 cm and 70 x 100 cm formats) that amount to a total of 35 sqm of designed space, the book is the result of 4 years of design and 12 years of research presenting linguistic finds that go back to the original Romanised population. Numerous icons and phonetic signs were designed to match the selected typography; and, based on three different historical templates, almost 8 sqm of the cartography were entirely redrawn, relabelled and linked to the content via coordinates and references. Featuring a cloth binding with embossed printing and a systematically, clearly arranged and reader-friendly layout, the design reflects the high content value of this compendium, which compiles knowledge transmitted through several generations.

Statement by the jury

»How can a topic such as this be visualised in an attractive manner, without the design becoming too dominant? The answer is a well-balanced layout that follows a highly self-contained approach in conveying the information. Be it through a congenially matched typography, outstanding maps and easy-to-understand icons – this book convinces in all aspects.«

client
Gemeinde Pfronten

design
designgruppe koop,
Nesselwang

creative direction
Andreas Koop

graphic design
Alexander Kählig

text
Bertold Pölcher,
Dr. Thaddäus Steiner

designer portrait
→ Vol.1: p.486

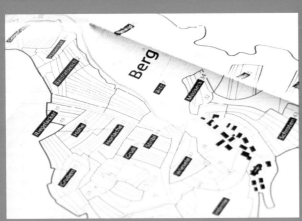

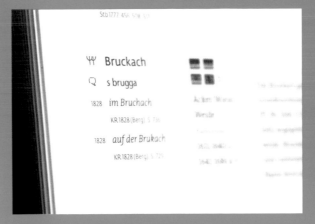

601 Artbook Project 2010
[Catalogue]

This book is the exhibition catalogue for the eighth edition of the 601 Artbook Project in 2010. Its title, "22 points", represents the different approaches taken by the 22 featured, award-winning artists, who are also represented on the cover by 22 dots of highly detailed and creatively designed patterns. These dots symbolise the uniqueness of the artists and, being stickers, can be attributed to the artists presented in the book. Thus, the book, which visualises the different artistic positions by presenting the works in different land-scape and urban space surroundings, gains a further playful character. This active inte-gration allows readers a different approach when perusing the works and the catalogue, featuring all type in a size of 22 points, can thus be received as a highly interesting and thought-provoking art book.

Statement by the jury

»Playful, interactive and aesthetically sophisticated. The works of the 22 artists in the book are presented following a visually consistent and interesting concept that turns it into an entertaining and engaging read. Furthermore, the book possesses an interactive character that invites readers to actively partake in and create the design of the book.«

design
601bisang, Seoul

creative direction/art direction
Kum-Jun Park

graphic design
Kum-Jun Park, Bon-Hae Koo

illustration
Kum-Jun Park, Ji-Hee Lee

photography
Kum-Jun Park, Ok-Hee Cho

publishing
Jong-In Jung

coordination
So-Youn Lee, Ji-Sun Song,
Jung-Hye Lee, Sung-Kwon Joe

designer portrait
→ Vol.1: p.458

Season Programme 2011/2012

The season programme of the Schauspielhaus Graz communicates both upcoming premieres and the theatre ensemble. The title is the result of a search for a common denominator of all plays and is inspired by the thematic notions of irritation, knowledge and ignorance. The graphic design realises this idea on a meta level: inspired by popular science magazines of the mid-20th century, the programme features fake editorial contributions about seemingly serious yet absurd scientific content, which are flanked by information graphics that, at first glance, seem to provide real evidence. In addition, a visual photographic concept was developed for the plays, in which theatre employees are the main actors. They are shown in utmost bizarre scenes, while the end of the book depicts the ensemble members as participants in a fictitious convention with, however, weird and absurd details. The programme thus manages to successfully convey the objective of the theatre: a radical turmoil of all certainties.

Statement by the jury

»This work is highly imaginative and funny. It possesses a bizarre touch in the most positive sense, as the photographs tell their very own, weird stories. What is special here is that this succeeds in creating a unique identity and that the members of this theatre thus achieve a similar kind of mediation and attention that they aim at through their work.«

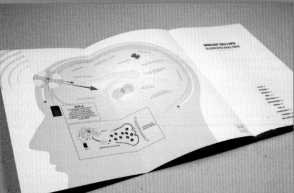

client
Schauspielhaus Graz GmbH,
Graz

design
EN GARDE OG, Graz

creative direction
Mario Rampitsch

art direction
Verena Michelitsch

concept
Philipp Kanape

graphic design
Valentin Zhuber-Okrog

photography
LUPI SPUMA Fine Photography

designer portrait
→ Vol.1: p.474

red dot: best of the best

White Green – ten projects in the great outdoors by White arkitekter

[Book]

The Swedish architectural firm White is one of the pioneers of green building design. The ten projects featured in this book document the firm's approach to and care for nature, analyse the implementation and consider how successful the results have been in practice. The cover is divided in two, with the top part being green and the bottom part being white, a division that runs all through the book and which underlines the strict balance between man-made architecture and nature. Cover two does not have a title or any lettering at all and, instead, conveys the name and content of the book via colours. Underlining the light footprint of these buildings, the contents pages show the sites without any visible structures. The same pictures are repeated later on in the book, in direct connection with the actual documentation showing the completed buildings, thus making clear how carefully these structures have been fitted into the landscapes. The top half of the pages tells the story of each architectural project, the bottom half shows drawings, models and plans.

Statement by the jury

»This book embodies a subtle yet highly accurate design implementation based on a sophisticated concept. The way the paper and alternating colours are used in the design follows an unusual path. The visual language consists of documentary photography and therefore is highly consistent.«

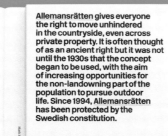

Allemansrätten gives everyone the right to move unhindered in the countryside, even across private property. It is often thought of as an ancient right but it was not until the 1930s that the concept began to be used, with the aim of increasing opportunities for the non-landowning part of the population to pursue outdoor life. Since 1994, Allemansrätten has been protected by the Swedish constitution.

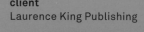

client
Laurence King Publishing

project leader
Mark Isitt

editor/author
Mark Isitt

design
Kazakoff Design, Stockholm

creative direction/concept
Igor Kazakov

graphic design
Igor Kazakov

designer portrait
→ Vol.1: p.484

02
Kastrup
Sea Bath
74__93

Das Rote-Faden-Buch /
The Red Thread Book

The Red Thread Book is part of a communication campaign which has as its primary goal to make Abtei, a manufacturer of dietary supplements, more accessible to a younger target group. Students in particular, given the high level of pressure put on them in their studies, were identified as the target group for this book, which was made available on bulletin boards at universities. The book features ten useful hints for preparing and giving a successful presentation, transforming and embodying the idea of a "red thread" one-to-one as seen by the ten guidelines which unfold as a single red thread from the very first to the last page and every page in between. Each letter and illustration in the book, without ever being cut or interrupted, are stitched from a single red thread which connects them all. The work itself is a visual reminder that reinforces the advertising message: Abtei Ginkgo Plus strengthens a person's memory and concentration.

Statement by the jury

»This book is truly remarkable and a real piece of craftsmanship in terms of how the red thread runs uninterruptedly through the entire book, forming typography and illustrations. The designers thus manage to make a strong and convincing statement.«

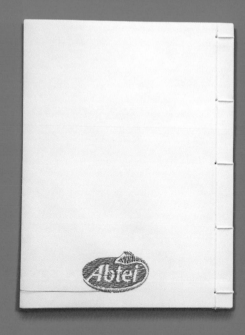

client
GlaxoSmithKline Consumer
Healthcare GmbH & Co. KG, Bühl

design
Ogilvy & Mather Advertising
GmbH, Düsseldorf

creative direction
Rob Bruenig

art direction
Sandra Prescher

text
Markus Bredenbals,
Katharina Kiklas

typography
Eleonore Bappert

designer portrait
→ Vol.1: p.493

Alape Katalog 2011 /
Alape Catalogue 2011

The Alape catalogue unites inspiration and information. The product portfolio of Alape is presented in the context of the new brand philosophy "emotional purism" and combines sensuality and objectivity into a harmonious whole. The photographs emphasise the geometric clarity and the emotional content of the products, technical sketches and material descriptions provide specific details. The transition from matte, coated to open paper enables the reader to feel the separation between both the inspiration and the information part in an optical as well as in a haptical way.

client
Alape GmbH, Goslar

design
Martin et Karczinski GmbH, Munich

creative direction
Peter Martin

art direction
Birte Helms

graphic design
Johannes Kemnitzer, Annabelle Lyhs

text
Wolfgang Wirsching

designer portrait
→ Vol.2: p.495

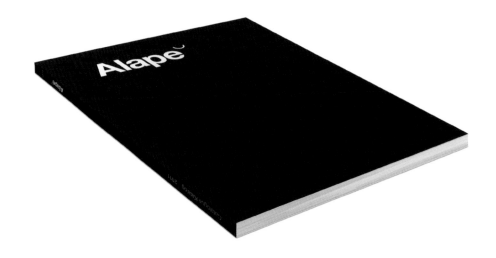

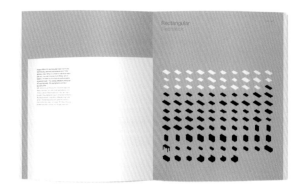

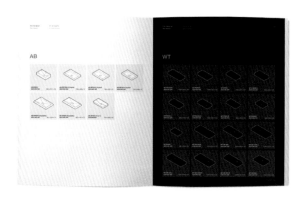

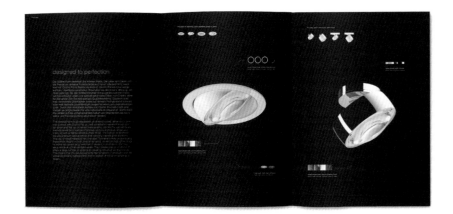

Occhio
Product Book Più

This image and product brochure provides comprehensive information about the Più spotlight series, which it presents as a consistent advancement of Occhio's portfolio. The design of the elegant black catalogue perfectly harmonises with the manufacturer's corporate identity, yet also emphasises the individual character of the spotlight series. The cover, refined by screen printing, and the hot foil stamping of the company logo underlines the high-quality appeal of this publication.

client
Occhio GmbH, Munich

design
Martin et Karczinski GmbH, Munich

creative direction
Peter Martin

art direction
Tobias Wibbeke

production
Christian Gieb

designer portrait
→ Vol.2: p.495

READ + PLAY

[Book]

The book "READ + PLAY" is targeted at both students and graduates and presents itself as a navigation guide through the jungle of expert knowledge on typography. It deals with pragmatic questions and issues of communication theory, featuring experts from the University of Applied Sciences in Mainz and providing short references on selected publications as well as links to further information. The clear and concise design of the reader is fully consistent with the subject matter and vividly illustrates the communicative function of a well thought-out typography.

client
Fachhochschule Mainz /
University of Applied Sciences
Mainz

design
Prof. Ulysses Voelker,
Peter Glaab

art direction/concept
Prof. Ulysses Voelker,
Peter Glaab

graphic design
Prof. Ulysses Voelker,
Peter Glaab

text
Prof. Ulysses Voelker

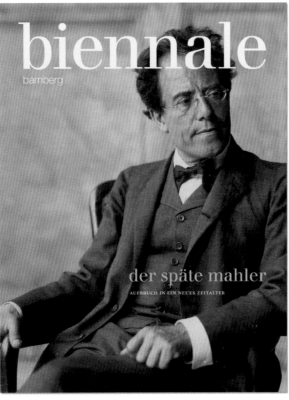

Biennale Bamberg 2010 – Der späte Mahler / *Biennale Bamberg 2010 – The late Mahler*

[Programme Magazine]

The Biennale Bamberg is a festival that every two years puts a composer or a specific work centre stage. The Biennale Bamberg 2010 was themed "Der späte Mahler" (The late Mahler). The accompanying programme magazine introduced Gustav Mahler's music in a historical context. With high-grade photographs and an unobtrusive design, which intelligently combines modern and classical elements, the magazine aims to present the time of Gustav Mahler to music lovers and enthusiasts in an exciting and entertaining manner.

client
Stiftung Bamberger Symphoniker – Bayerische Staatsphilharmonie, Bamberg

editorial work
Dr. Wolfgang Fink, Matthias Hain, Dr. Torsten Blaich

design
Simon & Goetz Design GmbH & Co. KG, Frankfurt/Main

creative direction/art direction
Bernd Vollmöller

graphic design
Bernd Vollmöller

project management
Kristin Janoschka

Heimat /
Homeland

[Product Catalogue]

client
Kraftstoff Handmade Bikes,
Dornbirn

design
Andreas Haselwanter
Grafik und Design, Dornbirn

head of marketing
Andreas Haselwanter

art direction
Andreas Haselwanter

graphic design
Andreas Haselwanter

text
Oliver Mösslang

photography
Marcel Hagen

printing
Druckerei Wenin

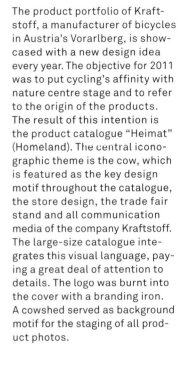

The product portfolio of Kraft-stoff, a manufacturer of bicycles in Austria's Vorarlberg, is show-cased with a new design idea every year. The objective for 2011 was to put cycling's affinity with nature centre stage and to refer to the origin of the products. The result of this intention is the product catalogue "Heimat" (Homeland). The central icono-graphic theme is the cow, which is featured as the key design motif throughout the catalogue, the store design, the trade fair stand and all communication media of the company Kraftstoff. The large-size catalogue inte-grates this visual language, pay-ing a great deal of attention to details. The logo was burnt into the cover with a branding iron. A cowshed served as background motif for the staging of all prod-uct photos.

AF Connection
Specimen

Conventional typesetting requires each letter to be surrounded by white space, in order to ensure legibility. The AF Connection font takes the opposite approach: every letter is connected with the next one, requiring the reader's eye to follow the connections in order to understand the text. This also allows for various possibilities regarding the layout of the text. This expressively designed specimen presents the three styles of AF Connection, strongly emphasising the creative potential of this font.

client
Acme Fonts, London

design
Dirk Wachowiak, London

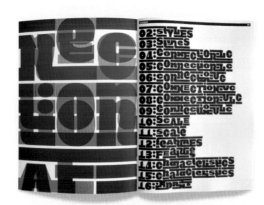

Freak/Show – Strategies for (Dis)engagement in Design
[Catalogue]

"Freak/Show – Strategies for (Dis)engagement in Design" is an exhibition on design that goes beyond standards and conventions, contrasting the work of ten unconventional designers. This exhibition catalogue presents itself as an equally unconventional companion to the exhibition: each of the ten designers is portrayed on an individual sheet made from a different type of paper. In combination, these individually designed sheets create a homogeneous whole, turning the printed catalogue into the 11th exhibit of the exhibition.

client
Helmrinderknecht contemporary design, Berlin

curator
Sophie Lovell

design
e-design+communication gmbh, Berlin

creative direction
Christiane Bördner

graphic design
Christiane Bördner

photography
Marcus Gaab, Stefano Galuzzi

designer portrait
→ Vol.1: p.472

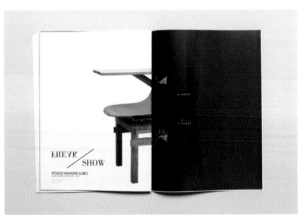

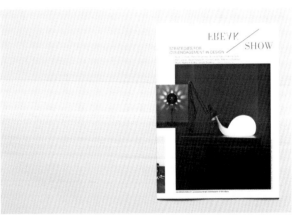

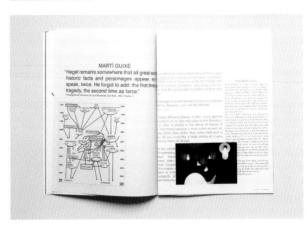

I AM

[Campaign Brochure]

The Auckland Museum holds the world's largest collection of Maori art along with art by other indigenous peoples of the Pacific region and is a natural history as well as a war memorial museum. As part of the development of a campaign identity and communications platform, this brand book showcases the campaign mark "AM" (an acronym for Auckland Museum) with the claim "I AM" as a place of identification. Formally reduced to essential elements, this publication fully articulates the new image campaign of the museum.

client
Auckland Museum, Auckland

design
Alt Group, Auckland

creative direction
Dean Poole

graphic design
Dean Poole, Shabnam Shiwan, Tony Proffit

text
Dean Poole, Ben Corban, Felicity Stevens

photography
Toaki Okano

print management
John Olding, GEON Print

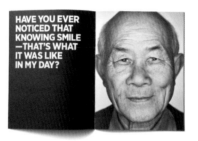

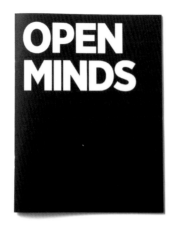
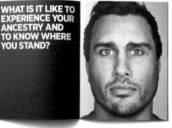

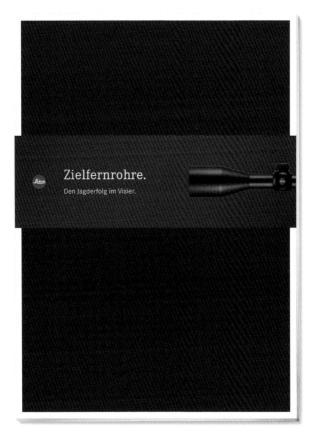

Leica Zielfernrohre /
Leica Riflescopes
[Product Catalogue]

Leica Camera, manufacturer of high-quality sport optics, introduces their first premium riflescope for affluent hunters. The catalogue uses the illustrations of the artist Marcello Pettineo to deliver all the romance of big-game hunting, with none of the shock. Using sensible and sparse design, the catalogue visualises the dream of any passionate hunter: to experience the harmony between man and nature.

client
Leica Camera AG, Solms

design
G2 Germany / Frankfurt

creative direction
Felix Dürichen (Art),
Jutta Häussler (Text)

art direction
Mona Pust

consultancy
Maik Hofmann, Anja Awater

illustration
Marcello Pettineo

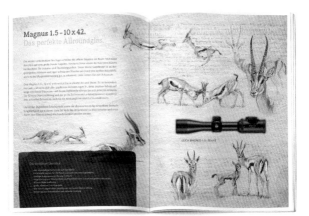

SVA Undergraduate Catalog 2011/12

The objective of the SVA Under-graduate Catalog 2011/12 is to show the high quality of art produced at the School of Visual Arts to prospective students. The large-size publication contains a wide variety of student works as well as comprehensive factual information on New York City and SVA. The expressive individual works are clearly and consistently arranged using a reduced typography and visual paths that guide through the book. Thanks to a heat-responsive coating, the cover reveals a map of the school when in contact with the skin.

client
School of Visual Arts, New York

design
Visual Arts Press, Ltd., New York

creative direction
Anthony P. Rhodes

art direction
Michael J. Walsh

graphic design
E. Patrick Tobin, Brian E. Smith, Suck Zoo Han

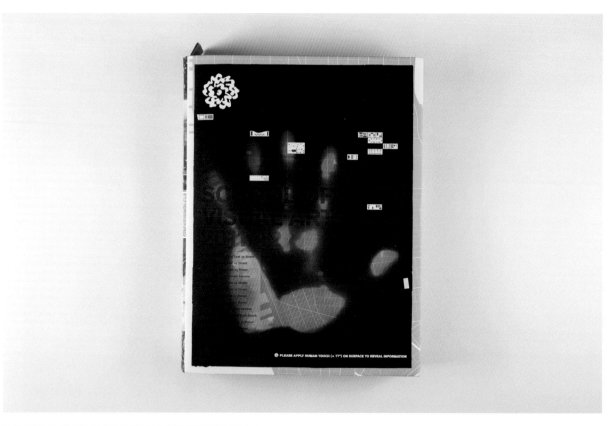

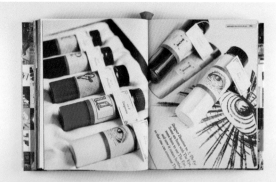

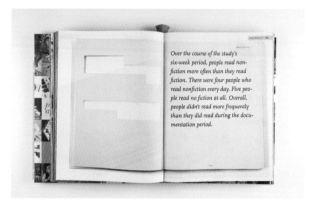

Orca Merino Lookbook

Orca is a sportswear brand that produces high-performance triathlon wetsuits and other clothing for triathletes. The new merino sports collection was inspired by the idea that "Life's a race". To illustrate the competitive mindset of the campaign, a two-word copy strategy was created as a series of poetic and rhythmically distinctive micro narratives, which complement and underline the product photos. In addition to high-quality studio photography, the series of images is complemented by a range of photographic styles including macro satellite images.

client
Orca, Auckland

design
Alt Group, Auckland

creative direction
Dean Poole

graphic design
Clem Devine

text
Clem Devine, Dean Poole

photography
Steven Tilley

Ernst Logar –
Invisible Oil

[Artist Book]

This extraordinary artist book documents the project "Invisible Oil" by artist Ernst Logar, who focused on exploring the oil industry and its socio-economic influences, with Europe's "oil capital" Aberdeen as example. The publication reflects on the issue of oil and the socio-political power of the oil industry in detail. It features an oily, black-brown CMYK colour that appears consistently throughout the entire layout of the book in form of monochrome "censoring" surfaces and oil-coloured threads.

client
SpringerWienNewYork, Vienna

design
Olaf Osten, Vienna

art direction
Olaf Osten

concept
Olaf Osten, Ernst Logar

graphic design
Olaf Osten

photography
Ernst Logar

printing
Holzhausen Druck GmbH, Vienna

designer portrait
→ Vol.1: p.495

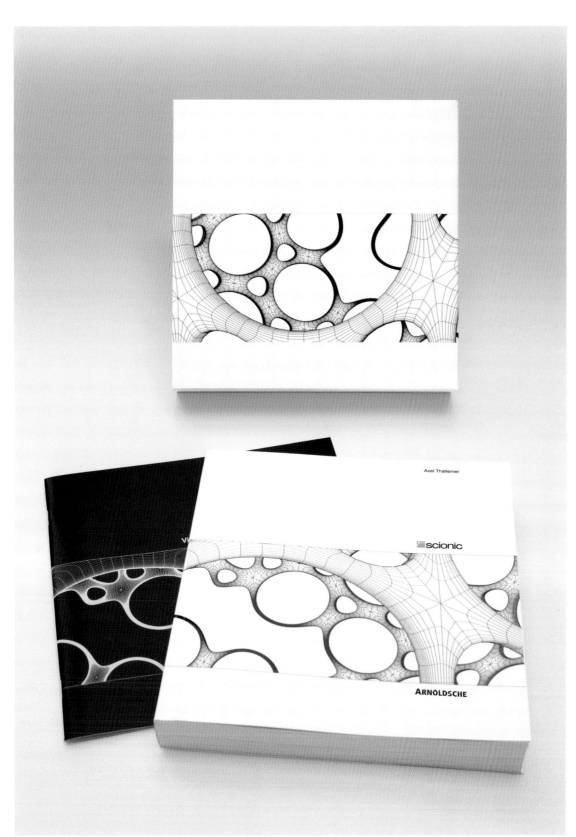

SCIONIC.
Purpose-driven Gestalt.
The End of Design?

[Brochure]

Creativity is presented in this publication not as a mysterious black box, but as a systematic approach. "SCIONIC" documents the workflow and problem-solving strategies of creativity professionals and design students. Tools such as the rapid prototyping are in this connection as important as creative thinking techniques. The design of this compendium fully represents the high demands on the content, combining academic accuracy with visual elegance into a harmonious synthesis.

client/publisher
ARNOLDSCHE Art Publishers, Stuttgart

design
scionic® I.D.E.A.L., Industrial Design, Linz

concept
Axel Thallemer

text
Axel Thallemer (scionic), Jens Reese (visual permutations annotations)

printing
Leibfarth & Schwarz, Dettingen/Erms

HDA –
Haus der Architektur
Reader 2010
[Yearbook]

This book is the first issue of a new annual series published by the HDA (House of Architecture) in Graz, Austria. It contains a documentation of the programmatic key aspects, interviews with experts and a presentation of the organisation's activities. The design of the yearbook is transparent and light. Layout and visual language accommodate the manifold photo and text material, combining it into a homogeneous entity. A typographically sophisticated directory system leads through the book, underlining the conceptional approach of the series.

client
HDA, Haus der Architektur / House of Architecture, Graz

design
gabriele lenz, büro für visuelle gestaltung, Vienna

creative direction
Gabriele Lenz

concept
Eva Guttmann, Christoph Marek

graphic design
Elena Henrich

project management
Elena Henrich

publishing
Metroverlag, Vienna

printing
Ueberreuter Print GmbH

FLACC 09

[Yearbook]

The publication "FLACC 09" documents the results of FLACC, a workplace for visual artists. The challenge for the design was to adequately document the results of the artists in English, French and Dutch, while avoiding to overshadow the photos with text. Thus, the original texts were printed in black, while the translations appear as italic spot-colour printing. The same difference in colour and printing technique distinguishes the artworks from the photos documenting the different processes.

client
FLACC vzw, Genk

design
Atelier Petit, Hasselt

printing
Cultura, Wetteren

designer portrait
→ Vol.1: p.461

b – No. 1 Magazin des Balletts am Rhein /
b – No. 1 Magazine Ballett am Rhein

With the beginning of the new season 2010/11 the first edition of the new magazine of the Ballett am Rhein was published. Essays, portraits and interviews introduced the choreographers, dancers and artists of the ballet company. In the centre of the magazine was an extensive image documentation that staged the performances b.01 to b.05 of the previous season. News and further information about the company can be found in the rear part of the magazine.

client
Ballett am Rhein,
Düsseldorf/Duisburg

**ballet director/
chief choreographer**
Martin Schläpfer

design
Markwald & Neusitzer
Kommunikationsdesign,
Frankfurt/Main

art direction
Nina Neusitzer,
Nicolas Markwald

editorial work
Anne do Paço

photography
Gert Weigelt

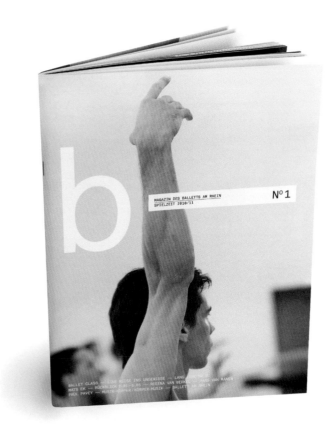

The Dream Room
[Exhibition Catalogue]

The catalogue accompanies the exhibition "The Dream Room" in the Liljevalchs art hall in Stockholm. 12 prominent experts of Swedish antiques staged the passion of collecting, each of them in their own gallery. They designed very personal rooms – dream rooms – that express the force that stands behind their passion. The catalogue contains interviews, essays and more than 40 images for each individual expert. The images kept in warm colours, document a deep relationship of the collectors to the objects.

client
Liljevalchs, Stockholm

design
Morris Pinewood Stockholm

creative direction/art direction
Mattias Frodlund, Hanna Moe

design team
Mattias Frodlund, Hanna Moe

printing
Elanders Fälth & Hässler, Sweden

designer portrait
→ Vol.1: p.490

phoenixmotion – Values in Style

[Brochure]

The paper manufacturer Scheufelen demonstrates in this publication the versatile uses of the phoenixmotion paper, which combines the feel of uncoated paper with the look and printability of coated paper. With affectionate texts, photographs and design the brochure illustrates the influence and importance of the paper choice for a successful visual design based on a wide and selected range of topics. It is refined by blind and hot foil embossing, special inks and a scented coating.

client
Papierfabrik Scheufelen GmbH
& Co. KG, Lenningen

design
Strichpunkt Design, Stuttgart

creative direction
Jochen Rädeker

art direction
Kirsten Dietz

graphic design
Julia Ochsenhirt,
Agnetha Wohlert

project management
Marc Schergel

photography
Niels Schubert,
Susanne Mölle

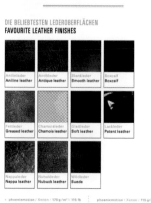

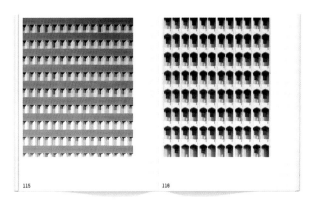

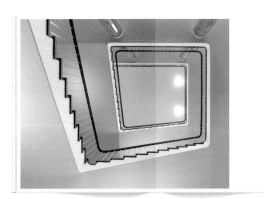

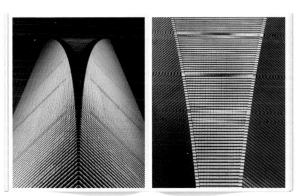

Commissioned Works
[Exhibition Catalogue]

The exhibition "Commissioned Works" and the catalogue of the same name show the works of architecture photographer Hans-Georg Esch, who produced them for national and international architecture firms during more than 20 years of his career. The layout with its monochrome colour scheme and the strict composition with only a few variations treat each project equally and put the works into an artistic context. An eight-page fold-out catalogues all 169 images.

client
HG Esch Photography,
Hennef Stadt Blankenberg

design
großgestalten
kommunikationsdesign, Cologne

design team
Tobias Groß, Jazek Poralla

photography
HG Esch

Bundesrasenschau /
Federal Lawn Show

[Art Book]

This art book is the accompanying documentation for an ephemeral work of art in a public space. Artist Ralf Witthaus cuts a three metres wide path through Cologne's inner greenbelt, revealing the city's architectural layout as a coherent form. The scale of the entire drawing, which is interrupted by houses and streets, is so large that it cannot be viewed in its entirety from any point, neither spatially nor temporally. When the circle is completed, only a memory of its origin lingers in the mind.

client
DIE NEUE SACHLICHKEIT,
kunst | buch | verlag, Lindlar

design
DIE NEUE SACHLICHKEIT,
kunst | buch | verlag, Lindlar

art direction
Christopher Schroer

concept
Christopher Schroer,
Ralf Witthaus

graphic design
Christopher Schroer

text
Gerhard Kolberg, Joachim Bauer

printing
Siebel Druck & Grafik, Lindlar

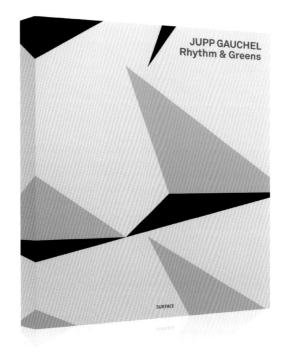

Jupp Gauchel – Rhythm & Greens

[Exhibition Catalogue]

The bilingual catalogue accompanies the exhibition "Rhythm & Greens" of artist Jupp Gauchel. He generates simple geometric drawings on his computer which are then carried out as laminate boards. The catalogue presents three laminate series with an introductory text, illustrates the reduced colour and texture palettes, and also contains an essay by Volker Fischer. Like the artist's working method the layout of the catalogue is based on a simple rational set of rules.

client
Jupp Gauchel, Karlsruhe

design
becoming – office for visual communication, Karlsruhe

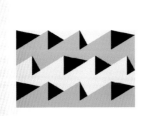

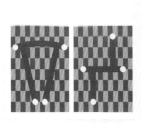

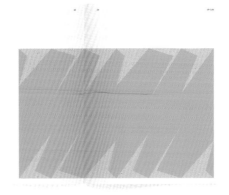

Smart in Your World

[Corporate Brochure]

The brochure "Smart in Your World" is based on the motto of the law firm Arent Fox and conveys it via an expressive visual language. In contrast to traditional publications in this industry, the brochure showcases the law firm with an eye-catching and "smart" design that makes use of clear structures and captivating contrasts. The oversized high-gloss magazine describes the most compelling cases of the firm and portrays some of its illustrious clients. A foil embossing provides additional refinement.

client
Arent Fox, Washington DC

design
DESIGN ARMY, Washington DC

creative direction
Jake Lefebure, Pum Lefebure

art direction
Pum Lefebure

graphic design
Charles Calixto

illustration
Tim Madle

printing
Worth Higgins & Associates

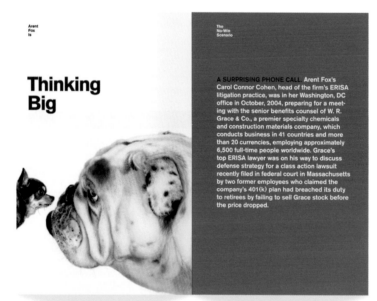

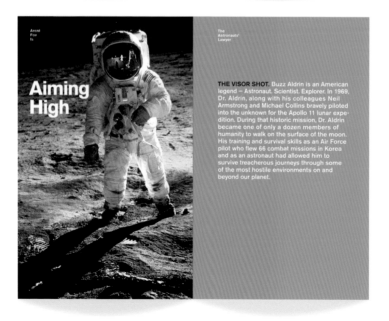

Christmas Tree Card

True to the motto "Big ideas come out of big pencils", the striking design of this Christmas card focuses on the logo of the Leo Burnett agency: the Big Black Pencil. The playful symbiosis of pencil and Christmas tree on the front surprises the addressee, creating curiosity and forming a harmonious visual balance with the distinctive corporate identity of the sender. This impression is further underlined by the use of high-grade paper. The unobtrusive layout of the text leaves enough space for personal words.

client
Leo Burnett GmbH,
Frankfurt/Main

design
Leo Burnett GmbH,
Frankfurt/Main

chief creative officer
Andreas Pauli

creative direction
Hans-Jürgen Kämmerer

art direction
Bjørnar Thorsen

illustration
Walter Pepperle

designer portrait
→ Vol.2: p.473

Ultras: Die Bühne
gehört uns –
Kinderstadt 2010 /
*Ultras: the stage is ours
– Children's City 2010*

[Documentation]

The new theatre projects of the
Thalia Theater in Halle focus on
exploring the problems of the
city and experimenting with new
forms of communication. This
series of books documents two
of these projects. The children's
city "Halle an Salle" was planned,
built and managed by children.
In the production "Ultras" soccer fans themselves performed
on stage. The publications are
printed on uncoated paper, feature a clear, easy-to-remember
typography and contain drawings
and photographs. A DIN A2-sized
poster serves as the book jacket.

client
Theater, Oper und Orchester
GmbH Halle, Sparte Thalia
Theater Halle

design
Neue Gestaltung GmbH, Berlin

design team
Pit Stenkhoff, Anna Bühler,
Eva Wendel, Nina Odzinieks

illustrations
Sebastian Schichel

designer portrait
→ Vol.1: p.491

Stadtordnung

§1 Die Kinderstadt „Halle an
Salle" ist dienstags bis samstags
von 10.00–18.00 Uhr im Zeitraum
vom 04.06.–11.07.10 geöffnet.

§2 Jedes Kind im Alter von 6–14
kann Bürger der Kinderstadt
werden. Um am Stadtgeschehen
teilnehmen zu können, muss ein
Eintrittsgeld gezahlt werden.

§3 Das einzig gültige Zahlungs-
mittel in der Kinderstadt sind die
„Hallörchen". Sie können nur in
„Halle an Salle" verdient und
ausgegeben werden.

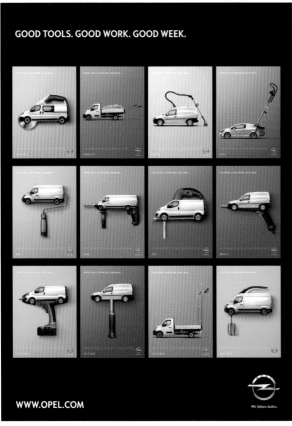

Opel LCV – Good Tools. Good Work. Good Week.

[Calendar]

The idea behind the motifs of this calendar was to showcase Opel's commercial vehicles with an emotionally appealing design that integrates the entire product range. The different target groups are individually addressed by connecting the vehicles to work equipment. Cars and tools form a harmonious combination in this image series, appealing to customers without alienating the actually promoted product.

client
Adam Opel AG, Rüsselsheim

head of advertising
Tamas Bator, Andrea Pfannmöller

design
brandtouch GmbH, Hamburg

creative direction
Günter Sendlmeier

art direction
Jonathan Sven Amelung,
Pedro Americo

photography
Christian Stoll

post-production
Ralph Hillert

Der Schriftenfächer – eine Entdeckungsreise /
The Fonts Displayer – A Discovery Tour

client
Zürcher Hochschule der Künste /
Zurich University of the Arts;
Berufsschule für Gestaltung
Zürich, Medien Form Farbe /
School of Design Zurich

head of project/initiation
Barbara Berger, Samuel Marty

creative direction/art direction
Richard Frick, Samuel Marty

concept/design/text
Richard Frick, Samuel Marty

cooperation
Erich Alb, Rudolf Barmettler,
Hans Rudolf Bosshard

printing
Eberl Print GmbH, Immenstadt

The Fonts Displayer aims to sensitise students of the Zurich University of the Arts and the School of Design Zurich to the topic "font". Against this backdrop, a handy compendium of typography was developed that proved to be a helpful medium at both schools. The high-quality Fonts Displayer was designed with great love for detail and comprises a comprehensive repertoire with a new classification of typefaces. A glossary of fonts with almost 400 terms replaces the classic sample texts. Distinctive features and characteristics of the fonts are thoroughly indicated and complemented by information about the type designers, the year of publication and distribution.

Lucida Serif | 114

24 pt
Typografie

8.5/12 pt
QUERBALKEN Horizontaler Strich bei den Buchstaben wie z.B. «H», «A» usw.
QUOTE Englischer Begriff für ein Zitat.
RANDABFALLEND Über das Seitenformat herausragende Elemente wie z.B. Abbildungen und Farbflächen (siehe →Beschnitt).
RAUSATZ Unbearbeiteter →Flattersatz mit teilweise unschönen Satzkanten (Treppen, Bäuche, Löcher usw.) oder Flattersatz mit kurz gehaltener →Flatterzone.

Lucida Std >(4)
Roman | Italic
Bold | **Italic**

Fedra Serif | 168

24 pt
Typografie

8.5/12 pt
HYBRID-SCHRIFTEN Von Hybrid spricht man bei Mischformen/-bildungen. In Bezug auf die Schrift gibt es zwei Möglichkeiten, um von Hybrid-Formen zu sprechen: Es handelt sich um Mischformen bei den Zeichen zwischen einer serifenlosen und einer →Serifenschrift wie z.B. «SemiSans» oder «SemiSerif», Bei den →Schriftsippen kann auch von Hybrid-Schriften gesprochen werden, wenn eine so erweiterte →Schriftfamilie aus zwei oder mehreren Schriftfamilien — →Antiqua, →Grotesk, →serifenbetonter Schrift — mit aufeinander bezogenen Formen und →Zurichtungen (gemeinsame →x-Höhe, →Laufweite usw.) besteht.

Fedra Serif A Std >(8+8)
Book | Italic
Demi | Italic
Medium | Italic
Bold | **Italic**
Weitere, nicht dargestellte Schriftschnitte
Familie: Fedra Serif B

---

15   Terminologie: Renaissance-Antiqua

1 Serife mit Kehlung zum Stamm und konkaver Basis
2 Schräge Achsenstellung
3 Querstrich
4 Schwacher Zug
5 Stamm, Hauptstrich, starker Zug
6 Fähnchen
7 Schräger Ansatz
8 Bauch
9 Übergang von der Serife zum Stamm
10 Überlauf
11 Scheitel
12 Gerundeter Endstrich

geschlossener Punzen   offener Punzen

---

31   Hinting

Hinting ist ein Verfahren, das zur verbesserten Schriftdarstellung bei niedrigauflösenden Ausgabegeräten eingesetzt wird (wie z.B. beim Bildschirm). Am stärksten kommt das Hinting bei kleinen Schriftgraden zur Geltung.
Hints (engl.: Hinweise) sind digitale Zusatzinformationen, welche der Outline-Beschreibung als Anweisungen für das Verhalten in bestimmten Punktgrößen beigefügt werden. Die Hints müssen für jeden Schriftgrad neu definiert werden. Daher ist das Hinting ein sehr aufwändiger Vorgang. So erstellte Schriften sind wesentlich teurer als jene ohne oder nur mit automatisch generiertem Hinting. Für weitere Informationen: www.typotheque.com/articles/hinting

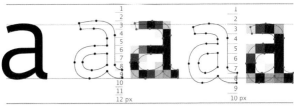

Originalschriftzeichen «a» der Fedra Sans | Outline auf die Pixelmatrix von 12 Pixel Schriftgröße hin optimiert | Outline über Pixelmatrix | Outline auf die Pixelmatrix von 10 Pixel Schriftgröße hin optimiert | Outline über Pixelmatrix

---

168   2-gliedrig   Fedra Serif

Peter Bil'ak, 2003–2006

Fedra Serif A Std
8 Schriftschnitte

Schriftsippe > 2-gliedrig
Antiqua > Renaissance [II]
----
www.typotheque.com

quadratisch, auf Spitze gestellter i-Punkt

Abschluss ohne Querbalken   schräg, gespreizte Schenkel   nicht geschlossener Punzen

5
16

55

22
2

ABCDEFGHIJKLMNOPQRSTUVWXYZ
abcdefghijklmnopqrstuvwxyz 1234567890 ?!;&©@

Schwarzkopf – Celebrating 50 years of color excellence

[Premium Calendar]

This manually riveted, limited calendar box was designed for the anniversary of IGORA, a Schwarzkopf Professional brand. The calendar features a flexible design consisting of three elements: in addition to calendar and month cards, original haiku were written, that allow users to put together both: their favourite motif and their favourite short poem for each month. The 12 photo prints are fit to plate embossing.

client
Schwarzkopf Professional, Hamburg

design
Paperlux GmbH, Hamburg

creative direction
Marco Kuehne

art direction
Hassan Haider

customer advisory service
Soraya Kuehne

project management
Sebastian Heberle

text
Nishant Peralta

printing
Officina Polychroma

PLAY!
Design for kids
[Calendar]

The design for this calendar is inspired by children's creativity and focuses on the experimental use of typography. "PLAY! Design for kids" contains the work of 53 designers and architects who combine concept and design with the joy of play to delight children. Produced by screen and embossed printing, the calendar is available in three different colours and aims to be an inspiring companion through the year 2012. Its designers gave their playful side free rein and let the inspiration from their children or their own childhood flow into the design of the typography.

client
EIGA Design, Hamburg

design
EIGA Design, Hamburg

creative direction
Elisabeth Plass

art direction
Henning Otto

graphic design
Nicola Janssen, Josefine Freund

printing
Mediadruckwerk Gruppe GmbH

designer portrait
→ Vol.1: p.473

zur nachahmung empfohlen expeditionen in ästhetik und nachhaltigkeit / *examples to follow! expeditions in aesthetics and sustainability*

[Exhibition Catalogue]

The touring exhibition "examples to follow! expeditions in aesthetics and sustainability", curated by Adrienne Goehler, showcases art projects and initiatives for maintaining our planet. The accompanying collection of publications contains the corresponding exhibition catalogue, ecologically innovative construction manuals, a reader and a draft for a sustainable fund concept. In accordance with the exhibition's theme, the publication is produced in an ecologically friendly way with a cover made of recycled textiles.

client
Adrienne Goehler, Stiftung Forum der Kulturen zu Fragen der Zeit, Berlin

editor
Adrienne Goehler

design
anschlaege.de – Atelier für Gestaltung, Lagé, Schuhmann & Watzke GbR, Berlin

creative direction
Axel Watzke

art direction
Steffen Schuhmann

concept
Christian Lagé

graphic design
Axel Watzke, Steffen Schuhmann, Christian Lagé

publishing
Hatje Cantz Verlag

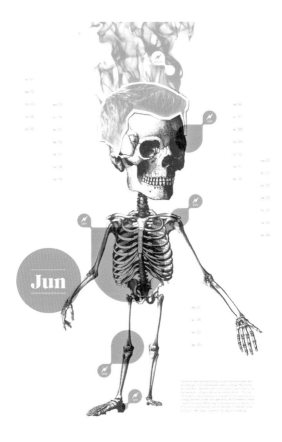

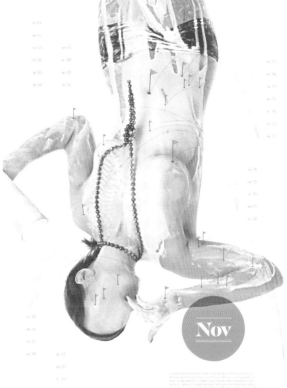

Zufallskalender /
Calendar of Coincidence

[Corporate Gift]

This calendar features 25 odd stories about coincidence and was created in a mostly aleatory process. The designers walked barefoot over colour charts, and the colours that coincidentally stuck to their feet defined the colour scheme for the calendar. For the design of the individual pages, dice rolling, random scripts and other principles of random coincidence were applied, leading to unexpected results. Pages were arranged in random order or printed with mixed-up colours. A making-of video can be found on the corresponding website.

client
Antalis, Frechen

design
Q Kreativgesellschaft mbH, Wiesbaden

creative direction
Thilo von Debschitz,
Matthias Frey,
Alexander Ginter

illustration
Matthias Frey, Alexander Ginter,
Moritz Stuebig

project management
Detlef Westenberger,
Komminform

printing
Volkhardt Caruna Medien

bookbinding
SYGO

designer portrait
→ Vol.1: p.497

Heimatseiten –
Wandkalender 2011 /
Homepages –
Wall Calendar 2011

In its wall calendar the Eberl
Media Group waives the presentation of its own products. Instead,
the calendar shows culinary
images from the Allgäu region –
from pickled nuts and farmhouse
bread to 500 old apple varieties.
The appetising images harmonise
with the modern and playful layout of the calendar. Additionally,
the calendar pages come with
exquisitely designed packaging
that can be reused right away for
wrapping original products at a
visit in the Allgäu region.

client
Eberl Print GmbH, Immenstadt

design
Strichpunkt Design, Stuttgart

creative direction/concept
Jochen Rädeker

art direction
Kirsten Dietz

graphic design
Agnetha Wohlert

project management
Peter Hoppe

photography
Susanne Mölle

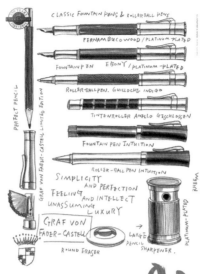

250th Anniversary of Faber-Castell 2011
[Calendar]

This calendar aims to worthily celebrate the 250th anniversary of the company Faber-Castell. For this purpose, all illustrations of the calendar were drawn with Faber-Castell products. Each illustration also shows the specific tool it was created with. With this expressive design the calendar represents the identity of the stationery maker and triggers curiosity for the promoted products. A Castell 9000 pencil was integrated into the unique binding of the calendar.

client
Faber-Castell Korea Branch (KOMOS International Co., Ltd.), Seoul

design
Heon Woo Lim,
Keimyung University, Daegu

creative direction
Heon Woo Lim,
Keimyung University, Daegu

illustration
Heon Woo Lim,
Keimyung University, Daegu

calligraphy
Dae Yeon Kim

Eternal Magnetic Calendar

This eternal magnetic calendar presents itself in a simple design and is usable in many ways. It consists of 63 individual pieces, delivered in a practical box, which also adhere reliably to each other. Beside the monthly and the daily chips, markers were designed that mark anniversaries, departures, arrivals or deadlines. Despite the high self-explanatory value, a concise manual is included in the box.

client
Dorogaya, Kiev

design
Chebotaryov Sergiy, Pinigin Igor, Dorogaya, Kiev

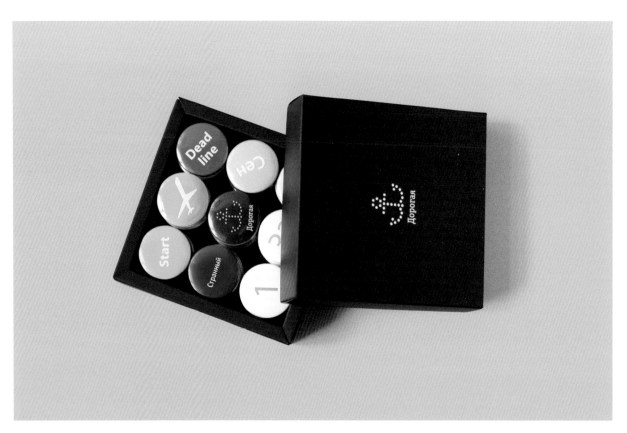

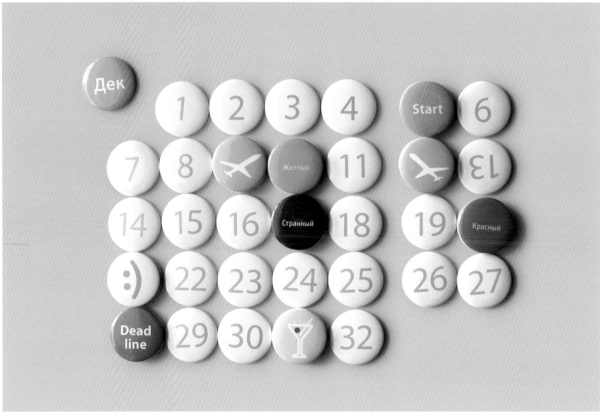

Trash Calendar

Sooner or later nearly every design product ends up in the trash. The Trash Calendar anticipates this – the trash can is its actual target. It consists of 12 rolls divided into quarters with 28 to 31 accordingly labelled garbage bags per month: one for each day. What lies behind this is that many ideas remain merely ideas, although they harbour quite a lot of potential to change the world. The Trash Calendar is supposed to make you think how each day was spent and why it was spent in this way and which ideas are worth continuing to exist.

client
Graphic design studio by
Yurko Gutsulyak, Kiev

design
Graphic design studio by
Yurko Gutsulyak, Kiev

art direction
Yurko Gutsulyak

graphic design
Yurko Gutsulyak

project management
Zoryana Gutsulyak

designer portrait
→ Vol.1: p.477

54th Venice Biennale – The Cloud of Unknowing (Singapore Pavilion) Catalogue

Ho Tzu Nyen presented Singapore at the 54th Biennale in Venice. His contribution, "The Cloud of Unknowing", is an audiovisual installation, which examines the different roles of clouds in art: as a historical object, as embodiment of emptiness, as exercise for imagination or a canvas for projections. It shows images from Ho's present and past works and offers essays on transparent and lightweight paper stock finished with roughened edges.

client
National Arts Council, Singapore

design
Asylum Creative Pte Ltd, Singapore

creative direction
Chris Lee

art direction
Cara Ang

graphic design
May Chiang

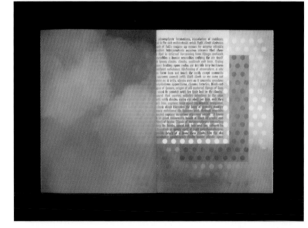

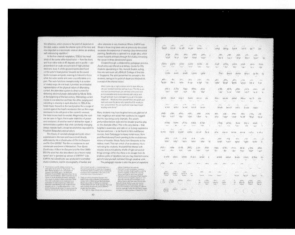

IDEE DING BILD REDE / *IDEA THING IMAGE SPEECH*

[Catalogue]

This catalogue is published for the exhibition "IDEE DING BILD REDE" (IDEA THING IMAGE SPEECH) – one of the most ambitious projects that the Magdeburg design forum has ever attempted. With a typographically and visually very distinctive design, the publication presents 12 individual objects of renowned artists and designers from Saxony-Anhalt, interpreting and documenting their development from conception to completion with photographic essays and texts.

client
Forum Gestaltung e.V., Magdeburg

design
Gina Louise Schmiedel, NORDSONNE IDENTITY GmbH, Berlin

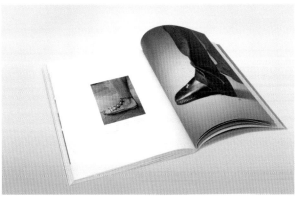

Drehbuch /
Turn-Around Book
[Paper Journal]

This unconventional paper journal
was developed for the Art Directors Club Germany. The Drehbuch
(Turn-Around Book) consists of
a black and a white part. The
book features a Z-shaped binding
which allows users to flip through
the white pages from one side
and through the black pages from
the other side. The Turn-Around
Book comes together with a
"turn-around pen" which writes
in both black and white. In this
way, positive people are allowed
to also have negative thoughts at
times, while it helps pessimists
to discover their positive sides.

client
Art Directors Club für
Deutschland (ADC), Berlin

design
brandbook.de, Frankfurt/Main

creative direction
Bernd Griese

text
Christoph Herold

project management
Sabine Kochendörfer

production
Dirk Mahlke

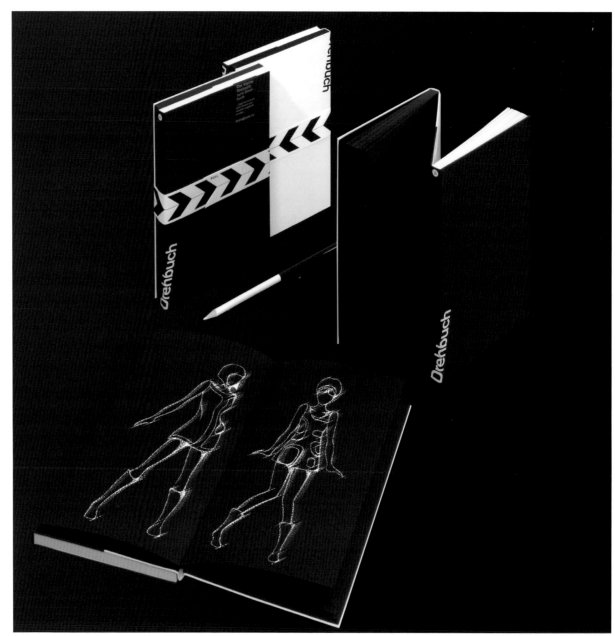

Swop Book
[Idea Book]

The Swop Book believes in the playful power of wild thinking and was conceived as attack on the fear of the blank page. With more than one hundred pictures from all fields of life it wants to replace emptiness with inspiration. The pictures tell little tales to spin off from and invite to scribble, draw or write. The Swop Book is complemented by a website that offers first inspirations for "swopping", uploaded sketches by users and a virtual edition of the book.

client
brandbook.de, Frankfurt/Main

design
brandbook.de, Frankfurt/Main

creative direction
Bernd Griese

text
Christoph Herold

project management
Sandra Elm

photography
Shutterstock

production
Sabine Kochendörfer

Forster & Uhl Architekten GmbH

[Documentation]

At first glance there seem to be only a few lines inside the brochure of the Forster & Uhl architecture office in Zürich. All pages show large-scale pictures of architectural projects realised by the office. Only the last page invites readers to open the perforations of the Japanese binding and take a look at the inner pages of the book. Printed in silver on black Chromolux paper, the drawings, plans and words explain the possible process-oriented methods of the architects.

client
Forster & Uhl Architekten GmbH, Zürich

design
Klauser Design GmbH, Zürich

art direction
Tobias Klauser

graphic design
Bruno Kaufmann,
Tobias Klauser,
Hans Peter Dubacher

text
Robert Roos, Lucerne

photography
Michael Freisager, Baar

printing
Köpfli & Partner AG, Neuenhof

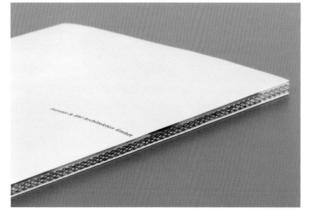

Advent Advent

[Advent Calendar]

"Advent Advent" is an Advent calendar in form of a book. The pages have a different colour for every week and feature typographically distinctive numbers. They are perforated on the margins and conceal absurdly profound illustrations inside. Conceived as a creative and memorable media of self-promotion, this Advent calendar every day directs the attention for a few moments to the giver. It surprises with an unusual form and with contents that are rather unconventional for the Christmas season.

client
Studio Delhi, Mainz

design
Studio Delhi, Mainz

art direction/concept
Manuela Rech,
Klaus Chmielewski

graphic design
Katrin Janka, Anika Obenland

illustration
Manuela Rech

This is Service Design Thinking

[Specialist Book]

This book is the outcome of an international, interdisciplinary design process with 23 co-authors and more than 80 online contributors. As a specialist book on the emerging field of service design it considers the reading experience a designable process. Thus, this publication presents itself as a service and focuses on the intangible service behind the mere object. The classic specialist book is complemented by an original pictographic language and a dramaturgy that is closely interwoven with the content.

client
Marc Stickdorn, Innsbruck

project management
Marc Stickdorn

text/content design
Marc Stickdorn

design
Jakob Schneider, Cologne

creative direction/art direction
Jakob Schneider

graphic design
Jakob Schneider

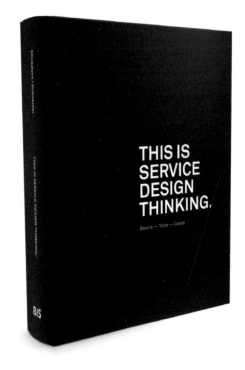

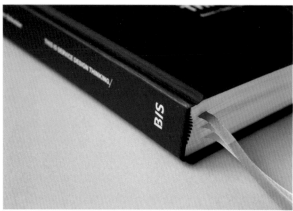

BasisBibel NT

[Book]

The BasisBibel was produced with the needs of readers of the 21st century in mind and closely linked to the original source, concisely written and cross-medially networked. It is specifically designed to be read as book as well as on screen. The design of the book itself is as concise as the translation. Everything is reduced to the cross, which, understood as central message of the New Testament, is being communicated like a brand. The bible is available in five limited edition colours and with partial colour edging.

client
Deutsche Bibelgesellschaft, Stuttgart

head of marketing
Florian Theuerkauff

design
gobasil GmbH, Hamburg

creative direction
Eva Jung

art direction
Oliver Schwartz

concept
Eva Jung, Nico Mühlan, Oliver Schwartz

printing
CPI – Clausen & Bosse, Leck

designer portrait
→ Vol.1: p.476

The Berlin Fashion-week Photodiary™ #2
[Documentation]

This documentation presents an authentic look behind the glamorous scenes of the Berlin Fashionweek. Models without make-up, garbage in the foyer, empty seats, exuberance and exhaustion after the show – these emphatic moments illustrate how much work and strain is behind the perfect surface of a fashion show. All photographs were taken with tiny rangefinder cameras and developed using analogue processes. The high-quality materials and a clear design lend the book the appeal of a timeless fashion accessory.

design
Joern Toellner Design, Berlin

creative direction/concept
Marc Schuhmann,
Joern Toellner

art direction
Joern Toellner

text
Jan Joswig,
Susanne Kaloff,
Bjoern Luedtke,
Campbell McDougall,
Hili Perlson,
Turid Reinicke

photography
Marc Schuhmann,
Karsten Friemel,
James Gregory Atkinson,
Chloé Richard

printing
Seltmann Druckereibetriebe,
Lüdenscheid

Pioniere des Reisens / *Pioneers of Travel*

[Book]

This book was designed in the context of the film "Pioniere des Reisens" (Pioneers of Travel), which tells the history of the MAIRDUMONT publishing company and the family history of its managing director Volkmar Mair. To do justice to the family's thirst for adventure, a large-scale format was chosen for the book. The open back, the uncoated paper and the red thread stitching emphasise the pioneering achievements. The photos are presented as filmstrips that run through the pages, creating interesting image sections, which are resolved only on the next page.

client
MAIRDUMONT GmbH & Co. KG, Ostfildern

project management client
Sabine Mack, Ute Lehre

text
Jens Bey, MAIRDUMONT

design
jangled nerves, Stuttgart

creative direction
Prof. Thomas Hundt, Ingo Zirngibl

graphic design
Stephanie Niewienz

project management
Gesina Geiger

eMPe nullneun

[Architecture Book]

The architecture book "eMPe nullneun" documents the ambitious project MP09 in the Austrian city of Graz from the first building plans to its completion, taking the visions and the premises, the individual participants and the construction process itself into account. The publication continues the aesthetic code of the building architecture conceptually and graphically and communicates the corporate philosophy along with the corporate architecture of the Michael Pachleitner Group in word, picture and graphic design.

client
Michael Pachleitner Group,
Graz

design
luffup, büro für
kommunikationsdesign

art direction
Tomislav Bobinec

concept
Tobias Federsel,
Tomislav Bobinec

graphic design
Tomislav Bobinec,
Ljubomir Sužnjević,
Volker Waldhauser

text
Tobias Federsel,
Manuela Hötzl

photography
Gerald Liebminger

printing
Platinium, Print & Druck

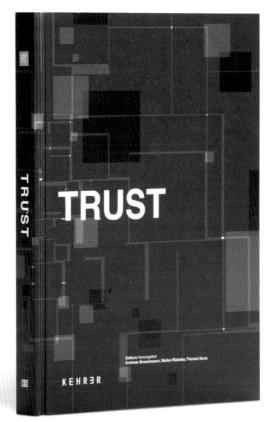

TRUST

[Exhibition Catalogue]

ISEA belongs to the most important international festivals for electronic art. As a project of RUHR.2010 – European Capital of Culture, it took place in Germany for the first time and presented the latest developments of international media art in Dortmund, Essen and Duisburg. Central topic of the design were picture elements that illuminate the connection and the fragmentation of media art. All communication media, including posters, print advertisements and the website, were designed with its own individual composition of pixels.

client
Andreas Broeckmann,
Stefan Riekeles,
Thomas Munz,
ISEA2010 RUHR,
Dortmund

design
labor b designbüro,
Dortmund

verbuendungshaus fforst – Eine Ermutigung / *an encouragement*

[Book]

Together with students from the European University Viadrina, the anschlaege.de design office opened the fforst house, a student-run, international dormitory in a "Plattenbau" building in Frankfurt/Oder, close to the Polish border, in 2006. The fforst book is a compendium in German and English. It tells about the practical experiences of self-administration, the collected knowledge and the discussions held in the fforst house. The various charts and images form a stimulating contrast to the clear typography and the vibrant illustrations.

client
verbuendungshaus fforst e.V., Frankfurt/Oder

design
anschlaege.de – Atelier für Gestaltung, Lagé, Schuhmann & Watzke GbR, Berlin

creative direction
Steffen Schuhmann

art direction
Axel Watzke

concept
Christian Lagé

graphic design
Axel Watzke, Steffen Schuhmann, Christian Lagé

publishing
Junius Verlag GmbH

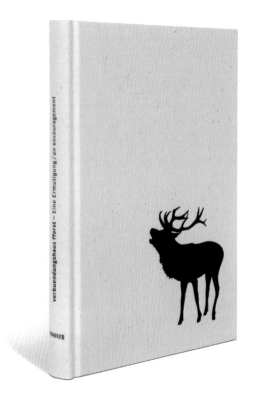

Vogelhausbuch / *Book of Birds*

[Editorial]

The colourful Görtz world of birds presents itself in all the Görtz sales areas set up for children's shoes. For this purpose, a lovingly designed birdhouse is of course indispensable: a big colourful book all about our feathered friends to play with and marvel at. Along with five different bird packagings for shoelaces, in the form of a sale special, it has served to increase customer frequency in the Görtz sales areas for children's shoes and to win over customers for the Görtz store card.

client
Görtz GmbH, Hamburg

head of marketing
Michael Jacobs

design
gürtlerbachmann Werbung GmbH, Hamburg

creative direction/concept
Uli Gürtler

art direction
Veronika Kieneke

project management
Anne Kukereit

illustration
Veronika Kieneke

text
Claudia Oltmann

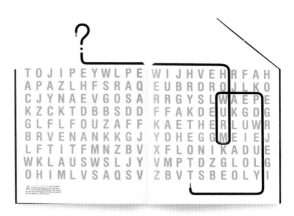

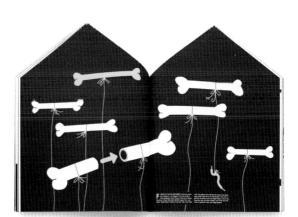

335

Presterende Bestuurders

[Book]

This book contains interviews with prominent politicians and articles about leaders. The authors analyse the challenges in public administration and formulated five of the most important requirements a politician must fulfil. The design puts great emphasis on utilising bold colours so it distinguishes itself from the usual, rather subdued look common in this field. Sensitive portraits complement the lively layout of this publication that was printed on uncoated paper.

client
Sdu Uitgevers /
HMS Management

design
Studio Marise Knegtmans,
Amsterdam

photography
Josje Deekens

printing
Drukkerij Wilco

andreas uebele – alphabet innsbruck

[Exhibition Catalogue]

Glowing characters, cast metal letters, sprayed-on messages – font types in public places are the visual fragrances of a city. The exhibition "alphabet innsbruck" reveals the hidden stories beyond the obvious semantics of the characters. This publication consists of typefaces and letters that were photographed in Innsbruck from unusual perspectives and then reproduced with the greatest possible accuracy. Thus, a documentation of the typographic web was created that captures the written culture of the city.

client
Prof. Andreas Uebele, Stuttgart; aut. architektur und tirol, Innsbruck

design
büro uebele visuelle kommunikation, Stuttgart

project management
Katrin Dittmann

graphic design/illustration
Katrin Dittmann

photography
Daniel Fels

copy
Georg Salden, Gretl Köfler, Andreas Uebele

Alkuin von York und die geistige Grundlegung Europas /
Alcuin of York and Europe's intellectual foundation
[Book]

This book was designed for the historical abbey library of St.Gallen. The objective was to reflect the historical tradition of the abbey and to combine it, at the same time, with contemporary design. For this purpose, a subtle typeface with classical proportions was selected which stands in coherent contrast to the unconventional layout of the footnotes. Supported by bold colours this book proves to be a successful synthesis between tradition and modernity.

client
Stiftsbibliothek St.Gallen

design
TGG Hafen Senn Stieger, St.Gallen

art direction
Dominik Hafen, Bernhard Senn, Roland Stieger

designer portrait
→ Vol.1: p.507

Die Mona Lisa von Trogen / *The Mona Lisa of Trogen*

[Book, CD]

In the 18th and 19th century the textile industry was a big branch of trade in Eastern Switzerland. Foundation of this work is an extensive portrait collection from this period. 15 authors and five musicians selected portraits to which they created prose or music pieces, to interconnect facts and fiction in an entertaining way with each other. The design manages to present the individual approaches in a consistent and very clear layout. The cover can be unfolded to a poster showing the different portraits.

client
Karin Bucher & Matthias Kuhn,
Trogen

design
TGG Hafen Senn Stieger,
St.Gallen

art direction
Dominik Hafen, Bernhard Senn,
Roland Stieger

designer portrait
→ Vol.1: p.507

Warmbronner Schriften Nr. 21 / *Warmbronn Scriptures No. 21*
[Book]

The 21st edition of the Warmbronner Schriften (Warmbronn Scriptures), titled "Wohin nun anders als nach Italien?" (Where else now than to Italy?), focuses on the literary processing of the travel impressions of poet Christian Wagner around 1900. In an unconventional way, Wagner's works are described with regard to the personal, historical and contemporary context and his progressive ideas. The large headlines look like old newspaper mastheads and divide the content into three chapters. The expressive poetry drafts and depicted postcards are reminiscent of a travel journal.

client
Christian-Wagner-Gesellschaft e.V., Leonberg

editor
Harald Hepfer

text
Prof. Dr. Burckhard Dücker

design
design hoch drei GmbH & Co. KG, Stuttgart

creative direction
Tobias Kollmann

art direction
Helmut Kirsten

graphic design
Lisa Jung

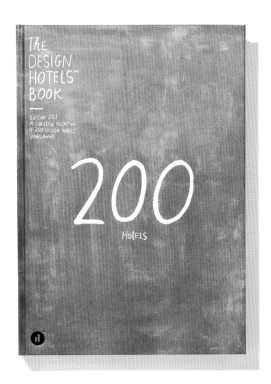

Design Hotels™ Books Collector's Edition 2011

With impressive images and detailed descriptions of 200 hand-picked member hotels this limited collection is intended to serve travellers, architects and designers as a source of inspiration. In 33 stories the visionaries behind the hotels are introduced. The high-quality finish and the elegant design support the content of the publication. The separation into two volumes creates more space for the two fields of product (member hotels) and brand philosophy (Made by Originals).

client
Design Hotels AG, Berlin

design
Design Hotels AG, Berlin

head of marketing
Bernd Neff

creative direction
Johannes Schwark, Berlin

art direction
Anne Prinz, Linda Kunnath, Berlin

text
Ken Baron, New York

project management
Steven Buttlar, Berlin

photography
Kerstin zu Pan, Steve Herud, Berlin

Reporting

[Book]

In corporate annual reports clinical numbers turn into charts and diagrams, which aside from providing information are also intended to whitewash the actual facts. This publication illuminates, how the disclosure requirement turns into the art of self-representation and how closely the numbers are related to the company's image. Clearly structured graphics, 1,300 images and a descriptive font emphasise the high information value of this publication, printed on special paper with phosphorescent colouring and embossing.

client
Strichpunkt Design, Stuttgart

design
Strichpunkt Design, Stuttgart

creative direction
Jochen Rädeker, Kirsten Dietz

art direction
Kirsten Dietz, Jochen Rädeker

graphic design
Kirsten Dietz

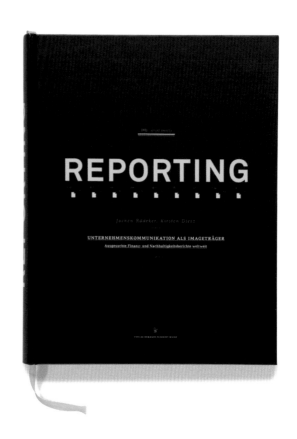

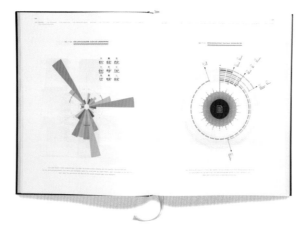

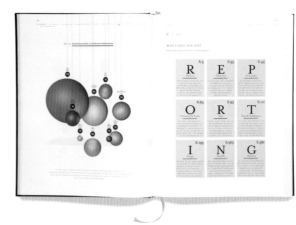

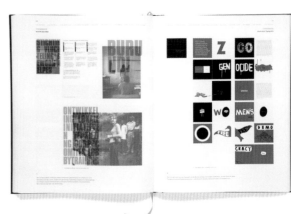

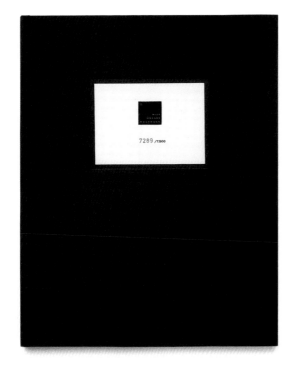

Moormann Gesamt-katalog Vol. 3 / *Moormann Complete Catalogue Vol. 3*

The Catalogue Vol. 3 by Nils Holger Moormann GmbH presents the current product range of the Chiemgau-based furniture manu-facturer. It comprises minimalist ambience pictures and a photo-graphic typology of the complete product range. Inserted pages, reduced in size, allow a glimpse behind the scenes of the company. Each copy is individually numbered on the cover label. Thus, all ad-dressees receive their personal copy, highlighting the handcrafted character of the furniture already in the communication medium.

client
Nils Holger Moormann GmbH, Aschau im Chiemgau

design
Jäger & Jäger, Überlingen

creative direction
Regina Jäger, Olaf Jäger

photography
Olaf Jäger

printing
Druck-Ring, Munich

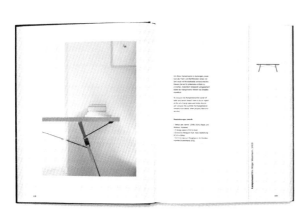

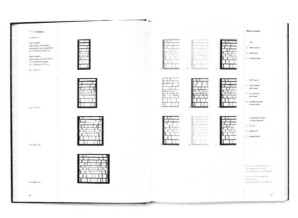

TypeFaces

[Book]

In typography a typeface is a set of one or more fonts, but this book takes a different approach: it interprets the term "typeface" literally. Each letter of the alphabet (type) is combined with the face of a child. This results in 26 "TypeFaces", illustrated with emotive photographs that form playful and inspiring contrasts to the imaginative design of the typefaces. In this way, children teach adults the alphabet and open their eyes to purity, beauty and unpredictability.

client
Verena Panholzer/Andreas Balon, Vienna

design
Verena Panholzer/Andreas Balon, Vienna

art direction
Verena Panholzer

concept
Verena Panholzer, Andreas Balon

text
Sibylle Hamtil, Verena Panholzer

photography
Andreas Balon

illustration
Verena Panholzer

printing
Theiss Druck

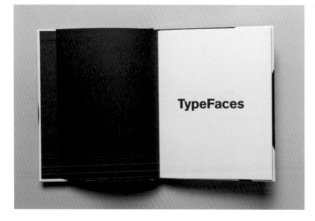

Taiwanese Snacks Notebook

[Snacks Guide]

The night markets are a central part of the Taiwanese culture. This travel guide contains not only general information about 118 night markets, but also advice about food, anecdotes and maps. It also defines itself as a notebook, in order to be used to note down own experiences. The design of the cover was inspired by the red and white plastic bags which are often seen at the night markets. Two folded leaflets, 155 cm long and attached to the beginning and the end of the book, provide introductions and recommendations for the four most well-known markets in Taiwan.

client
MIIN Design Co., Ltd., Taipei

design
MIIN Design Co., Ltd., Taipei

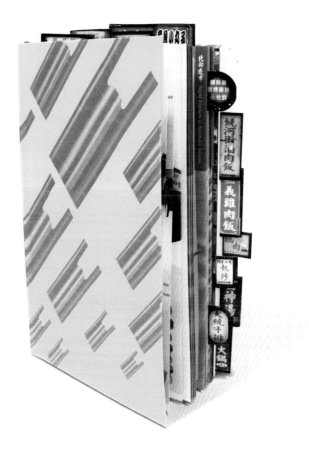

Atlas der Brutvögel Vorarlbergs /
Atlas of Breeding Birds in Vorarlberg
[Scientific Book]

This scientific publication presents the diversity of birds in Austria's most Western state. The book is characterised by a clear structure and an unusual high standard of production. It features a cloth binding with three-coloured screen printing. The atlas thus is not only fully consistent with the high scientific standard, but thanks to numerous colour photos and illustrations also realises an appealing design.

client
Birdlife Vorarlberg

design
Kurt Dornig Grafikdesign & Illustration

concept
Kurt Dornig

graphic design
Kurt Dornig

printing
Bucher Druck und Verlag

mapping
DI Jürgen Oberressl, Landesvermessungsamt Vorarlberg

image editing
Günter König, prepressstudio König

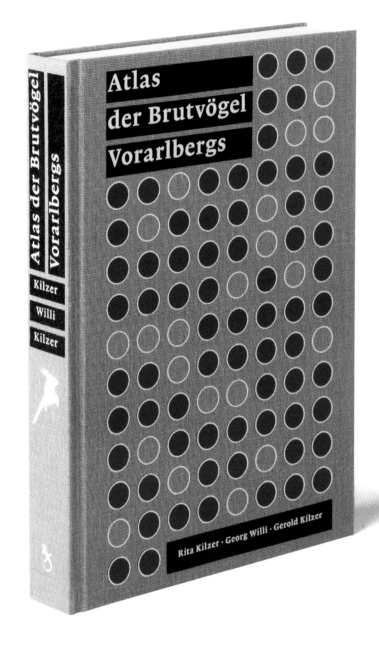

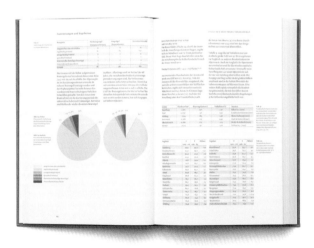

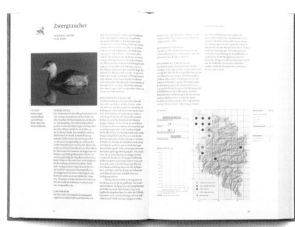

346

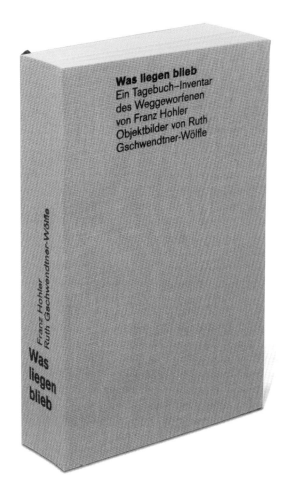

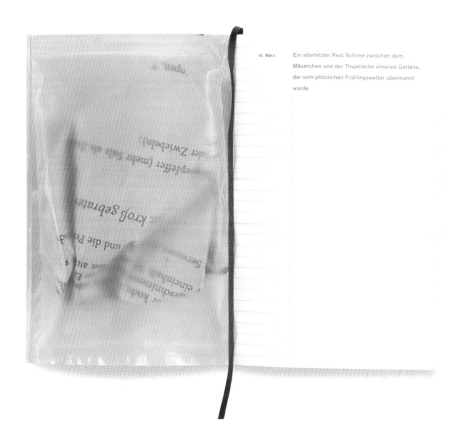

Was liegen blieb / *What was left*

[Artist Book]

This book unites two artists, who dedicated themselves to one topic. "Was liegen blieb" (What was left) is about ordinary, day-to-day found items. While Swiss author Franz Hohler describes his daily found item in a diary, Austrian artist Ruth Gschwendtner-Wölfle places a picture of a found item opposite to his text. The book, completely finalised in digital print, is 800 pages strong and encourages the reader to record their own found items and thoughts.

client
Ruth Gschwendtner-Wölfle

design
Kurt Dornig Grafikdesign
& Illustration

concept
Ruth Gschwendtner-Wölfle,
Kurt Dornig

text
Franz Hohler

graphic design
Kurt Dornig

photography
Günter König

printing
Mayr Record Scan

Antalis Diary 2011

"Each day is valuable, enjoy life, unique encounters must be captured for eternity" – this journal presents thought-provoking impulses and utilises an unusual typography and very minimalistic illustrations, that can also stand alone. Short worldly wisdoms, instructions on behaviour or simply single words are given a lot of space on one double-page spread each, in order to achieve their full effect. Explanatory commentaries in small print complement these illustrations.

client
Antalis (Hong Kong) Ltd.,
Hong Kong

design
Eric Chan Design Co. Ltd.,
Hong Kong

creative direction
Eric Chan

art direction/concept
Eric Chan, Iris Yu

graphic design
Eric Chan, Iris Yu, Andries Lee,
Sandi Lee, Miva Tsang

illustration
Miva Tsang, Iris Yu

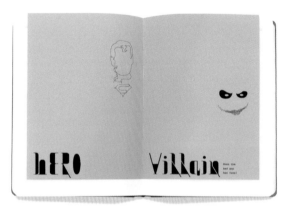

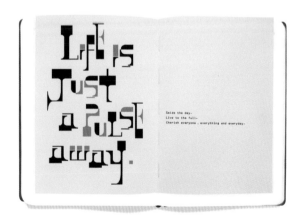

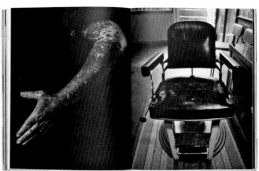

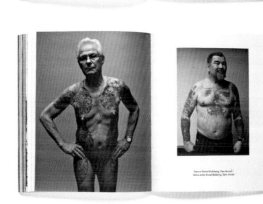

Danish Tattooing

[Book]

The book "Danish Tattooing" documents the history of Danish tattoos from 1895 to the present. Special attention was paid to the golden age of the 1960s with its many, fascinating stories from the underground. The book presents anecdotes and historical photographs of legendary personalities and tattoo centres at that time. 14 portraits of contemporary tattooists and their unique access to this art build a bridge to the present.

client
Nordstrøms Forlag, Copenhagen

head of marketing
Jon Nordstrøm

text
Jon Nordstrøm

design
Designbolaget, Copenhagen

creative direction/art direction
Claus Due

graphic design
Claus Due

concept
Jon Nordstrøm, Claus Due

designer portrait
→ Vol.1: p.470

The Graduation Exhibition 2010. The Funen Art Academy

[Catalogue]

client
Funen Art Academy, Odense

design
Designbolaget, Copenhagen

creative direction/art direction
Claus Due

concept
Claus Due

graphic design
Claus Due,
Henriette Kruse Jørgensen

designer portrait
→ Vol.1: p.470

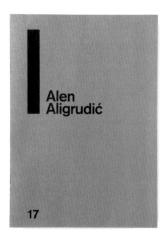
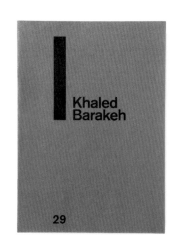

77

Mia
Helmer

89

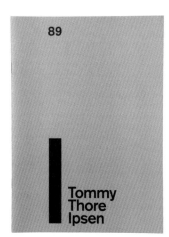

Tommy
Thore
Ipsen

101 Marie
Irmgard

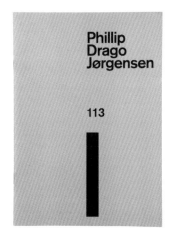

Phillip
Drago
Jørgensen

113

125

Michael
Würtz
Overbeck

Pelle
Møller
Schiødt

137

Tak /
Thank you

In spring 2010 eleven graduates of the Funen Art Academy presented their works in the Brandts art gallery in Odense, Denmark. In addition to the exhibition a catalogue was published that introduces the eleven artists and their works. The task was to portrait each artist individually, yet, at the same time, achieve a harmonious, comprehensive publication. Individuality was achieved by offering the artists to design their entries personally on the double-pages and most of them taking advantage of this option. The self-contained look of the publication was achieved with the chapter front pages for each artist's entry: each of them displays a single graphic element that can be found on the cover of the catalogue.

Dymaxion Car
Buckminster Fuller
[Book]

client
Ivorypress Spain, Madrid

text
Norman Foster, Jonathan Glancey,
David Jenkins, Hsiao-Yun Chu

design
Thomas Manss & Company

design team
Thomas Manss, Tom Featherby

printing
TF Artes Gráficas

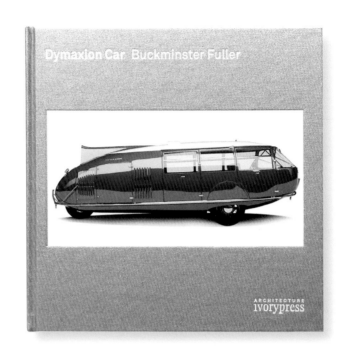

Marinero, maquinista, pensador global, emprendedor, creador, estudioso de tendencias, editor técnico, empresario, ángel, estratega, profesor de universidad, crítico, seminarista experimental, elemento aleatorio, verbo, diseñador completo, inventor, ingeniero, arquitecto, cartógrafo, filósofo, poeta, cosmogonista, coreógrafo, visionario, científico, unidad de valor, matemático, piloto de aviones, teniente de la armada, genio afable, geómetra, pensador inconformista, revolucionario amable, genio adorable, antiacadémico, doctor en ciencias, doctor en las artes, doctor en diseño, doctor en humanidades, amigable lunático, profeta, el custodio de un recurso vital.

Listado de las actividades de Buckminster Fuller, Richard Buckminster Fuller: An Autobiographical Monologue/Scenario, 1980

With the streamlined Dymaxion Car the American inventor and architect Buckminster Fuller realised his vision of the automotive future. The car drove on three wheels, was steered by a single rear wheel and could turn within its own length – a revolutionary concept that was abandoned due to a severe accident. In 2008 Norman Foster, an architect like Fuller, resurrected the car. The bilingual book illustrates the history and the serious accident of the Dymaxion. It presents extensive material – from historical documents and photographs to the newest construction sketches – and provides an insight into the two-year long manufacturing process.

BIKINI BERLIN

[Brochures]

client
Bayerische Hausbau Immobilien
GmbH & Co. KG, Munich

design
Gregor & Strozik Visual Identity
GmbH, Bochum

creative direction
Thorsten Strozik, Bernhard Klug

art direction
Nina Küpper

concept
Thorsten Strozik, Bernhard Klug

customer advisory service
Tina Hesse

illustration
Maike Teubner

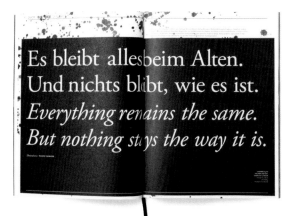

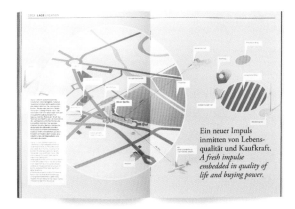

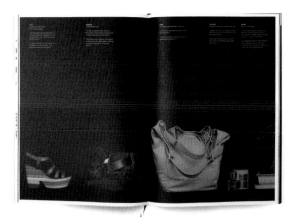

Various publications introduce a West Berlin real estate project with international ambition. The novelty of the concept, the appeal and the complexity of the idea are reflected in the diversity of the contents and the variety of the design. Interviews, image series of inspiring places and products, as well as hand-drawn illustrations aim to make the idea tangible. A few scribbles and renderings illustrate what the finished project will look like. A magazine presenting the whole project is complemented by booklets advertising the retail and office sectors and by other summarising publications. This conveys the spirit and capacity of the project to convince potential tenants of the idea's attractiveness.

Audi Urban Future Award –
The Publications

[Books]

"The Publications" comprises all publications of the Audi Urban Future Award 2010. It aims to communicate the interaction of mobility, architecture and urban development with a precise vision of the future. The publications document the different stages in the development of all contributing architects from the first briefing to the exhibition at the Architecture Biennale in Venice in August 2010. The covers of the three volumes "The Process", "The Conference" and "The Award" were inspired by geometrical forms, underlining this complex topic.

client
AUDI AG, Ingolstadt

design
Antonia Henschel,
SIGN Kommunikation GmbH,
Frankfurt/Main

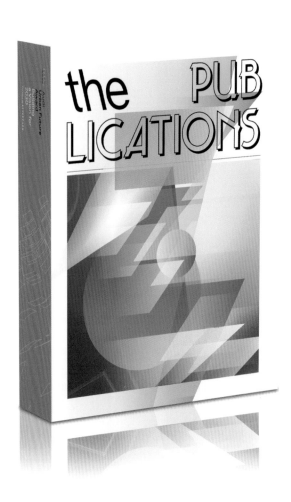

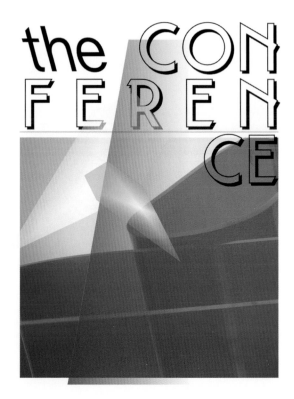

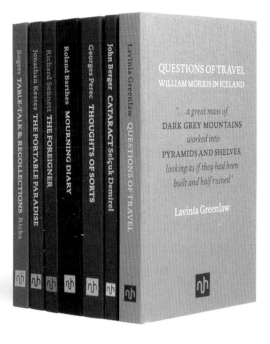

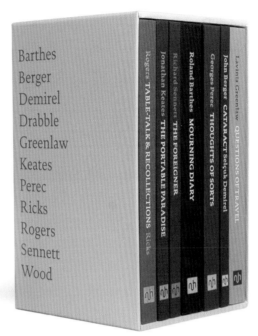

Notting Hill Editions

[Books]

The London publisher Notting Hill Editions aims to revive the literary genre of the essay with this high-grade gift box. Providing an inspiring and appealing spectrum of topics, it presents a selection of authors from a wide range of disciplines and eras. The books, featuring a cloth binding and a classic typography, were manufactured in Germany, underlining the publisher's high demands on design and production. In addition to the book design, an entire visual identity, website and further communication materials were developed for the publishing house.

client
Notting Hill Editions Ltd, London

design
Flok Design Communication GmbH, Berlin

creative direction/art direction
Garvin Hirt

graphic design
Garvin Hirt, Matthias Richter, Marie Wocher

project management
Garvin Hirt, Fiona Buckland, Jess Lawrence

typesetting
Garvin Hirt, Matthias Richter; CB Editions, London

printing
Memminger MedienCentrum

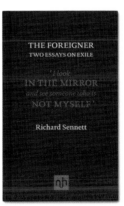

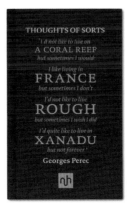

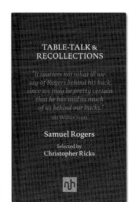

Atlas der abgelegenen Inseln / *Atlas of Remote Islands*
[Book]

The "Atlas der abgelegenen Inseln" (Atlas of Remote Islands) depicts places which probably only few people will ever set their eyes on. It contains maps and anecdotes of 50 islands, most of which are only a few square kilometres in size and scattered far away across the oceans of the world. The emotive graphic design and the carefully selected texts combine into a poetic synthesis of the arts which turns the most remote islands of this world into centres of human desires. The atlas is available in five special colours and features a half-cloth binding.

client
mareverlag GmbH & Co. oHG, Hamburg

project management
Sandy Weps

design
Judith Schalansky, Berlin

art direction/concept
Judith Schalansky

graphic design/illustration
Judith Schalansky

text
Judith Schalansky

Warmbronner Schriften Nr. 22 / *Warmbronn Scriptures No. 22*
[Book]

In the 22nd edition of the Warmbronner Schriften (Warmbronn Scriptures), titled "Der Autor und sein Biograf" (The author and his biographer), the correspondence between the poet Christian Wagner and his friend and benefactor Richard Weltrich from 1886 to 1912 is examined. Already the cover illustrates in its feel the fleetingness of an envelope. The graphic citation of a postmark leads with its finely curved lines into the lively dialogue. The sections of each letter writer are being highlighted with fine straight and wavy lines, and a considerate typography provides orientation between the author's comments and the letter quotes.

client
Christian-Wagner-Gesellschaft e.V., Leonberg

general editor book series
Harald Hepfer

editor/text
Ulrich Wilhelm Weiser

design
design hoch drei GmbH & Co. KG, Stuttgart

creative direction
Tobias Kollmann

art direction
Helmut Kirsten

graphic design
Diana Müller

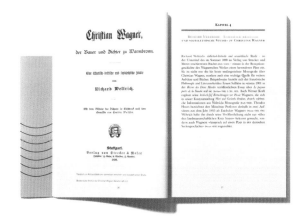

Digital Theory

[Book]

"Teoria Digital" (Digital Theory) was created for the 10th anniversary of FILE – Electronic Language International Festival – and presents a collection of theoretical material that has been produced since its first edition. The graphic project explores non-linear navigation systems of digital media, starting with the cover which presents an overview of the content by showing selected keywords and their occurrence. Inside the book, each text is preceded by a lead page featuring a synoptical table that illustrates how often and on which page the main keyword appears.

client
FILE – Electronic Language International Festival, São Paulo

design
ps.2 arquitetura + design, São Paulo

creative direction/art direction
Fábio Prata, Flávia Nalon

graphic design
Fábio Prata, Flávia Nalon, Guilherme Falcão

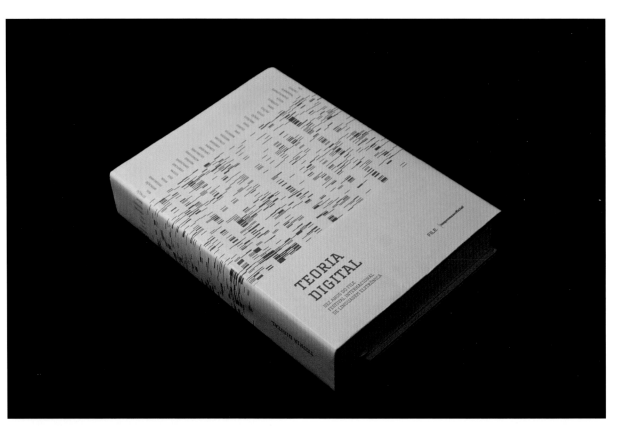

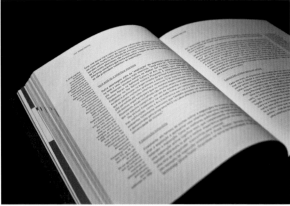

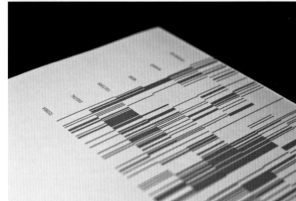

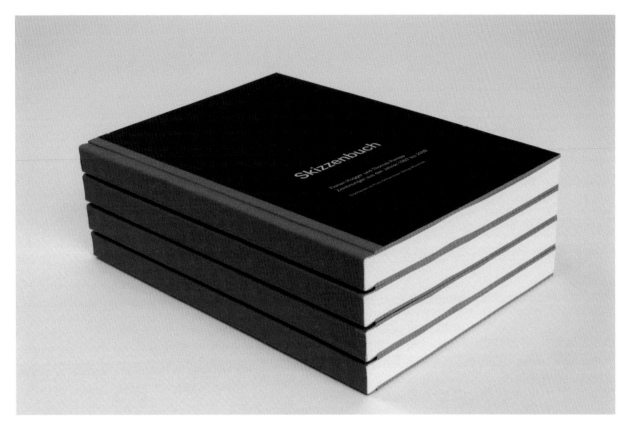

Skizzenbuch /
Sketchbook

This book with a classic appeal was developed within a simple and clear design framework and features a considerable proportion of hand-drawn sketches. It was developed by a design and an architecture office with the objective of creating a valuable present for their clients, which establishes a personal relation to the offices' owners. The choice of materials and its characteristic appeal are inspired by the sketchbooks of the draftsmen. The sketches could thus be taken from the original sketchbooks without losing their individual character and origin.

client
ediundsepp
Gestaltungsgesellschaft,
Florian Hugger und Thomas
Rampp GbR, Munich

design
ediundsepp
Gestaltungsgesellschaft,
Florian Hugger und Thomas
Rampp GbR, Munich

art direction/concept
Florian Hugger, Thomas Rampp

graphic design
Charlotte Binder

team
Johanna Hermenau

drawings/sketches
Florian Hugger, Thomas Rampp

text
Florian Hugger, Thomas Rampp

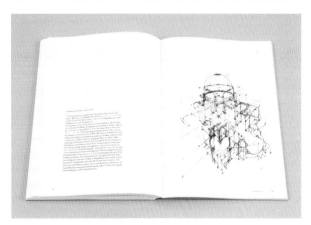

Sonderpostwert-
zeichen – Für die
Wohlfahrtspflege 2011
4 Motive von Loriot /
*Special stamps – For
welfare work 2011
4 themes from Loriot*

With four appealing motifs, this
German series of 2011 special
stamps, sold to benefit welfare
work, display famous scenes
from Loriot's skits, including
"Das Frühstücksei" (The Break-
fast Egg), "Herren im Bad" (Men
in the Bathtub), "Der sprechen-
de Hund" (The Talking Dog)
and "Auf der Rennbahn" (At the
Track). To lend the stamps a
unified appearance, the illustrations are set against a sky-blue
background. The stamp's value,
plus the donation amount, is
displayed in a highly unobtrusive
manner so as to not impair the
humorous picture language. A
discreet lower caption refers to
the welfare work.

client
Bundesministerium der Finanzen,
Referat Postwertzeichen, Berlin

design
Hans Günter Schmitz,
Wuppertal

illustration
Vicco von Bülow (Loriot)

JUBILEUMPOSTZEGELS 2011

ORGANISATIE VOOR ECONOMISCHE SAMENWERKING EN ONTWIKKELING
DE OESO ZET ZICH AL 50 JAAR WERELDWIJD IN VOOR GROTERE WELVAART EN WELZIJN VAN MENSEN DOOR NAUWE SAMENWERKING TUSSEN LANDEN. WWW.OECD.ORG

KONINKLIJKE NEDERLANDSE BILJARTBOND
DE KNBB BESTAAT IN 2011 100 JAAR EN IS DE NATIONALE SPORTBOND VOOR BILJARTSPORT DIE ALLE KEUSPORTEN (POOL, CARAMBOLE, SNOOKER EN DRIEBANDEN) VERTEGENWOORDIGT. WWW.KNBB.NL

KONINKLIJKE NEDERLANDSE DAMBOND
DE KONINKLIJKE NEDERLANDSE DAMBOND (KNDB) IS EEN SPORTBOND MET 6.000 LEDEN EN PROMOOT HET DAMSPEL IN DE RUIMSTE ZIN. WWW.KNDB.NL

SLOT LOEVESTEIN
MÉÉR DAN EEN MUSEUM! SLOT LOEVESTEIN IS EEN VAN DE BEKENDSTE KASTELEN VAN NEDERLAND. VOORAL DOOR DE SPECTACULAIRE ONTSNAPPING IN EEN BOEKENKIST VAN HUGO DE GROOT. WWW.SLOTLOEVESTEIN.NL

GENOOTSCHAP NEDERLANDSE COMPONISTEN
HET GENOOTSCHAP VAN NEDERLANDSE COMPONISTEN, IS EEN BEROEPSVERENIGING DIE DE DIRECTE EN INDIRECTE BELANGEN BEHARTIGT VAN NEDERLANDSE COMPONISTEN. WWW.GENECO.NL

AANVANG VERKOOP 2 MEI 2011
ARTIKELNR 310561

Anniversary Stamps

Common to all four postage stamps within this series from the Netherlands is an abstract visual language that purposefully avoids traditional imagery. Thanks to versatile design ideas, the specially conceptualised typography manifests as actual illustrations. The design of the lettering is inspired by the content of the series, conveying the anniversary theme. Pool balls, for example, are used instead of zeros and the letter "o", referring to the 100th anniversary of a billiard association. Or for the anniversary of a composer, an artistic font is set against a background ornamented with staff lines.

client
PostNL, Julius Vermeulen,
The Hague

design
Samenwerkende Ontwerpers,
Amsterdam

creative direction/art direction
André Toet

concept
André Toet

graphic design
André Toet

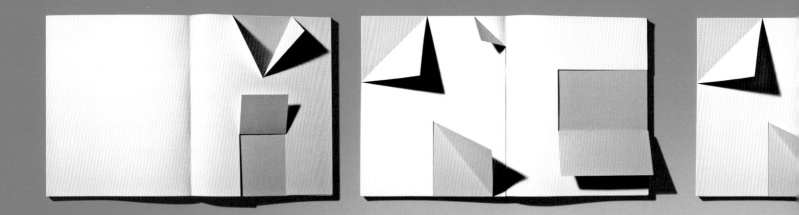

MAKE IT RUSTLE, SMELL IT, FEEL IT. Nothing is more outdated than yesterday's newspaper. Achievements that are new, creative and unparalleled, however, are acknowledged every year. Be it a newspaper or magazine design: sophisticated typography, unusual motifs and surprising colour concepts are convincing.

Smart designers know exactly why and for whom they create what. They are not influenced by stereotypes, but instead dare to explore new paths.

red dot: grand prix

Quart Heft für Kultur Tirol Nr. 15/10 / *Quart Cultural Magazine for Tyrol No. 15/10*

Quart is a cultural magazine published biannually in Innsbruck. Focusing on a strong regional footage and showcasing images and texts produced exclusively for the relevant edition, the magazine has another special asset in store: each volume comes with an "original supplement" – exclusive pieces of art which directly appeal to the enthusiastic collectors among the readership. The cover pages are a designated "art zone", with the title usually occupying only a minimum of space. The magazine's underlying design principle was created by chemist and typographer Walter Pamminger, who interprets book design as a conscious arrangement of reading spaces: all right-hand pages are reserved exclusively for text edited in a clearly legible style, while the opposite pages leave space for an "echo" of free associations and cross connections. In volume 15, this echo space presents several graphical analyses in black and white. This high-profile magazine, each volume of which features a cover created by a contemporary artist, also has the courage to leave a double-page or two almost untouched, except for a minimal highlight near the centrefold.

Statement by the jury

»The magazine Quart represents more than the branding of a region. It is the manifestation of a true statement both in terms of content and design: it follows a highly individual approach in presenting the culture of the region and, at the same time, complements it by self-sufficient thoughts and images that open up an entirely independent level.«

Lichtverhältnisse am Berg

Restbestand

client
Kulturabteilung des Landes Tirol,
Innsbruck

design
Circus. Büro für Kommunikation
und Gestaltung, Innsbruck

concept
Walter Pamminger

graphic design
Norm

cover artwork
Markus Schinwald

designer portrait
→ Vol.1: p.467

Neugier.de – Made in India

[Newspaper in Slipcase]

Neugier.de is a new newspaper that picks up on the original human drive to be curious about the world and presents its topics with a fresh approach to both text and image. The first issue is dedicated to India, since people there look optimistically into the future and think positively about progress – quite different than many people in Germany. Highly engaging reports on green genetic engineering, Bollywood, youth culture and career opportunities open up a wide spectrum of current topics which are complemented by an impressive image series and offer readers multifaceted and fascinating insights into this country. Featuring a vivid layout that alternates between two and three columns and photographs of different sizes, the newspaper turns into an entertaining read reflecting on the dynamic progress of this country and, at the same time, aims to present a change in perspective regarding the view on Germany.

Statement by the jury

»This newspaper distinguishes itself through a sophisticated and inspiring layout. The photographs of different sizes and formats are complemented by an outstanding typography and together convey the message in a versatile and fascinating manner.«

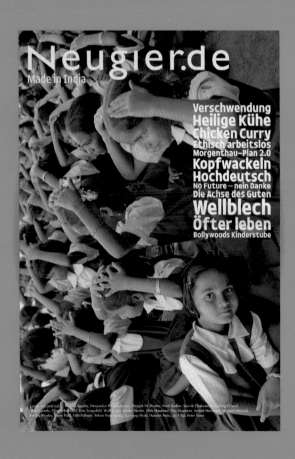

client
stadt land fluss GmbH, Berlin

design
stadt land fluss GmbH, Berlin

creative direction/editorship
Dirk Maxeiner, Fabian Nicolay

art direction
Fabian Nicolay

concept
Dirk Maxeiner, Fabian Nicolay

graphic design
Fabian Nicolay

text
Henryk M. Broder, Vera Lengsfeld,
Wolf Lotter, Marco Martin,
Dirk Maxeiner, Michael Miersch,
Fabian Nicolay, Udo Pollmer

photography
Tim Maxeiner, Fabian Nicolay,
Jay Ullal, Peter Vann

printing
europrint medien GmbH, Berlin

designer portrait
→ Vol.1: p.492

red dot: best of the best

zwei

[Doctors' Magazine]

The magazine zwei by pharmaceutical company Pfizer is targeted at 16,000 doctors in Germany and surprises not only through its choice of content, but also through its overall appearance. Constantly reinventing itself, each issue of the magazine features a different main theme such as "Me", "Happiness" or "Time". What is special about it is that doctors are the protagonists of most of the articles. The layout stands out on its own as an independent bearer of ideas, providing irony or setting counterpoints. Thus, the cover of the "Me" issue, for example, is a mirror for readers to see themselves reflected in, and the "Happiness" issue features the appearance of a gambling machine. Well-researched articles and profiles of people with unusual journeys through life offer entertainment on a high level, which is further enhanced by the layout, as it captivates readers through distinctive illustrations and original photographs.

Statement by the jury

»This concept is highly surprising and daring as it is for a magazine of a pharmaceutical company. Both in terms of content and design it goes way beyond the ordinary. Featuring contributions on specific topics in professionally designed layouts with hilariously humorous illustrations and informational diagrams, the magazine possesses both lightness and ingenuity.«

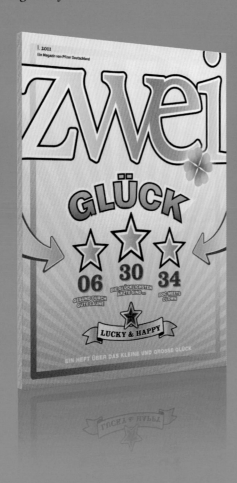

HERR PROFESSOR HÜTHER,
WO SITZT DAS GLÜCK?

client
Pfizer Deutschland GmbH,
Berlin

design
Bohm und Nonnen,
Darmstadt

creative direction
Theo Nonnen,
Bohm und Nonnen

art direction
Steven Dohn,
Bohm und Nonnen

concept
Henning Hesse,
Kirsten Wörnle

text
Henning Hesse;
Kirsten Wörnle,
Kairos Redaktionsbüro

designer portrait
→ Vol.1: p.464

„Ich" ruft und fühlt es in uns – doch wo steckt sie denn nun, die Seele eines Menschen?

Hat das Ich einen Ort?

Seit Jahrhunderten zerbrechen sich Gelehrte darüber den Kopf, während Naturvölker einfach Fakten schaffen. Eine Auswahl.

WO WOHNT DAS ICH?

in der Brust

im Gehirn

im Atem

im Auge

im Samen

im Kopf

im Nirgendwo

im Herz

in den Nervenzellen

in den Haaren

Lamborghini Magazine

[Customer Magazine]

The concept of the Lamborghini customer magazine is based on the brand identity's core pillars: Italian, uncompromising and extreme. Apart from cars, the content focuses on topics from the areas of lifestyle and design. In each issue, the monothematic magazine concept examines a special facet of the brand personality so that readers may experience its air of fascination. In accordance with the selected topic, each issue is characterised by a suitable colour taken from the vehicles' current colour range.

client
Automobili Lamborghini S.p.A.,
Sant'Agata Bolognese

head of marketing
Fintan Knight

design
köckritzdörrich GmbH,
Reutlingen

creative direction/art direction
Lutz Suendermann,
köckritzdörrich GmbH

concept
Michael Köckritz,
köckritzdörrich GmbH

graphic design
Jonas Kriegstötter,
köckritzdörrich GmbH

customer advisory service
Christian Westenhöfer,
köckritzdörrich GmbH

strategic planning
Berthold Dörrich,
köckritzdörrich GmbH

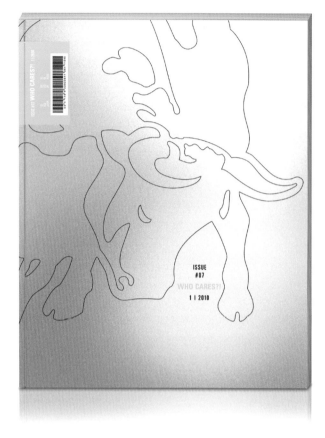

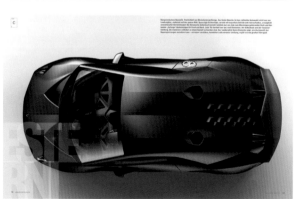

Adeyaka Magazine
[Customer Magazine]

As the customer magazine of the Japanese premium automotive brand Infiniti, Adeyaka portrays a brand world of multifaceted elegance. Dynamic colourfulness is combined with a focus on the essentials, with emotionally moving photo sequences supplemented by short texts. Conceived for a successful, confident and cosmopolitan target group, the magazine is divided into the sections "Lobby", "Lounge" and "Gallery". It utilises brand partnerships and offers further multimedia reading experiences on the Internet.

client
Infiniti Global,
Rolle/Nashville

head of marketing
Andreas Sigl, Patrice Virte

design
köckritzdörrich GmbH,
Reutlingen

creative direction
Lutz Suendermann,
köckritzdörrich GmbH

art direction
Lutz Suendermann,
köckritzdörrich GmbH

concept
Michael Köckritz,
köckritzdörrich GmbH

customer advisory service
Christian Westenhöfer,
köckritzdörrich GmbH

strategic planning
Berthold Dörrich,
köckritzdörrich GmbH

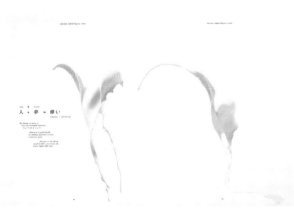

fluoro8

[Biannual Design Publication]

fluoro8 is a biannual cultural guide published in Australia, which provides a comprehensive perspective on design, art, fashion and culture. The editorial concept includes extensive coverage of avant-garde topics in particular, with the team discussing emergent innovation through in-depth articles. The well-suited layout is characterised by gripping imagery as well as versatile typography, creating a formally convincing connection with the introduced topics, products, brands and artists.

client
Fluoro Publications Pty Ltd, Melbourne

head of marketing
Audrey Bugeja

editor
Nancy Bugeja

design
housemouse, Melbourne

creative direction
Miguel Valenzuela

graphic design
Arron Curran (Senior Designer)

printing
PrintLinx

fahrstil –
Das Radmagazin /
fahrstil –
the bike magazine
[Magazine]

The bicycle-culture magazine fahrstil (German for "riding style") has been conceived as a magazine whose demands clearly exceed that of typical special-interest publications. Neither readers nor bicycles are split up into different categories; instead, the whole world of cycling is examined. Thrilling reports mirror the individualised and ambitious lives of the readers. The design is tailored to each individual article in order to give the content at hand the space and appearance it deserves. Large-format photographs create an emotional connection with the reader.

client
velonauten UG, Göttingen

editorship
Gunnar Fehlau, H. David Koßmann

photography
Kay Tkatzik, Martin Häußermann

design
echtweiß | Corporate Design, Heidelberg

art direction
Janna Marten, Sven Marten

graphic design
Katharina Haaf, Sofia Bertolini

I love you No. 5

[Magazine]

With fairy-tale imagery, issue No. 5 of the magazine "I love you" examines every little girl's dream of being a princess. Full-page illustrations against pastel-coloured backgrounds create an independent character, appealing to its target group with a strong sense of irony. Individual articles, for instance, accompany an actress along the streets of New York and shed light on the tragic lives of the six wives of King Henry VIII. A recipe for baking a fairy-tale castle is also included, featuring a large number of illustrations.

client
e-design+communication gmbh, Berlin

design
e-design+communication gmbh, Berlin

creative direction
Christiane Bördner

graphic design
Lea Delion, Mirka Laura Severa

designer portrait
→ Vol.1: p.472

I love you No. 6

[Magazine]

"I love you" is an independent art and fashion magazine for women with a focus on design and photography. The magazine is conceived as a conceptual, topic-oriented journal with a personal and emotional perspective on themes such as fashion and lifestyle. Issue No. 6 is dedicated to the topic of motherhood. Large-format photo spreads foster a space of respect for strong types of women. In the commentary, life as a mother is captivatingly presented – from a subjective point of view – as an appealingly authentic lifestyle.

client
e-design+communication gmbh, Berlin

design
e-design+communication gmbh, Berlin

creative direction
Christiane Bördner

designer portrait
→ Vol.1: p.472

MMM –
Maison Moderne
Magazine

[Magazine]

client
Maison Moderne Publishing,
Luxembourg

design
Maison Moderne Design,
Luxembourg

art direction
Maxime Pintadu

concept
Mike Koedinger

text
Boz Temple-Morris

photography
Anoush Abrar

illustration
Lyndon Hayes, Tim Eun Kim

designer portrait
→ Vol.1: p.488

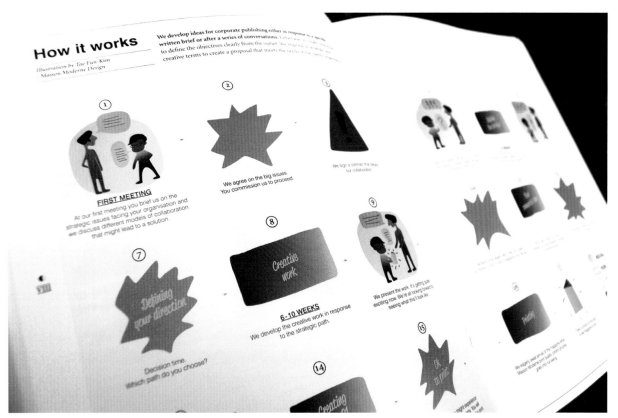

MMM (Maison Moderne Magazine) represents an annual snapshot of the publishing industry, presenting best practices as well as the latest innovations in content and design. The first issue contains interviews with key players about current practices and trends, including, for example, an interview with the photographer who took the picture gracing the cover. The powerful image, which speaks for itself, remains uncovered by text or graphic elements thanks to a paper band. Underlining the high standards of this magazine are details such as distinctiveness in paper quality and rounded corners. The magazine itself consists of two parts, with a current summary of activities embedded in the middle of the magazine. Both parts differ in layout, format and paper selection.

NICO –
Interviews & Fashion
[Magazine]

client
Maison Moderne Publishing,
Luxembourg

design
Maison Moderne Design,
Luxembourg

art direction
Maxime Pintadu

editor-in-chief
Mike Koedinger

text
Mike Koedinger, Philippe Graff,
Angelina A. Rafii, Duncan Roberts,
Cynthia Schreiber

photography
Sebastien Agnetti, Christian
Aschman, Eric Chenal,
Amber Gray, Andres Lejona,
Jussi Puikkonen, Anoush Abrar &
Aimée Hoving, Steeve Beckouet,
Anne Combaz, Wayne Kahn,
Rosa und Gerlinde, Edwin Tse

illustration
Kustaa Saksi

designer portrait
→ Vol.1: p.488

The magazine "NICO – Interviews & Fashion" focuses on strong editorial content and presents talent from the fields of fashion, photography, art, design and illustration. It offers the reader a mix of progressive pop culture, exclusive and honest interviews as well as inspiring photo shoots. Photos and illustrations are an important component of the layout. Every article has its own art direction customised to the topic, with a focus on matching typography. In general, the layout aims to be non-disruptive in order to give photographs and illustrations the space they deserve. A flexible design grid, which nevertheless offers structure, provides the published texts with an appropriate framework.

Dear Dave, 9

[Magazine]

Dear Dave is an artistic publication dedicated to photography and writing. It celebrates the community of visionaries with humorous affection and publishes idiosyncratic and original work that deserves closer attention. Issue No. 9, dedicated to swim fashion, pays homage to the annual Sports Illustrated swimsuit issue, though here the swimsuits are depicted in highly unconventional ways using imaginative photo settings and surprising illustrations.

client
School of Visual Arts,
New York

design
Visual Arts Press, Ltd.,
New York

creative direction
Anthony P. Rhodes

art direction
Michael J. Walsh

project management
Eleanor Oakes (Managing Editor),
Kimberlee Venable

editor-in-chief
Stephen Frailey

Modular
Festival Magazine
[Event Programme]

The Modular youth festival offers its visitors a broad spectrum of events. In order to lend structure to the programme's multifariousness, a festival booklet with a distinct look was developed. The cover shows a key visual comprised of basic geometric shapes in a stacked arrangement. For better orientation, the colour-coded forms were paired with a snapshot photo concept suited to the target group. The playful use of typography intentionally pushes the boundaries of readability.

client
Stadtjugendring Augsburg KdöR, Modular Büro, Augsburg

design
KW Neun Grafikagentur, Augsburg

creative direction
Artur Gulbicki

art direction
Mara Weyel, Christoph Sauter

strategic planning
Tobias Sommer

photography
Mara Weyel, Christoph Sauter, Max Diederich

Horst und Edeltraut

[Lifestyle Magazine]

Horst und Edeltraut is an independent urban-lifestyle magazine from Berlin in which young people from all around the world present their undistorted views on fashion, art and culture. The bilingual magazine offers international young talent a presentation platform. In addition, the target group is provided with daily news from the metropolises of Berlin, New York, London and Rome via Facebook and a blog. Each issue focuses on a main topic through interviews, photo essays and articles as well as background stories.

client
Horst und Edeltraut,
Berlin

editor-in-chief
Cosima Bucarelli,
Johanna Moers

design
muehlhausmoers
corporate communications

art direction
Pascal Schöning

project management
Jürgen Jehle

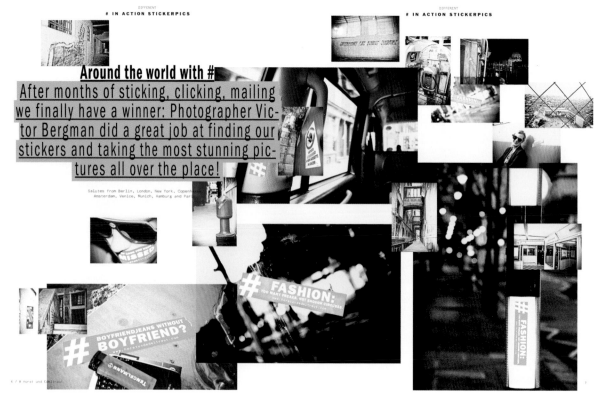

PICNIC # 05 – Lithostar LP-82, Plate Manager Galileo VXT & Co.

[Magazine]

PICNIC is a magazine by Trademark Publishing that serves as a forum for graphic designers, photographers and illustrators and covers a wide variety of topics. Issue No. 5, "Lithostar LP-82, Plate Manager Galileo VXT & Co.", is dedicated to printing machines and their names. Presented here is a selection of devices from the printing industry, ranging from time-honoured to state-of-the-art machines. Photographed, illustrated and colour separated, the magazine manages to provide entertaining insight into the world of publishing.

client
Trademark Publishing, Frankfurt/Main

design
Samuel Roos, SIGN Kommunikation GmbH, Frankfurt/Main

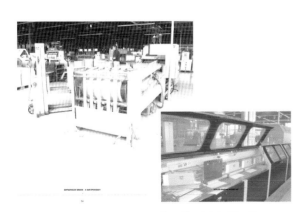

SAP SPECTRUM

[Customer Magazine]

client
SAP AG, Walldorf

design
grasundsterne Werbeagentur und
Corporate Publishing GmbH,
Munich

art direction
Iris Fuchs

concept
Markus Elsen, Tim Grasmann

graphic design
Pia Härle, Jan Meyer,
Veronika Schmidt

printing
Colordruck, Leimen

THE WORLD IS
MY LAB

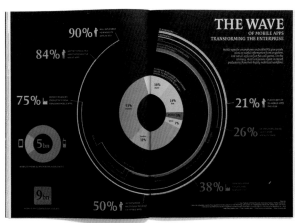

THE WAVE
OF MOBILE APPS
TRANSFORMING THE ENTERPRISE

INTELLIGENCE
ON THE MOVE

In terms of design approach, SAP SPECTRUM – unlike most IT and business magazines – hones in on the content-related meta-level: instead of typical imagery from the IT world, its conceptual as well as design focus offers a surprisingly new perspective on each topic (from software solutions to business strategy). A large share of specifically created image content – implemented through emotionally charged photographs, compositions, illustrations and typographic design – characterises the independent overall look. In the spirit of sustainability, the magazine is made of ecologically friendly paper using FSC-certified, carbon-neutral printing.

A SYSTEM
THAT KEEPS
ON
GROWING

WEALTH
IN WASTE

KAP #5

[Customer Magazine]

The KAP magazine is published by the KAP Forum communication platform, initiated by several companies based at the Rheinauhafen harbour in Cologne. In line with the location, the subject of this particular issue is water. The magazine typography echoes the rhythm and order of H_2O molecules, while the illustrations are based on the use of a wave-like tilde. This generates tension between rhythm and dynamics. The use of silver as a special colour element, with its iridescently reflecting expression, supports this effect.

client
KAP Forum, Cologne
(Alape, Carpet Concept, Dornbracht, Gira, Silent Gliss, Wilkhahn, Zumtobel Licht)

design
großgestalten
kommunikationsdesign, Cologne

design team
Tobias Groß, Martin Schüngel

illustration
Dominik Kirgus, Daniela Herweg

editorial work
Inken Herzig

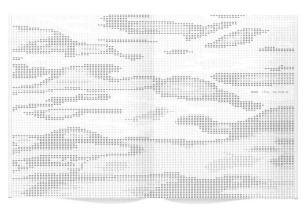

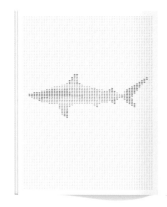
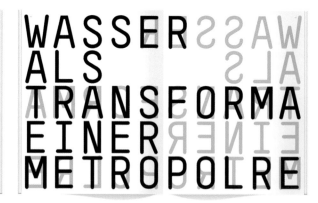

221 plus
[Customer Magazine]

Sal. Oppenheim is one of Germany's leading private banks. The objective was to create a premium, attention-grabbing and entertaining magazine that communicates the bank's sophisticated self-image. With its classic, representative character, the design communicates the values lived by the bank: tradition, individuality and exclusivity. An unobtrusive layout supports the informative editorial concept, which offers its readers a unique perspective on interesting topics.

client
Sal. Oppenheim jr. & Cie.,
Cologne

design
Simon & Goetz Design GmbH &
Co. KG, Frankfurt/Main

creative direction
Bernd Vollmöller

art direction
Dörte Fischer, Bernd Vollmöller

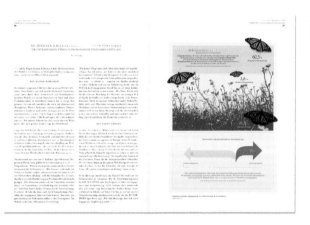

ZUNDER

[Magazine]

The agency magazine ZUNDER (German for "tinder") deals with all varieties of neuromarketing, design and advertising in an entertaining, unusual and surprising way. With this issue, which focuses on the topic of sweets, readers are holding a magazine that gives them an intense impression of how neuromarketing works, simply through the experience of unwrapping. All articles in the magazine – from an interview with a neurobiologist to an article on a chocolate brand from Berlin – have been extensively researched and professionally written while also featuring a creative layout.

client
red pepper, Gesellschaft für neurowissenschaftliche Markenverankerung mbH, Bremen

design
red pepper, Gesellschaft für neurowissenschaftliche Markenverankerung mbH, Bremen

art direction
Erik Wankerl

graphic design
André Spiehs, Jennifer Fischer

text
Emina Seifert, Sabine Weier

project management
Juliane Grzonka

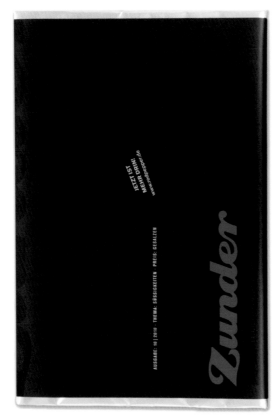

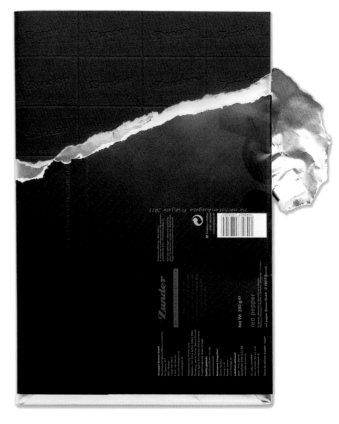

Nike Sportswear Autumn/Winter 2011

[Catalogue]

The 2011 autumn/winter collection by Nike Sportswear is presented by means of a catalogue which, thanks to its editorial content, has the character of a photo-illustrated book. The main focus of this season was running, which led to the conceptual approach of interviewing different artists about their running experiences. Accordingly, the catalogue was split into two parts: one narrative section and one for products, with these typographically differentiated from one another. In the interview segment, the dynamic energy of the still lifes is underlined by water splashes.

client
Nike Inc., Beaverton

design
e-design+communication gmbh, Berlin

art direction
Christiane Bördner

photography
Marcus Gaab, Tim Barbor

designer portrait
→ Vol.1: p.472

CREATIVE AND STRONG IN CONCEPT. Poster design is one of the supreme disciplines in the world of design – the virtuosic play with letters, the signalling effect of imagery and a perfect use of space – each element poses a challenge with each new design.

Vividly coloured, minimalist or humorous in design, they all create fascinating and individual worlds that captivate and impress beholders leaving a lasting effect.

Premiere Posters
Theater Erlangen

The poster series has the aim of portraying Theater Erlangen as a place of cultural dialogue and discussion, as well as a place of experiences and emotional richness. The posters advertise the theatre's multifaceted repertory of debut performances, commissioned plays and new theatrical concepts – the theatre's signature approach. Although the posters vary in their subject, they all feature the same plain font and a black silhouette of an abstract figure. This figure almost looks like a black board on which the theatre works are announced in thin majuscule letters of different sizes. The figures on all posters are easily identifiable through their shape, but always reveal a curious detail at closer inspection, such as a dog's fifth leg. The design thus maintains an appearance that is immediately recognisable, yet also attracts attention with each new poster by inviting people to spot and unravel the curious element.

Statement by the jury

»These theatre posters stand out from others because each single one of them reflects an individual approach without ever losing sight of the content. They thus work well both on their own and as parts of a series, emphasising the distinctive identity and brand image of Theater Erlangen. The silhouette figures serve as icons which, complemented by a skilfully embedded typography, convey to beholders a first impression of the play they advertise.«

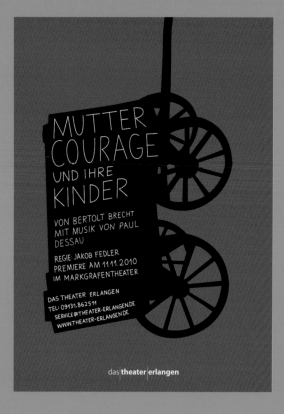

client
Theater Erlangen

design
Neue Gestaltung GmbH, Berlin

design team
Anna Bühler, Nina Odzinieks,
Pit Stenkhoff, Eva Wendel

designer portrait
→ Vol.1: p.491

red dot: best of the best

Research

[Poster Series]

The poster series Research announces six lectures held at the Academy of Art and Design Offenbach by communication designers on the topic of design research and its different approaches. The posters show stick figure illustrations of simple and reduced design to create an imagery that reflects at a glance the different hypotheses and individual theories. These ironic and inventive sketches – such as the one on the topic of "Vorglühen, Aufglühen, Verglühen!" ("Pre-heat, glow, burn!"), which shows one stick figure trying to give a light to another but producing a huge flame instead – aim at raising curiosity and interest. The colours of black and white suffice to spark the vivid imagination of the viewer and direct the attention to information presented in an equally minimalist design on the bottom edge of the posters.

Statement by the jury

»The beauty of this series of six black-and-white posters lies in the simplicity of the dash-line illustrations in combination with a harmoniously matched typeface on the one hand, and the original and distinctive appeal thus achieved on the other. The six skilfully rendered motifs put the topic of design research in a humorous light and aim at sparking dialogues about the different positions and approaches followed within the institute.«

RESEARCH TWO

09_12_2010 RALPH HEINJOHN ////////////////
VORGLÜHEN ¡ AUFGLÜHEN ¡ VERGLÜHEN ! ///////
HFG OFFENBACH ¡ SCHLOSSSTR_31 //////////////
RM 101 ¡ 18 UHR ///////////////////////////////

RESEARCH ONE

02_12_2010 SPEZIELL_NET ///////////////////////
ZWISCHEN EXPERIMENT + MARKTFÄHIGKEIT ///
HFG OFFENBACH ¡ SCHLOSSSTR_31 //////////////
RM 101 ¡ 18 UHR ///////////////////////////////

RESEARCH THREE

16_12_2010 FLORIAN BÖHM ////////////////////
VIEWS ///////////////////////////////////////
HFG OFFENBACH ¡ SCHLOSSSTR_31 //////////////
RM 101 ¡ 18 UHR ///////////////////////////////

RESEARCH SIX

27_01_2011 JOHANNES BERGERHAUSEN /////////
UNICODE ¡ MEGA—NISCHE ¡ DIGITALE KEILSCHRIFT
HFG OFFENBACH ¡ SCHLOSSSTR_31 //////////////
RM 101 ¡ 18 UHR ///////////////////////////////

client
Hochschule für Gestaltung
Offenbach / Academy of Art
and Design Offenbach

head of marketing
Prof. Peter Eckart

head of advertising
Ulrike Grünewald

design
Hesse Design GmbH, Düsseldorf

graphic design / illustration
Klaus Hesse

designer portrait
→ Vol.1: p.480

red dot: best of the best

Chairligraphy Series I
[Poster]

While the Chinese art of calligraphy has inspired generations of artists for centuries, the starting point of this poster series was the designer's fascination with chairs – two subjects that seem to be incompatible at first, but which the designer made the themes of his artistic creations. Set against a black background and recognisable only upon closer inspection, the posters reveal the subtle three-dimensional shapes of several hand-drawn chairs, which have been superimposed with old Chinese characters in white to create a strong contrast. Interestingly, the two-dimensional characters thus acquire a three-dimensional effect, causing the eye to constantly switch between two layers of perceived depth. As a combination of Ming-style chairs and classic Chinese calligraphy, "Chairligraphy" was created in the hope that the viewer could sense and feel the smoothness and strength of the calligraphic stroke.

Statement by the jury

»This poster series distinguishes itself through the skilful merging of Chinese roots with personal taste and the combination of typography with construction techniques. Both forms of expression enter into a kind of dialogue, alternately tracing the lines of the characters or those of the chairs. The actual coalescence effused is not only about beauty but also has a deeper meaning, inspired by Ming Dynasty aesthetics.«

唐一楷椅

client
Kan & Lau Design Consultants,
Hong Kong

design
Kan & Lau Design Consultants,
Hong Kong

creative direction/art direction
Freeman LAU, Siu-hong

concept
Freeman LAU, Siu-hong

designer portrait
→ Vol.1: p.483

2010/2011
Theatre Posters

The classic movie Metropolis, number one topic of the season 2010/2011 of the Schauspiel Stuttgart, is closely related to Stuttgart 21. Ten posters combine themes of the film, the corresponding repertoire of the Schauspiel Stuttgart, and scenes from the city in an off-theatre look and position the theatre in the centre of the controversy over a liveable city. Without using polemics or catchwords, the state theatre presents itself in a differentiated way and still sets a clearly visible sign with its revised logo, a neon-green clenched worker's fist.

client
Schauspiel Stuttgart

design
Strichpunkt Design,
Stuttgart

creative direction
Jochen Rädeker

art direction
Kirsten Dietz

graphic design
Julia Ochsenhirt

project management
Alexandra Storr

Ruhrtriennale Posters

For the second season of the Ruhrtriennale cultural festival, with the theme of "migration", photographs depicting the venues with people in vivid motion were used for the illuminated, large billboard and in-house poster series. Continuing the key visual of the last season, the human handwriting, streaks in space symbolise sequences of movement and represent the interaction between human beings and buildings, physicality and spirituality. The colours used for the posters are reserved and subtle, the paintbrush logo functions as a hybrid of the number "3", standing for "Triennale", and an "R", standing for "Ruhr".

client
Kultur Ruhr GmbH,
Gelsenkirchen

design
Strichpunkt Design,
Stuttgart

creative direction/concept
Jochen Rädeker

art direction
Julia Ochsenhirt

graphic design
Julia Ochsenhirt,
Agnetha Wohlert

strategic planning
Jochen Rädeker

Seit 110 Jahren
in der Kritik. /
*Has come under
criticism for 110 years.*
[Posters]

client
Deutsches Schauspielhaus
in Hamburg

head of marketing
Olaf Bargheer

design
Leagas Delaney Hamburg GmbH,
Hamburg

creative direction
Hermann Waterkamp

art direction
Patrik Hartmann

graphic design
Björn Byns, Sona Krude

text
Michael Okun

illustration
Patrik Hartmann, Björn Byns,
Sona Krude

designer portrait
→ Vol.2: p.490

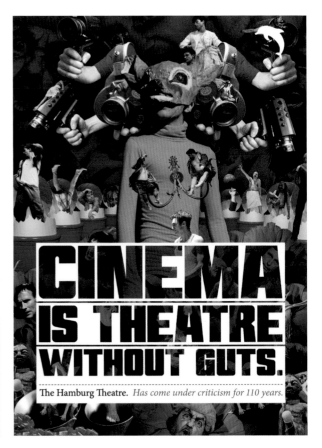

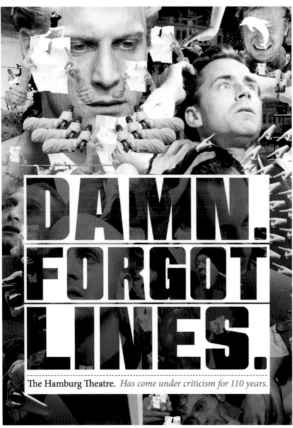

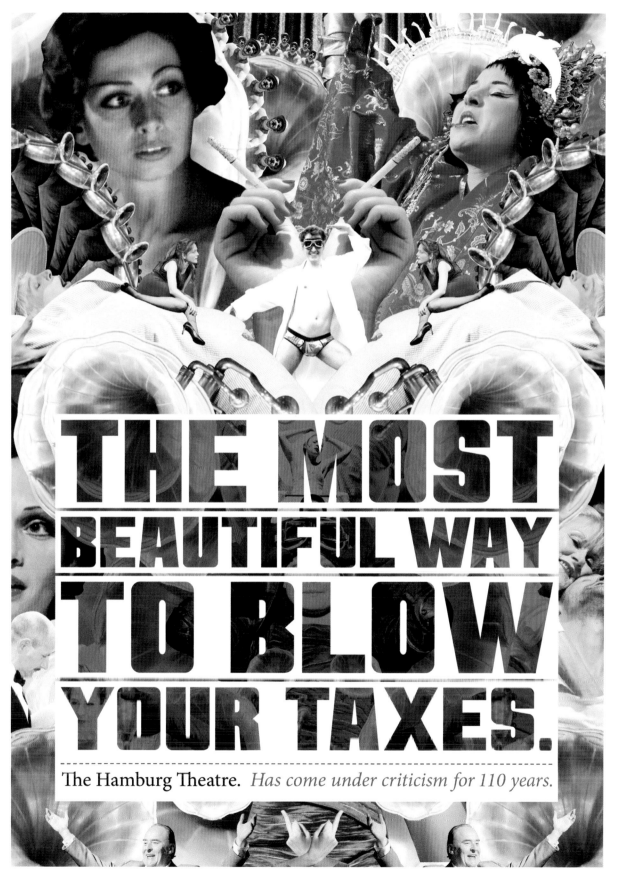

On the occasion of the 110th anniversary of the Hamburg theatre Deutsches Schauspielhaus, the design of this poster series focuses on its eventful history. Collages, assembled from film and theatre scenes, celebrate the fact that the Deutsches Schauspielhaus in its long history inflamed the critics and the audience time and time again with its daring productions, unusual interpretations and provoking performances. Thus the anniversary provided a welcome opportunity to celebrate the controversial position of the theatre in its hometown.

LATE Posters

The Auckland Museum is a natural history and war memorial museum in the process of repositioning itself and improving their relationship with visitors. The posters serve to announce the monthly event LATE and highlight the fact that the museum is opened longer on this day. Neon lights were chosen as an appropriate visual metaphor to illustrate that point. Each letter, made from fluorescent tubes, is aligned with the typography of the AM campaign (AM is an acronym for Auckland Museum) and positioned in a perspex cube. Thus, the letters could be set up in different configurations.

client
Auckland Museum,
Auckland

design
Alt Group,
Auckland

creative direction
Dean Poole

graphic design
Dean Poole, Shabnam Shiwan,
Jinki Cambronero, Tony Proffit,
Aaron Edwards

photography
Toaki Okano

printing
Phantom Billstickers

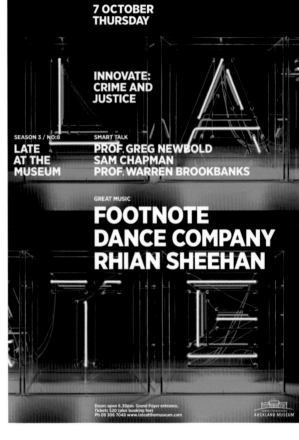

Verses

[Poster Series]

This poster series, combining expressive typography with dynamic photography, was developed for the contemporary Pacific dance company Black Grace. The central motif of the campaign combines images of the artists and important visual elements of their performances as a triptych. The incorporation of a custom typeface – combining a classic modernist font with the form of traditional Samoan tattoos – allows the image to still be clearly visible through the typeface.

client
Black Grace,
Auckland

photography art direction
Neil Ieremia

design
Alt Group,
Auckland

creative direction
Dean Poole

graphic design
Shabnam Shiwan

photography
Duncan Cole

MKO Season 10/11

[Poster Series]

The theme of the season 2010/
2011 of the Münchener Kammerorchester was architecture. The
poster series comprises eight
posters for the subscription
concerts, one season poster as
well as some for special concerts,
and implements the wish for a
non-representational design
aesthetic by arranging the elements sound, space and light into
a multi-layered design and by
creating various seasonal motifs
with strong recognition value. The
motifs were created by pictures
of objects being manipulated
in colouring and light mood via
technical procedures such as
flash, inversion or digital colour
processing.

client
MKO, Münchener Kammer-
orchester, Munich

design
Schmidt/Thurner/
von Keisenberg, Munich

graphic design
Prof. Gerwin Schmidt

designer portrait
→ Vol.1: p.501

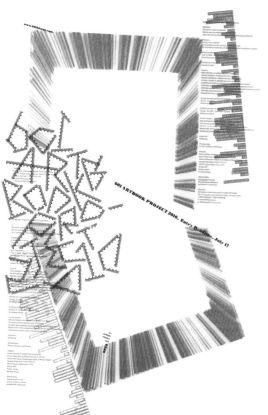

601 Artbook Project 2010

[Poster Series]

The design of the posters for the 601 Artbook Project 2010 pursues a book's structure that provides its content in an open and accessible way to readers. The title as well as the typography are intended to highlight this and to bring the creativity and the narrative style to life. The design of the title, looking as if little birds are conquering the world, is eye-catching. The exhibition poster "22 points" depicts 22 dots created by unique patterns and a geometrically shaped human silhouette merging typographically with a graphic illustration of the exhibition place.

client
601bisang, Seoul

design
601bisang, Seoul

creative direction/art direction
Kum-Jun Park

graphic design
Kum-Jun Park

illustration
Kum-Jun Park, Ji-Hee Lee

designer portrait
→ Vol.1: p.458

David Sandlin
Subway Posters

The New York School of Visual Arts utilises a series of posters which has continually been in use as an important vehicle for their advertising and self-presentation since the 1950s. The posters, which in the past have been designed by designers and illustrators like Milton Glaser, Paula Scher, George Tscherny and James Victore, are displayed in the New York subway. The 2010 poster was designed by David Sandlin, a renowned painter, printmaker and cartoonist, who has published and exhibited widely in both Europe and the United States.

client
School of Visual Arts,
New York

design
Visual Arts Press, Ltd.,
New York

creative direction
Anthony P. Rhodes

art direction
Michael J. Walsh

illustration
David Sandlin

Gedanken / *Thoughts*

[Print Campaign]

This print campaign demonstrates how the illness cancer features in the mindset of children, illustrating how children suffering from cancer are affected by a disease without morale or conscience – the inevitability of death collides with their naiveté. The intention is to let viewers of the posters experience the perspective of the children and relive the injustice, viciousness and brutality of cancer. The purpose of the campaign was to evoke real emotions which encourage people to help.

client
Hilfe für krebskranke Kinder
Frankfurt e.V., Frankfurt/Main

head of marketing
Eva-Maria Hehlert

design
Leo Burnett GmbH,
Frankfurt/Main

chief creative officer
Andreas Pauli

creative direction
Andreas Stalder,
Ulf Henniger von Wallersbrunn

art direction
Ulf Henniger von Wallersbrunn,
Benjamin Röder,
Juliana Paracencio

text
Andreas Stalder,
Leonardo Assad

illustration
Aki Röll

designer portrait
→ Vol.2: p.473

Höchstleistungen /
Peak Performance

[Posters]

Peak performances as the focus of this poster series describe the high standards of paper manufacturer Scheufelen. The design concept uses the visualisation of human and physical peak performances, for example the deepest dive, the creation of the brightest beam of light and a representation of the building of the most powerful telescope, to create a direct analogy to the performance capacity of this company and to communicate their values to the client: high standards, independence and creativity.

client
Papierfabrik Scheufelen GmbH & Co. KG, Lenningen

design
Strichpunkt Design, Stuttgart

creative direction
Jochen Rädeker

art direction
Kirsten Dietz

graphic design
Julia Ochsenhirt,
Agnetha Wohlert

project management
Marc Schergel

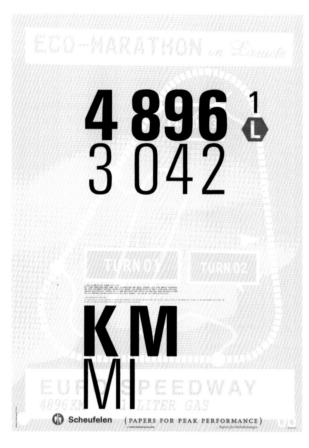

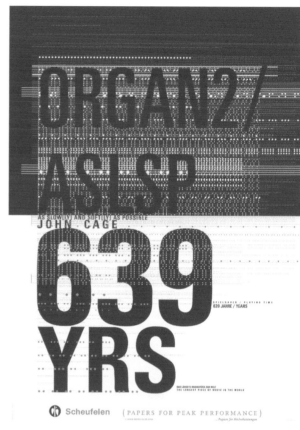

Loewe 3D

[Posters]

Loewe meets the trend towards 3D television that harbours a lot of potential for the home entertainment area with its own premium concept. Within a large-scale teaser campaign for the planned introduction of a new generation of 3D TVs in Full-HD LCD technology with LED backlighting in the first quarter of 2011, these clearly designed posters are supposed to awaken the interest of a demanding target group. Typographical and architectural 3D elements visualise the new technology in a very distinctive way.

client
Loewe Opta GmbH, Kronach

design
Scholz & Friends

head of advertising
Martin Pross

creative direction
Matthias Spaetgens,
Wolf Schneider

art direction
Gito Lima (Freelancer),
Juergen Krugsperger

graphic design
Désirée Denner

designer portrait
→ Vol.2: p.503

LOEWE Individual 3D – a new reality.

LOEWE.

LOEWE Individual 3D – a new reality.

LOEWE.

Jetons / *Chips*
[CLP Advertising Column]

The casino Spielbank Hamburg was one of the hosts of the satellite tournaments of the 18th German poker championships 2010 in Texas Hold'em No Limit – a poker variety with no stake limit. Prior to the tournament two premium city-light columns were converted into coloured metre-high chip towers. Visible to car drivers and passers-by from far and in conjunction with the message, "Bet, as high as you wish!", they attracted numerous participants and visitors.

client
Spielbank Hamburg Jahr + Achterfeld KG, Hamburg

head of marketing
Gunda Windberger

design
gürtlerbachmann Werbung GmbH, Hamburg

creative direction/concept
Mirco Kukereit

art direction
Mirco Kukereit

project management
Anne Kukereit

text
Claudia Oltmann

Opel LCV – Good Tools. Good Work.

[Campaign]

To unite the entire range of Opel's commercial vehicles into one single campaign, a comprehensive system was developed. The idea is to address the target groups with their own everyday work tools while additionally introducing the vehicle. The look of the final "work tool" was created by combining the vehicles with the various work tools of the core target groups. Work tool and commercial vehicle form a unit without alienating the actual product, the vehicle, itself.

client
Adam Opel AG,
Rüsselsheim

head of advertising
Tamas Bator,
Andrea Pfannmöller

design
brandtouch GmbH,
Hamburg

creative direction
Günter Sendlmeier

art direction
Jonathan Sven Amelung,
Pedro Americo

photography
Christian Stoll

post-production
Ralph Hillert

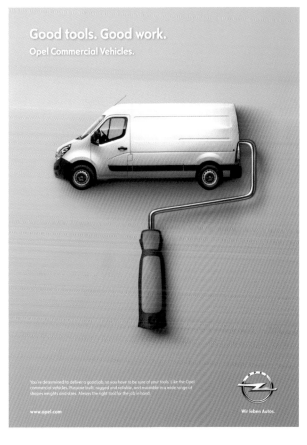

413

EXPO 2012
YEOSU KOREA

[Poster]

The design of these two posters represent the vision of the EXPO 2012 in Yeosu, "The Living Ocean and Coast", in focusing on the relationship between man and nature as a theme. The lifeline of the human hand symbolises the idea of a new beginning, which becomes possible through wise utilisation and protection of the earth. The second poster uses the symbol for Yeosu, the camellia, and combines it with the organic shape of two merging bodies. These again symbolise the connection between the sea and the coast.

design
601bisang, Seoul

creative direction/art direction
Kum-Jun Park

graphic design
Kum-Jun Park

illustration
Kum-Jun Park, Soo-Hwan Kim

project management
Seung-Yeon Jeong

account executive
Jin-Ho Choi

coordination
Jong-In Jung, Na-Won You

designer portrait
→ Vol.1: p.458

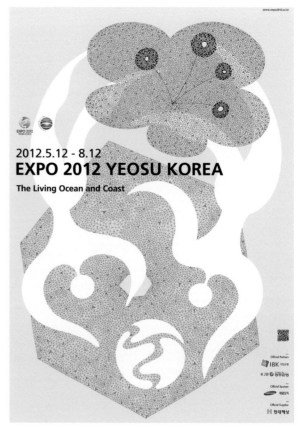

Pulchri Studio
[Exhibition Poster]

This poster promotes the annual spring exhibition (Voorjaarssalon) as well as the over 100 years old artist society Pulchri Studio as an active organisation and exhibition space with room for both established artists and young talents. The arrangement of natural elements in the poster design reflects the way visual artists structure and manipulate elements from the world around them in their work. The tinge of colour accenting the lily petals references new life arising in spring.

client
Pulchri Studio, The Hague

design
Studio Dumbar, Rotterdam

graphic design
Liza Enebeis, Studio Dumbar

photography
Denise Collignon

designer portrait
→ Vol.2: p.506

Ezio

[Poster]

Georg Friedrich Händel's opera is about a deadly intrigue against Roman commander Ezio, who is nearly brought down by accusations of alleged treason. In their basic constellation, the main protagonists are inspired by Roman history. The poster communicates the subject matter, using an intense, bold type font and knocking the letters which build the name of the eponymous hero off balance. The injury Ezio receives is indicated by the tilting sharp-edged Z.

client
Theater Biel Solothurn

head of marketing
Beat Wyrsch, Florian Schalit

design
Atelier Bundi AG, Boll

art direction
Stephan Bundi

graphic design
Stephan Bundi

printing
Serigraphie Uldry

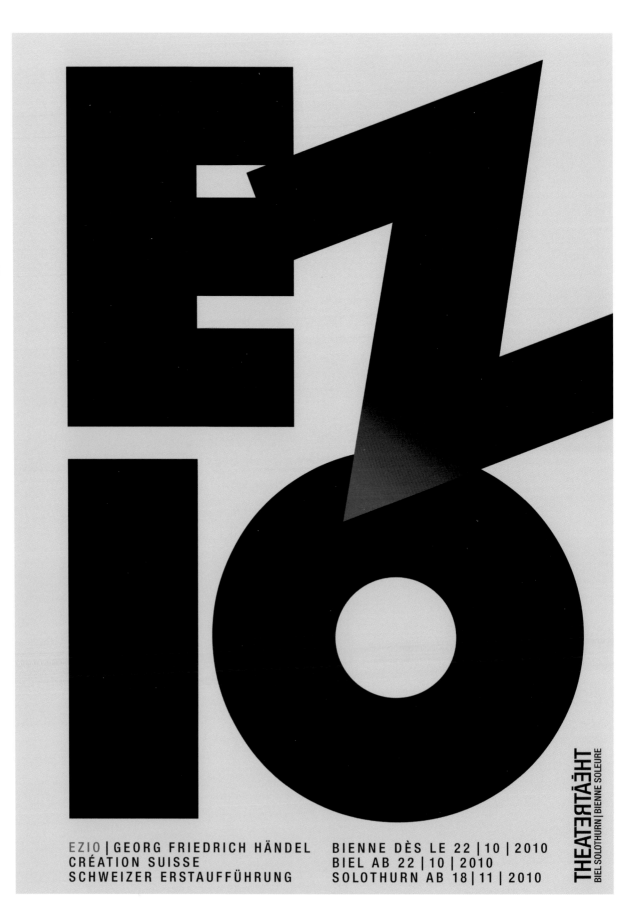

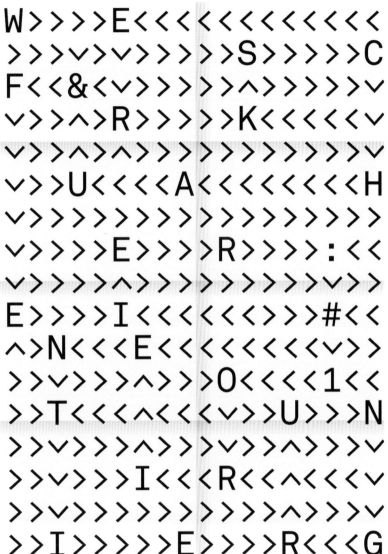

großgestalten werkschau
[Invitation Poster]

The invitation of the agency großgestalten to their "Werkschau #1 Orientierung" was a typographic Monospace labyrinth. The visitors were told to find their own way through the maze of letters and characters. Starting from the letter "W", they had to follow the arrows, orient themselves and playfully decipher the invitation in this way. To remain consistent with the name of the agency (which literally means "tall figures"), the invitation was generously designed in DIN A1.

client
großgestalten
kommunikationsdesign, Cologne

design
großgestalten
kommunikationsdesign, Cologne

design team
Tobias Groß, Jazek Poralla

The backbone of your office.

[Poster]

The design for the client König + Neurath, a manufacturer of high-quality office furniture for the most different fields of work, required an idea that would visualise their extensive competency in seating furniture ergonomics. The aim was to communicate to specialised traders that each single model is based on continuous ergonomic research as well as innovative seating concepts and mechanics. The design solution features a striking line in the shape of the human spine consisting of 24 different chairs of the manufacturer.

client
König + Neurath, Karben

design
Scheufele Hesse Eigler,
Frankfurt/Main

creative direction
Oliver Hesse

art direction
Corinna Zeidler

graphic design
Katrin Janka

text
Oliver Hesse

strategic planning
Frank Eigler

project management
Christian Flöck

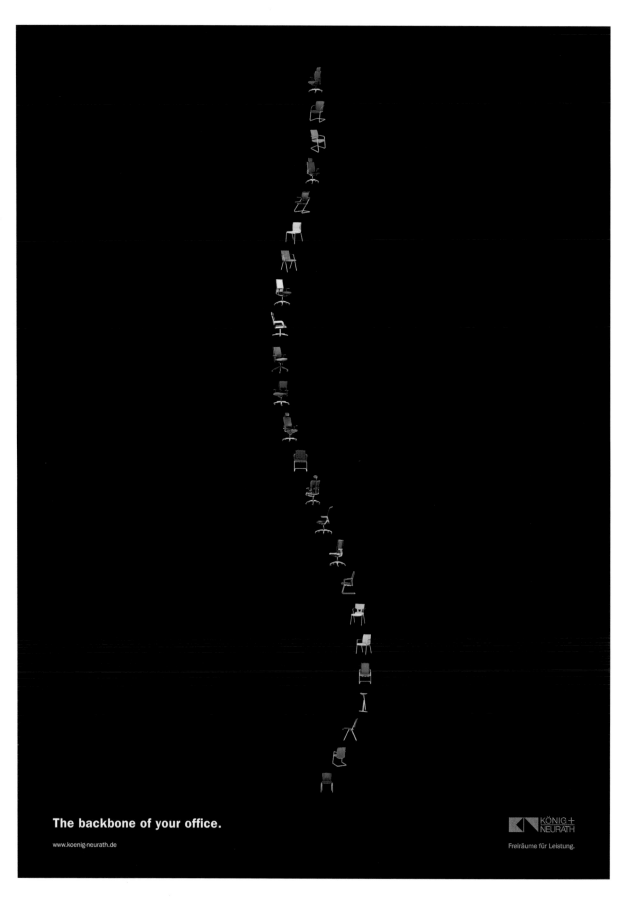

The backbone of your office.

www.koenig-neurath.de

KÖNIG + NEURATH

Freiräume für Leistung.

Fremd?! / *Stranger?!*

[Poster]

The poster conveys the transcultural character of the educational theatre project "Fremd?!" ("Stranger?!") by and for adolescents and young adults mainly by using typographical elements. The diversity of modern society and the cultural backgrounds of the participants were highlighted by arranging the names of the participants into the shape of continents. The design directly addresses the different target groups of the event, teenagers as well as their families, and also the urban population that has an interest in the topic.

client
Transkulturelles Theater- und Bildungsprojekt „fremd?!", Basel

design
Bureau Dillier, Basel

Die fiftyfifty
Galerie Plakate /
The fiftyfifty
Gallery Posters

[City Light Posters]

A street gallery was the solution to the task of promoting an art gallery run by the homeless charity fiftyfifty. The proceeds of the event were supposed to go to people in need. The idea was implemented by putting up 200 city light posters in the urban area of Düsseldorf. The gallery presented works of renowned international artists, such as Thomas Ruff or Otto Piene. Merely small price tags, featuring the fiftyfifty logo instead of a price, informed about the event. 60,000 euros of donations were generated this way.

client
fiftyfifty Obdachlosen-
organisation, Düsseldorf

design
Euro RSCG Düsseldorf

creative direction
Felix Glauner, Martin Breuer,
Martin Venn

art direction
Ingmar Krannich

graphic design
Michel Becker, Franziska Lopau
(Freelancer)

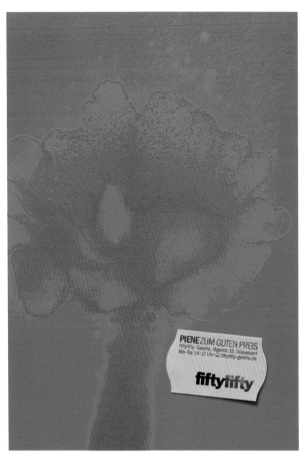

Hinz&Kunzt Handcrafted Cardboard Illustrations

On the occasion of local elections, a campaign against vacancies drew attention to the fact that in the affluent metropolis Hamburg thousands of people were living in the streets while more than 1.4 million sqm of living and office space remained vacant. Key elements of the entire campaign are posters made from corrugated cardboard with portraits of homeless people carved into the top layers and powerful slogans added with markers. The handcrafted posters were attached extensively to the front facades of vacant buildings. Additionally floor posters were on display in shopping streets.

client
Hinz&Kunzt gGmbH, Hamburg

head of marketing
Isabel Schwartau

design
JWT Germany GmbH, Hamburg;
Isabelle Göntgen,
Isabelle Illustration,
Zell unter Aichelberg

creative direction
Till Hohmann

art direction
Regina Groffy

graphic design
Ainara del Valle Perez-Solero

text
Michael Muck

421

Help

[Poster]

The designers, whose motto is "winning over people", felt it was their obligation to help people and designed an appeal for donations in the form of a poster, which they provided to charitable organisations for free, and in this way they could support the Japanese population after the earthquake and the tsunami. The design, inspired by the world-wide recognisable images of drones, utilises a top view of the destroyed nuclear plant and modifies the topographic layout of the plant as well as the steam to create the letters "HELP" for the appeal.

client
SHE for Japan,
Scheufele Hesse Eigler,
Frankfurt/Main

design
Scheufele Hesse Eigler,
Frankfurt/Main

creative direction/concept
Oliver Hesse

graphic design
Katrin Janka, Maria Michel

text
Oliver Hesse

project management
Katharina Fritz

illustration
Francesco Strazzanti

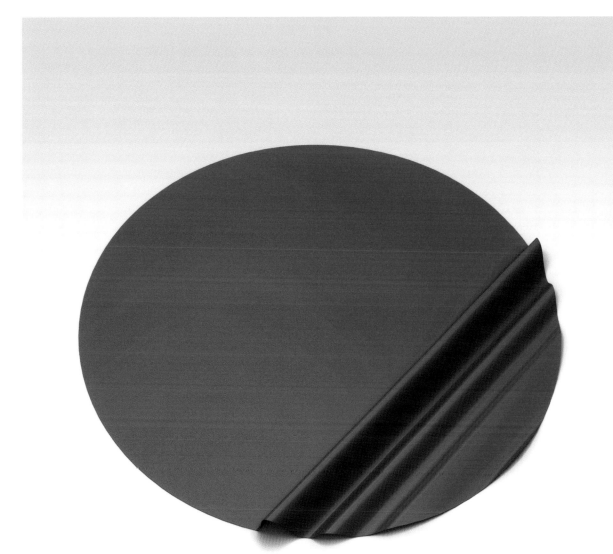

HELP JAPAN

Help Japan
[Donation Poster]

The Help Japan poster visualises the tsunami that hit Japan on March 11th 2011, causing a nuclear disaster. The Japanese flag, a red disk on a white rectangular banner, symbolises the consequences of the flood in a straightforward and distinctive manner by using simple pleats on one side of the disk. Designed as an appeal for donations with the title "Help Japan", it communicates the message in the tradition of Japanese simplicity and purity, which can be understood without any mental detours.

client
HOME^Agentur für
Kommunikation, Gelsenkirchen

design
HOME^Agentur für
Kommunikation, Gelsenkirchen

creative direction
Klaus Trommer

graphic design/illustration
Klaus Trommer

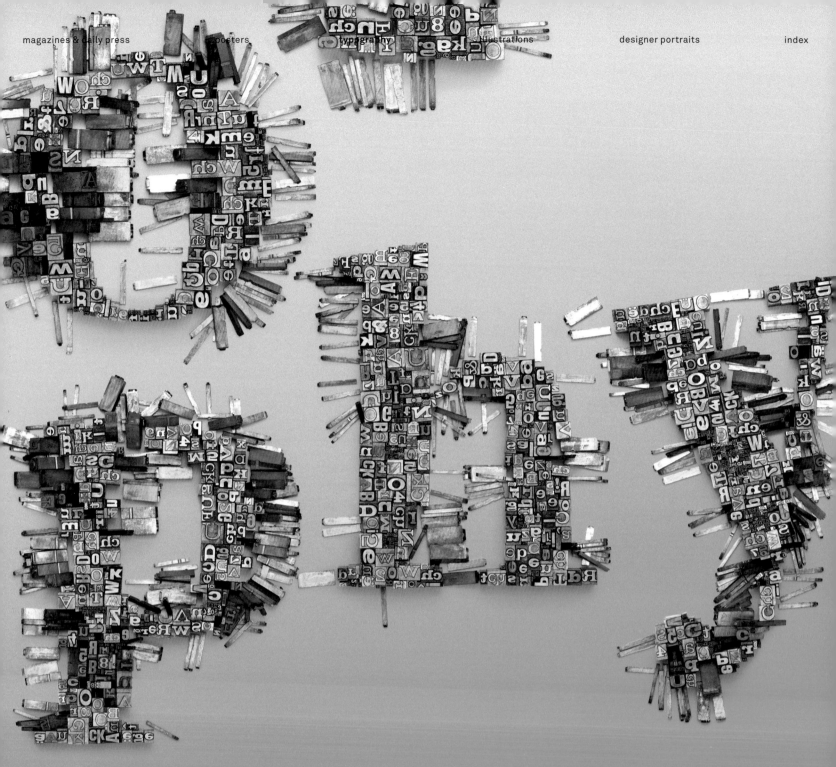

TRIGGERING THE IMAGINATION. Text is not only a means of communication, it is also an important design element. Some designers utilise typical creativeelements such as dots, lines and forms consistently, others take a more playful approach towards them.

The goal-oriented use of fonts to trigger emotions, pictograms that inform and perfect calligraphy are the key to producing an outstanding typography.

Die BMW Lightwall /
The BMW Light Wall

The task was to promote the BMW M3 Coupé at Hamburg Airport with an expressive and distinctive idea. The solution was a very special billboard in form of a 50 x 2 metre light wall set up in the middle of the arrivals hall. Its special feature is that only one half of the letters of the majuscule claim "EXCEED MAXIMUM" is displayed. The other half is added by the shiny stone floor: it reflects the letters and completes the claim. Enhanced by the light, the claim thus gains the effect of travellers paying attention to it immediately and instinctively, as they get curious to learn what this wall is about. Thus, the message of the light wall simultaneously showcases an automobile that technically exceeds familiar limits through a typographical poster that pushes the limits of formal representation.

Statement by the jury

»'EXCEED' means to 'go beyond limits' and, in doing so, to 'exceed expectations'. The designer convincingly managed to visualise this message for the BMW M3 Coupé on a 50 x 2 metre billboard. The idea to integrate the reflective quality of the long gangway floor into the presentation is outstanding. Through simple typographic means, the word 'MAXIMUM' thus takes shape and passers-by can experience this fascinating product staging by becoming part of it.«

client
BMW AG, Munich

design
serviceplan, Hamburg

chief creative officer
Alexander Schill

creative direction
Maik Kaehler, Christoph Nann

art direction
Roman Becker, Manuel Wolff

graphic design
Savina Mokreva,
Maximilian Kempe

text
Andreas Schriewer

designer portrait
→ Vol.1: p.503

red dot: best of the best

Mandarin Phonetic Symbols (Series)

[Poster]

The efforts and activities of the green economy industry have depended, since its beginnings, on innovative and broadly conceived advertisement methods, which convey to as many people as possible the different approaches and projects, the idea of a corporate management and the concept of peace. This poster series features an exclusively typographic design and aims to educate the next generation on how to develop a green environmental awareness as early as possible, and to give them a better understanding of fair trade and organic food. Thus, the posters are inspired by and pick up on the first thing taught in school: the alphabet. Through the phonetic symbols of Mandarin and the characters of the Latin alphabet, between which the name of the company is hidden, the campaign aims to convey that the concept of environmental protection and, thus, the concept of the Green at Heart company has become a natural and essential part of human life.

Statement by the jury

»The meaning of this mysterious poster series lies hidden in a footnote: 'We believe: Environmental friendliness is the universal language. Education leads us to live Green at Heart.' The cryptic, typographic message of the different alphabets underlines this universal demand with a poetic appeal. Realised as 'concrete poetry', the design possesses a quality that is as self-sufficient as it is surprising.«

client
Green at Heart, Hong Kong

design
Hufax arts

creative direction / art direction
Fa-Hsiang Hu

concept / text
Alain Hu

graphic design
Fa-Hsiang Hu, Fei Hu, Di Hu

account management
Kai-I Lee

designer portrait
→ Vol.1: p.482

ㄌㄩˋㄙㄜˋㄒㄧㄣㄧˋ

lu se xin yi

我們深信：文字符號只能傳達我們的主意，綠色生活則是表達對地球的心意
We believe: Phonetic symbols deliver the language;
the lifestyle of Green at Heart delivers our concern for the world.
www.greenatheart.com.hk

red dot: best of the best

Typeface Design for the "Christian Garden" in Berlin

This project comprises the typeface design for an architecture that consists entirely of letters set up in the "Christian Garden" inside Berlin's recreational park "Gardens of the World". Inspired by medieval cloisters, the 33 cm high letters form an arched walkway that is built from texts of the Christian-Occidental tradition. Various alternative letter shapes of different widths create a highly homogeneous web of text, which is capable not only of transmitting the high static loads evenly to the ground but also prevents, due to the highly varying number of glyphs per line, particular lines from looking too compressed or too wide. Up to three alternative forms – majuscule, minuscule and special characters – serve to create a highly lively composition without being repetitive in appeal. The font supports 13 written languages, including ancient Greek and Cyrillic, and creates a typeface design of a sculptural appearance.

Statement by the jury

»This Babylonian confusion in the form of an arched-covered cloister has a high aesthetic appeal and is typographic architecture at its best. Developing an original typeface that supports no less than 13 written languages, including ancient Greek and Cyrillic, is an outstanding accomplishment. The typography inside the entire construction, thus, acquires a unique visual as well as spatial appearance.«

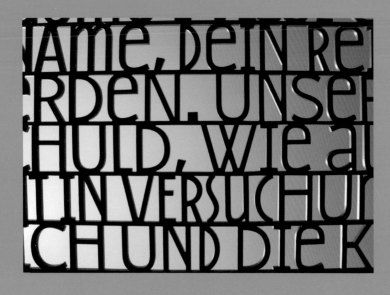

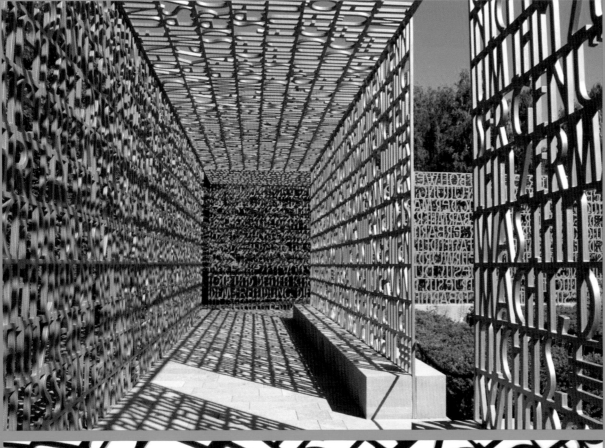

design
xplicit Gesellschaft für
visuelle Kommunikation mbH,
Berlin

typeface design
Alexander Branczyk

typography
Annette Wüsthoff

structural engineering
Schlaich Bergermann
und Partner

general concept/architecture
relais Landschaftsarchitekten,
Berlin

designer portrait
→ Vol.1: p.510

Typescape

[Booklet Series]

Typescape is a project which delves into typography beyond paper. Exploring how a text may have vitality beyond the scope of paper, the aim is to facilitate new forms and meanings through all kinds of experiences within time and space. Typescape fosters a different view of letters, like those displayed on a moving railroad car or an automobile. The constellations in the night sky may likewise be read in the form of letters. Sometimes lettering in Typescape is shown in three-dimensional space.

client
GT Press, Seoul

design
Hankyong National University

graphic design
Namoo Kim

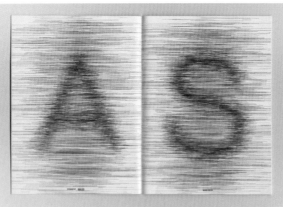

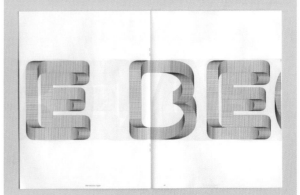

decodeunicode – Die Schriftzeichen der Welt / *decodeunicode – The world's writing systems*
[Book]

The book decodeunicode investigates the unknown glyph treasures, which, according to the author, lie within the depths of the keyboard, and sends the reader within its 600 pages on a typographical journey around the world and through time. decodeunicode understands itself as a key to all the existing glyphs in the world and presents 109,242 of them. Additionally it documents an enormous multitude of different scripts and integrates extinct, frequently used ones as well as niche scripts. The book awakens the passion to discover unfamiliar scripts and encourages creative interaction with them.

client
Verlag Hermann Schmidt Mainz

design
decodeunicode, Cologne

creative direction / art direction
Prof. Johannes Bergerhausen,
Prof. Ilka Helmig, Siri Poarangan

text
Prof. Johannes Bergerhausen,
Siri Poarangan

project management
Prof. Johannes Bergerhausen

software development
Daniel A. Becker

printing
Universitätsdruckerei Mainz

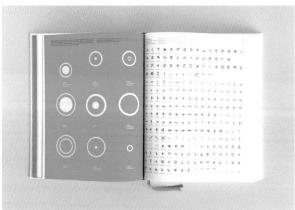

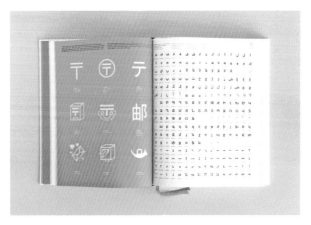

EDG
Pictogram System

This concise pictogram system has been developed for the Dortmund-based waste disposal company EDG to inform citizens about the replacement of the previous Yellow Bin with the Re-cycling Bin within information campaigns and exhibitions. It visualises different kinds of waste, such as small electrical appliances, metals and plastics, which now can also be collected and recycled. The pictogram system harmonises with the existing typeface of the client. Eventually the symbols for or-ganic, paper and residual waste were added to the system.

client
EDG, Entsorgung Dortmund GmbH, Dortmund

design
Paarpiloten, Düsseldorf

creative direction
Christopher Wiehl, Nanni Goebel

art direction/concept
Christopher Wiehl

graphic design
Stefanie Marniok

designer portrait
→ Vol.1: p.496

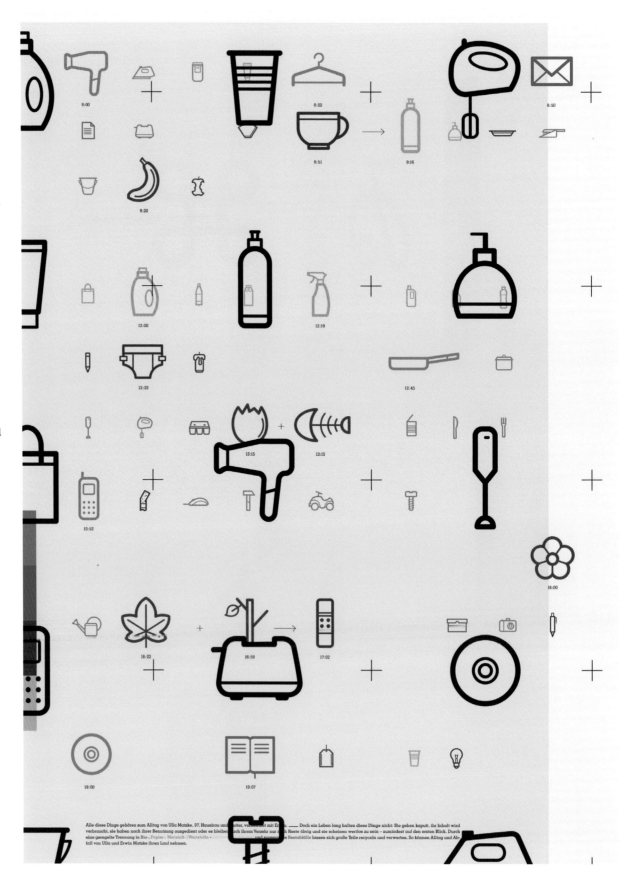

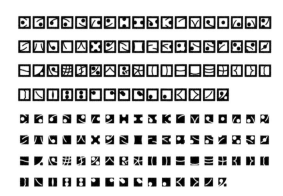

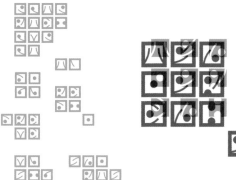

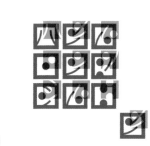

BGY-aPaT

[Typography]

Corresponding to the difference in temperature of the work of the artist Wassily Kandinsky and the cubism of Pablo Picasso, this typography has been inspired by three different shapes and the cubism. They describe three different kinds of temperature: an equilateral triangle means "hot", a circle symbolises "cold" and a square means "not too hot and not too cold – lukewarm". Accordingly, the figures become the base of this typographical work as they start from the relation between emotion and temperature. The letters consist of dots and lines (straight lines and curves) in each base respectively.

client
Young-Il Seo, Daegu

design
Young-Il Seo, Daegu

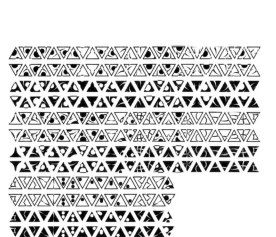

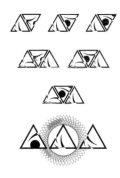

Alphatool

[Alphabet]

The innovative Alphatool concept combines the semantic meaning of letters with a highly functional design. Alphatool is an alphabet upon which you can sit. These letter-shaped chairs are a fun experience for children and offer a new level of playful and didactic learning. By engaging with the chairs and building words with them, children become familiarised both with the letters of the alphabet and with their alphabetical order.

client
Lenoirschuring, Amstelveen

design
André Toet,
Samenwerkende Ontwerpers,
Amsterdam

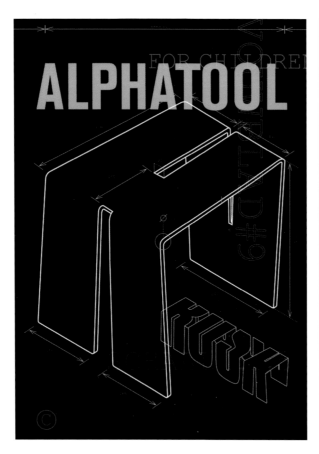

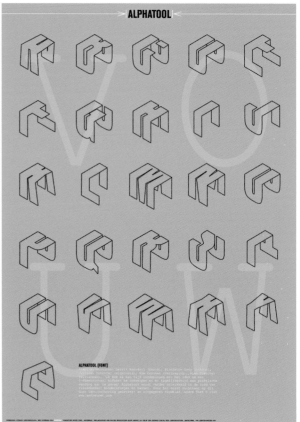

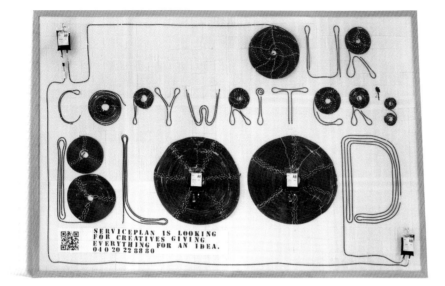

Posters of Passion: Blood, Sweat & Tears

These posters tangibly communicate this agency's dedication to its ideas. The use of "blood, sweat and tears" becomes the design "resource". A blood donation carried out in a hospital, for instance, provides the ink for a poster where blood-filled tubing pens the textual message. For another poster, the designers' sweat was collected in a sauna and then applied to black fabric using a spray bottle and stencil; the typography thus takes form from the dried salt residue.

client
serviceplan, Hamburg

design
serviceplan, Hamburg

chief creative officer
Alexander Schill

creative direction
Maik Kaehler, Christoph Nann

art direction
Savina Mokreva, Manuel Wolff

graphic design
Christoph Kueckner,
Maren Wandersleben,
Christoff Strukamp

programming
Steffen Knoblich, plan.net

designer portrait
→ Vol.1: p.503

Chinese Surname Totem

[Typography]

client
Denro International Co., Keelung

design
Chin-Shun Wang

head of marketing
Chin-Min Wang

text
Yu-Fen Wang

project management
Yu-Jie Wang

designer portrait
→ Vol.1: p.508

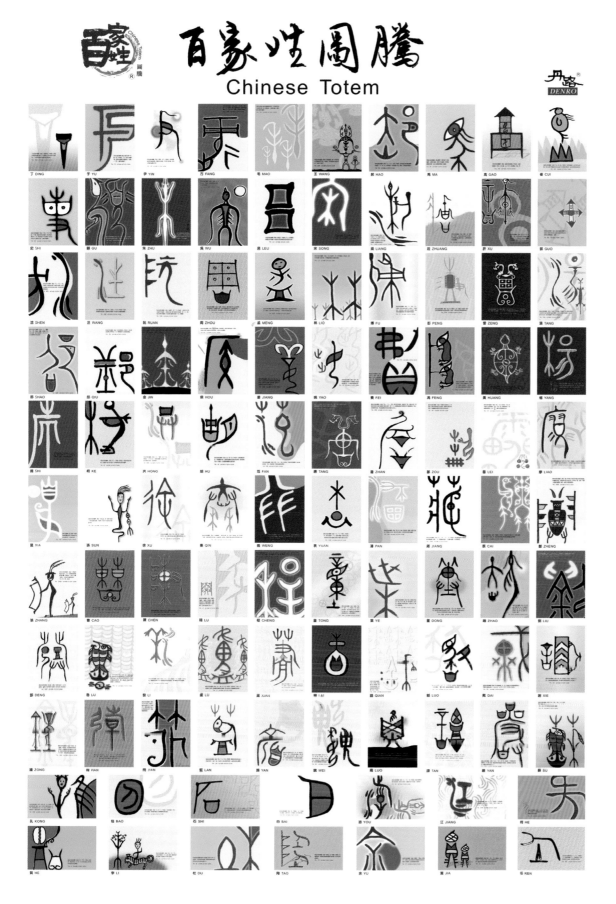

Chinese Totem

Chinese surnames originate from ancient totem figures and each one of them has its own history. The totem of a clan represents a social structure, a belief and a tradition, but also a primitive form of art. Using calligraphy is a way to express the beauty of those totem figures. This print is an exemplary compilation of 104 different totem figures of Chinese family names. Each of them is based on the study of historical characters as well as legends about the family names and displays the lines and totem figures in a strictly calligraphic way. To combine the traditional calligraphy with modern art, the colour patterns of artists like Picasso, Miró or Warhol were used with the individual works so the historical totems received a new contemporary layout.

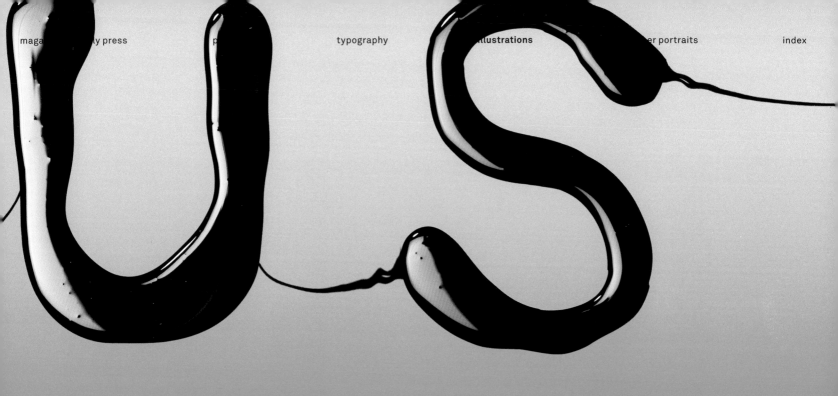

THE SPECIAL MARK. Print and digital media achieve a distinctive identity through illustrations that emerge from a wealth of outstanding ideas and a passion for imagery and storytelling.

Interactive animations, films and advertisements gain life through expressive images whose content is brought to the fore in an eye-catching manner. Their implementation can be classic, out of the ordinary or even highly humorous.

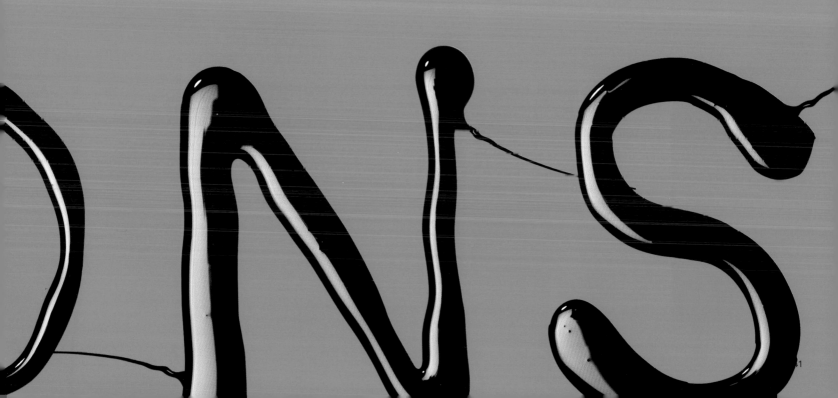

red dot: best of the best

Big Business 3

[Illustrations]

This book continues the series of Big Business issues and, inspired by the book's title, features illustrations that are a collage of banknotes. The use of this means of financial circulation plays on the dual character of brand, business and currency – with the aim of providing a new vision of understanding brand and identity and inviting people to rethink the influence of money and desire on human beings. It introduces a selection of 222 global brand designs from the 500 leading companies worldwide. The featured face illustrations, which were handcrafted lovingly by arranging countless small snippets cut from real banknotes into collages, take on expressions of sadness or happiness, tragedy or comedy, depending on the viewing angle. Richly detailed and filigree in design, the illustrations thus convey the message in a vivid and innovative manner.

Statement by the jury

»The illustrations of faces made of money address the beholder directly. The how, why and what is not answered immediately at first sight, but their beauty appeals to us, and the answers follow by themselves. They might be different for each individual, but one common denominator remains: the thought of how money rules over the world and us. In an impressive manner, the illustrations manage to shed a light that is both fascinating and unsettling onto the commercial world of brands and business.«

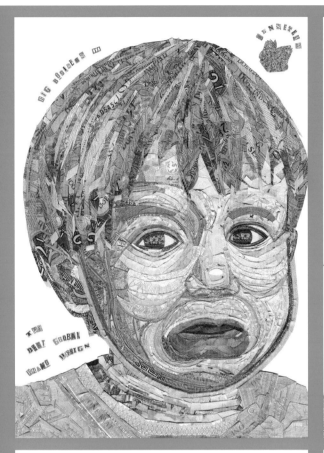

client
SendPoints, Guangzhou

design
SenseTeam, Shenzhen

graphic design
Hei Yiyang, Wang Xiaomeng

illustration
Hei Yiyang, Wang Xiaomeng,
Zhao Xinyu, Liu Haiyan,
Zhang Chi, Chen Silin

designer portrait
→ Vo.1: p.502

red dot: best of the best

45th Dimitria Festival

[Illustration]

A total of 16 characters were illustrated as the main elements of the complete visual identity for the 45th Dimitria Festival. Taking place annually in Thessaloniki and Northern Greece, this cultural festival is the largest of its kind in Greece and covers all the arts including music, dance and theatre. Humorously kept in black-and-white, these characters have reference in the local traditional culture of engraved art as well as the Greek shadow theatre featuring the main character of hunchbacked Karagiozis. The illustrations were used in many different applications, such as merchandise and publications, and as three metres high wooden installations that were placed at hotspots and historical places around the city. The themes of the illustrations are related to each place they were installed at: a character in a prop-driven aircraft, for example, is placed at the airport, an owl near the university area and a fisherman is sitting on the seaside. These easily recognisable motifs thus promote the festival in an inviting manner.

Statement by the jury

»The mix of performances that characterise the Dimitria Festival is conveyed through a series of icons that support the message in a distinctive and original manner. Following an individual and humorous design approach, the implementation embodies an outstanding solution.«

client
Municipality of Thessaloniki,
Department of Culture and Youth,
Thessaloniki

design
Beetroot Design Group,
Thessaloniki

creative direction
Yiannis Charalambopoulos,
Alexis Nikou, Vangelis Liakos

art direction
Mixalis Rafail

photography
Kostas Pappas

illustration
Alexis Nikou

designer portrait
→ Vol.1: p.463

Hollywood

[Book]

Illustration, typography and design are merged into one graphic unit in this book about film. Cinematic elements, such as titles and credits, end title credits, zoom shots and narrative image sequences, are rendered into the medium of a book. Scenes done in bright Technicolor recount the story of the breakthrough of colour film. The graphic style, the choice of typeface and fonts used in the titles are inspired by old film posters of the 1930s. A golden, screen printed linen hardcover is supposed to underline the glamour of this defining era of film history.

client
Gerstenberg Verlag,
Hildesheim

design
Robert Nippoldt, Münster

art direction
Robert Nippoldt

concept
Robert Nippoldt,
Daniel Kothenschulte

graphic design
Robert Nippoldt

text
Daniel Kothenschulte

illustration
Robert Nippoldt,
Christine Goppel

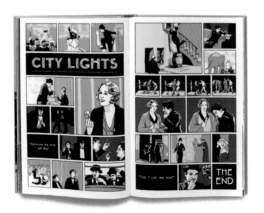

Leica Zielfernrohre / *Leica Riflescopes*

[Product Catalogue]

Leica Camera, manufacturer of high-quality sport optics, introduces their first premium riflescope for affluent hunters. The catalogue uses the illustrations of the artist Marcello Pettineo to deliver all the romance of big-game hunting, with none of the shock. Using sensible and sparse design, the catalogue visualises the dream of any passionate hunter: to experience the harmony between man and nature.

client
Leica Camera AG, Solms

design
G2 Germany / Frankfurt

creative direction
Felix Dürichen (Art),
Jutta Häussler (Text)

art direction
Mona Pust

consultancy
Maik Hofmann,
Anja Awater

illustration
Marcello Pettineo

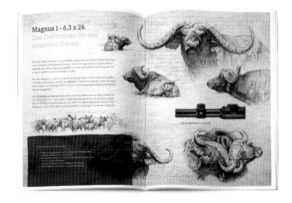

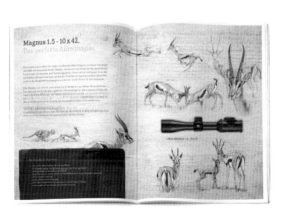

TypeFaces
[Letter Illustration]

TypeFaces reflects the uniqueness of a child and the individual character of its name. 26 children's faces (Faces) in combination with unusual illustrations of the 26 initials of their given names (Types) form expressive pairs. Each "TypeFace" stands for a letter and teaches grown-ups to view the alphabet from a child's perspective. The eye is sharpened for the pure, beautiful, innocent and unpredictable along with the questions, "Who would you like to be?" and "What name would you like to have?".

client
Verena Panholzer /
Andreas Balon, Vienna

design
Verena Panholzer, Vienna

art direction
Verena Panholzer

text
Sibylle Hamtil,
Verena Panholzer

photography
Andreas Balon

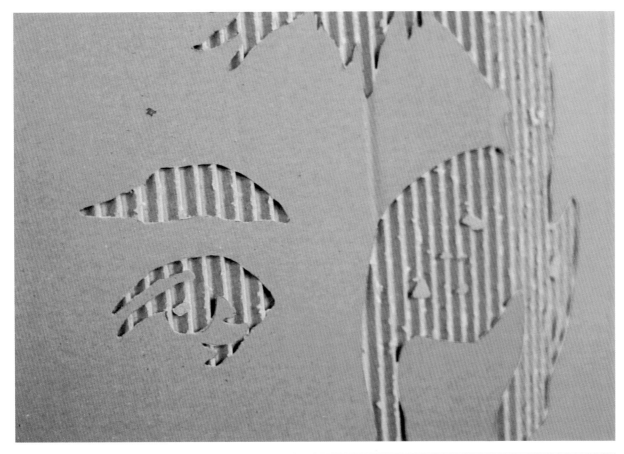

Hinz&Kunzt Handcrafted Cardboard Illustrations

On the occasion of local elections, these cardboard carvings drew attention to the fact that in affluent Hamburg thousands of people were living in the streets while more than 1.4 million sqm of living and office space were vacant. Corrugated cardboard in a very illustrative design replaced the usual election posters: portraits of homeless people were cut into the top layers and catchy slogans were added with markers. The handcrafted posters marked vacant buildings and floor posters were spread on shopping streets; even a 300-sqm variation was used.

client
Hinz&Kunzt gGmbH, Hamburg

head of marketing
Isabel Schwartau

design
JWT Germany GmbH, Hamburg;
Isabelle Göntgen,
Isabelle Illustration,
Zell unter Aichelberg

creative direction
Till Hohmann

art direction
Regina Groffy

graphic design
Ainara del Valle Perez-Solero

text
Michael Muck

Gegen den Strom /
Against the tide
[Film]

client
Fish & More GmbH,
Friedrichshafen

design
Leagas Delaney Hamburg GmbH,
Hamburg

creative direction
Stefan Zschaler,
Florian Schimmer,
Michael Götz

art direction
Florian Schimmer,
Robert Westphal

graphic design
Felix Boeck,
Nadine Hoenow

text
Michael Götz,
Heiko Franzgrote

illustration
Veronika Kieneke

animation
Absolute Post, London;
Marcel Wilkens,
Ronald Mau,
Leagas Delaney Hamburg GmbH

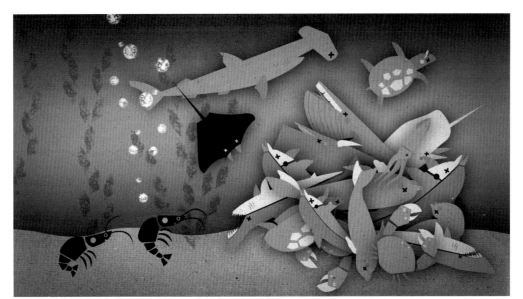

With friendly illustrations reminiscent of pictures in children's books, this corporate movie conveys the message that our oceans are already overfished to their limits. With seemingly naive sequences but without attaching blame, the film communicates that the awarded brand followfish consequently engages in sustainable fishery and for that purpose raises awareness by providing extensive information. Thus, "Gegen den Strom" (Against the tide) does not only intend to reveal the alarming scale of overfishing, but also wants to convince the audience that it is not too late for a change of course yet.

HIDE AND SEEK

[Illustrations]

These illustrations weave the cycle of life and the co-existence of the human world in contrast to the world created by God to a complex and touching tale. Filigree and imaginatively illustrated images tell of people of 13 different nations existing in an additional dimension who have dug a tunnel to get to the other world. Because of a blind spot they can't get any further. Only the character "Joker" is able to jump between tunnels without any problems.

design
Ting-Yi Hsu, Taipei

advisor
Prof. Chun-Huang Cheng,
Prof. Li-Jun Sun

designer portrait
→ Vol.1: p.481

Enduro Untamed – Motocross Enduro Magazine
[Illustrations]

The Motocross Enduro magazine Enduro Untamed focuses on unbridled action, which is characteristic for this kind of sport. The magazine addresses especially the target group of adventurous bikers, who ride harder, jump higher and are wilder than others. The expressive illustrations of the magazine series were developed for print ads. They feature graphically modified motorbikes, reminiscent of wild animals and communicate the central message in a very concise way.

client
serviceplan, Munich

creative direction
Oliver Palmer

text
Oliver Palmer

design
Eat, Sleep + Design.
Frank Gräfe & Daniel Reiss GbR, Berlin

art direction
Frank Gräfe

illustration
Frank Gräfe

Audi quattro

[Advertisements]

client
AUDI AG, Ingolstadt

design
kempertrautmann gmbh,
Hamburg;
Liga_01 Computerfilm GmbH,
Munich

These ads were designed to demonstrate the leading technological position of Audi in the field of four-wheel drives and to win back the image leadership. The aim of the campaign is to depict the customer value and the functionality of the new quattro generation with a simple and memorable analogy. The most significant feature of the advertisement is a high-tech gecko embodying a smart combination of mechanics and electronics.

THE PROFESSIONALS. Who are they, what exactly are they doing and how do they look like? In the portraits on the following pages the designers and design studios whose extraordinary and creative design achievements and realisations convinced the jury, consisting of internationally acknowledged branch experts, are introduced with vita, interview and photo.

Awarded works
→ Vol.1: p.223,
p.278–279, p.407,
p.414
→ Vol.2: p.144

601BISANG
KUM-JUN PARK
— "22 points" contains the unique viewpoints of 22 artists symbolised in 22 points (dots).

Kum-Jun Park, born in 1963, graduated from Hongik University with a master's degree in advertising and public relations. In 1998, he founded the design company 601bisang, and has been its president since. He has planned and designed a variety of art books, including "Calendars are Culture", "2note:time.space", "601 SPACE PROJECT" and "Eoureum – the uniting of two".

In 2003, he initiated the competition "601 Artbook Project", which has since made a significant contribution to both design education and the genre of art books. From 1999 to 2005, he lectured on communication design at his alma mater. He is a member of the AGI and has won numerous international awards.

What inspires you?

It is hard to pinpoint one source from which I am inspired – I am inspired by history, the works of other people or various experiments. Taking a new approach to familiar matters or putting myself in an unusual situation abroad is also very stimulating. There is a moment when the little things around me feel very familiar and cosy.

I started to see a story behind an empty can on the street, or behind the little twig that I saw on my way up a mountain, and so forth. Every day has been a gift for me ever since.
My drawers are full – from small gadgets that I purchased on my trips abroad to dry tree roots and discarded stuff that I picked up in some narrow corridor. I collect these things because I see myself in them. All things around me inspire me.

ACT&REACT

— *Neues Denken.*
(A Novel Approach)

act&react was founded in March 2000 in the adopted city of Dortmund, a creative hub in the German Ruhr area. The studio focuses on creating concepts and visual communication displaying novel ideas and perspectives.

Since 2006 the act&react studio has concentrated on strategic communication concepts, and since 2008 on individualised marketing. While the offices for the team led by Thomas Szabo, born in 1976, had to be extended, the agency continues to champion the communication of authentic design reduced to essential elements.

What has been your greatest challenge in a project so far?

Persuading people that the Internet can be turned into a "noise protection wall".

What inspires you?

To observe the world and absorb it like a sponge.

What do you understand by good communication design?

Creating emotion through images, convincing through content.

What kind of project would you like to realise once?

Any project that requires one to boldly embark on new paths.

Awarded works
→ Vol.1: p.235
→ Vol.2: p.381

AMMUNITION
BRETT WICKENS,
JEREMY MATTHEWS

— *Launching one of the world's most advanced toilets.*

Ammunition is a product, identity, and interaction design company. Based in San Francisco, USA, the firm is led by its founder, industrial designer Robert Brunner, and his partners Brett Wickens and Matt Rolandson. Its team is comprised of designers, engineers, and brand strategists dedicated to creating product, service, and brand experiences that matter. The company has capabilities in industrial design, graphic design, design strategy, brand development, packaging, engineering, web development, user interface, prototyping and production implementation.

Which trends do you currently recognise in your field?

The shift away from the "solitary designer" toward multidisciplinary teams necessary to solve some of the more complex communication design challenges we face. The role that technology now plays in communication design means that the landscapes for messaging are more complicated and thus require distinct – and frequently evolving – areas of expertise.

ATELIER PETIT
KEVIN REYNAERT

— I've always liked the quote from Thomas Alva Edison: "A diamond is a piece of coal that stuck to the job."

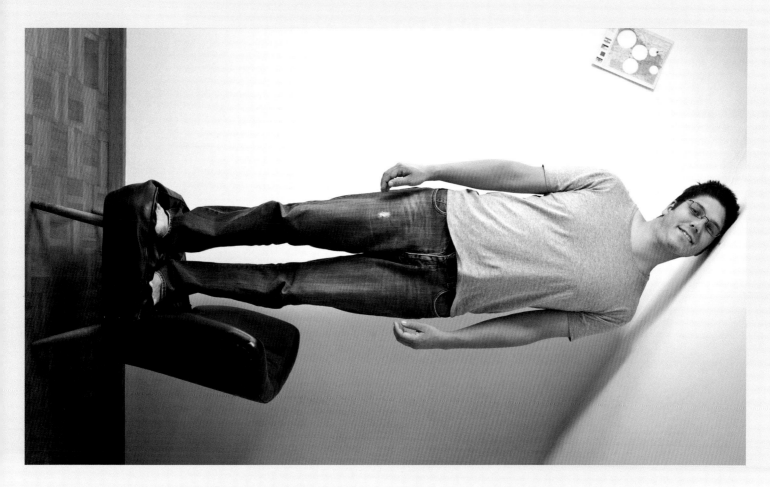

Kevin Reynaert, born in 1982 in Vilvoorde, Belgium, grew up in Siegburg, Germany, and currently lives in Hasselt, Belgium. He founded the creative studio Atelier Petit, which specialises in illustration and graphic design projects. On an irregular basis, he also publishes editions under the name "Another Papercut".

His interest in design grew from childhood passions such as skateboarding, music and street art. This evolved into his current work, which is located between fine and applied arts, following an intuitive, direct approach in which form, colour, lines, shapes and experimentation gain the upper hand. His work encompasses drawing, painting, illustration, graphic design, printing and collage.

What has been your greatest challenge in a project so far?

Trying to give an impression of Edison's life in a 20-metre hallway mural, because there is so much in his body of work to show.

Which trends do you currently recognise in your field?

I've always appreciated a DIY approach, sustainable design and the older handicraft techniques.

What do you understand by good communication design?

For me, good design is a result of dialogue and pleasure in the work, but it must still focus on function.

What kind of project would you like to realise once?

All projects are interesting in their own way, but a collection of stamps have always been my "little boy's dream".

BCCARD DESIGN TEAM
— *A credit card platform for creating true works of art / Beyond Card, BCcard.*

Hojae Lee, Sehoon Oh and Kyung Hee studied industrial design and graduated from Hongik University. Today, they are working as design managers at Korean credit card company BCcard. The senior designer Hojae Lee has developed and accumulated extensive expertise in designing credit cards for 13 years and is recognised by many bankers as a veteran manager. Senior designer Sehoon Oh has hands-on experience and know-how through working in various advertising agencies, in Korea's largest franchise company and in a computer manufacturing company. He joined the team of BCcard in 2007 and has since worked on 11 credit card designs and promotional productions in progress.

What has been your greatest challenge in a project so far?

To respond to the desire for mobile payment systems, a desire emerging out of the distress that the overall paradigm shift of an active society moving towards a mobile lifestyle poses.

What inspires you?

Trends that are inspired and triggered by another trend.

Which trends do you currently recognise in your field?

We see more convenient mobile payment systems with better interface design.

What kind of project would you like to realise once?

We prefer projects with a clear conception, clear goals and a clear sense of direction.

BEETROOT DESIGN GROUP

— Beetroot = the most intense of the vegetables.

Awarded works
→ Vol.1: p.165,
p.444–445
→ Vol.2: p.160–161,
p.300

Beetroot is an award-winning design group based in Thessaloniki, Greece. All team members are design enthusiasts with expertise and skills in the creative field. The company has won prestigious distinctions in competitions all over the world, some of which are: European Design Awards Agency of the Year 2008, and three times Agency of the Year in the Greek Design Awards in 2006, 2008 and 2010. Beetroot has been seeking new ways of expressing creativity and providing design solutions since September 2000.

What has been your greatest challenge in a project so far?

Every project is a new challenge. Creativity never stops, you just need to push yourself in new paths and re-evaluate your thoughts about design. We need challenges to keep us motivated. The greatest challenge we feel is overcoming ourselves every time we create something successful or we win a prize.

What inspires you?

We are inspired by anything original. It could be a fairy tale, a dream, a conversation, fine art, or technological achievements and, of course, we get inspired by nature.

What do you understand by good communication design?

One that works. It is about communicating a message successfully to an audience. It is that simple but yet so complicated.

BOHM UND NONNEN

CHRISTIANE BOHM,
THEO NONNEN, STEVEN DOHN

— Design is challenging and fun!

For over 20 years, Bohm und Nonnen has provided design and consulting services in corporate communication, as well as corporate and graphic design. The Darmstadt-based agency, under the helm of its founders Christiane Bohm and Theo Nonnen, works in a team of communication designers and photographers for clients such as Cairo, creative inneneinrichter, Bilfinger Berger, Pfizer, Abbott, and the German third-world charities Brot für die Welt and Menschen für Menschen. The agency's strengths lie in its intensive exchange of ideas with its clients. Steven Dohn, who has been with Bohm und Nonnen for six years, mainly looks after editorial projects to which he brings his extensive experience as a photographer.

What has been your greatest challenge in a project so far?

The next project is always the greatest challenge – always having to surprise, but nonetheless deliver substantive content.

What inspires you?

The world out there – in all its complexity and beauty.

Which trends do you currently recognise in your field?

An alignment and standardisation of messages that we convey. All communication appears to be "sustainable" and "emotional". I would like to see more courage, clarity and differentiation in the way in which clients see themselves.

What do you understand by good communication design?

Design that does not force itself on people, but is clear and understandable.

BOROS
INGO MAAK
— Each client, each task calls for dedication.

Ingo Maak, born in 1964 in Wuppertal, lives in Cologne and works in Wuppertal as well as in Berlin. He is art director at BOROS.

What has been your greatest challenge in a project so far?

It depends. That varies.

What inspires you?

Everything.

Which trends do you currently recognise in your field?

Trends come and go. Quality remains.

What do you understand by good communication design?

As little as possible.

What kind of project would you like to realise once?

The visual identity of the Catholic Church.

Awarded works
→ Vol.1: p.164,
p.168–169

CDR ASSOCIATES
SUNGCHUN KIM
— *Harmony of reality and ideal.*

Sungchun Kim, born in 1963, is the CEO of CDR Associates, one of the first identity design companies in Korea established in 1973. He graduated from Seoul National University and has since implemented national and international identity design projects for representative Korean companies such as Hyundai Motor Group, Kia Motors and S-Oil, as well as for Korean government organisations such as the National Assembly and the National Museum of Korea, and created international projects including the Incheon Asian Game 2014 and the IAAF World Championships. He was selected as a representative designer in identity design in the Creative Design Awards 2006, and is currently the chairman of the Korea Design Firm Association.

What has been your greatest challenge in a project so far?

Grafting the space and brand in the S-Oil project.

What inspires you?

All the strange things that I see while travelling and on the street inspire me.

What do you understand by good communication design?

Good communication makes people understand the mind of a matter, not its logic.

CIRCUS.
BÜRO FÜR KOMMUNIKATION
UND GESTALTUNG
— *The aim obstructs the path.*

The design and communication agency Circus, with offices in Innsbruck and Vienna, was founded by Andreas Schett in 1996. Alongside exhibitions and books, the studio creates communication design for large cultural businesses (among others Tyrolean Festival Erl and the music label "col legno"), service providers (such as the Austrian Alpine Association) and small handicraft businesses (including the imperial royal court's shoemaker Scheer in Vienna).

Circus is in charge of the content and editorial design of the Tyrolean magazine Quart, which has already been honoured with several awards. For this project, Circus collaborates regularly with other design offices as well as acclaimed fine artists.

What has been your greatest challenge in a project so far?

A constant challenge we face is to make the high calibre of the content (or artistic expression) congruent with a certain demand for mass appeal.

What inspires you?

The fine arts (the muses of Parnassus).

What kind of project would you like to realise once?

The communication design for a good opera house.

CONTRUST [DESIGN]
SIMONE STENGER, STEPHAN RUH
— *Rendering the complex comprehensible.*

Simone Stenger and Stephan Ruh both studied communication design at the University of Applied Sciences in Darmstadt. After graduating together in 1995, they worked for various agencies and went on to found contrust [design] in 2003. The agency advises, conceives and creates corporate designs, brands, signage, Internet presences, videos, exhibitions and adverts and works for customers from the technology, scientific and cultural sectors. The designers believe their task is to read between the lines, to structure and analyse information and to visualise essential messages in an emotional, functional and aesthetically appealing way – both for the customers and their target audiences.

What has been your greatest challenge in a project so far?

That is precisely the fallacy – as if there were only one great challenge in the life of a designer. Each project has its own particular greatest challenge. We need to recognise and solve them – that's all.

Which trends do you currently recognise in your field?

Creativity is becoming the most important commodity in Europe. The creative sector the most important employer. Creativity is our equity and our future. Creatives form a network of specialists and connect with each other anew for every fresh project. Old values and institutions have lost people's trust. The winners will be those who manage to communicate with credibility.

Awarded works
→ Vol.1: p.60, p.96,
p.109
→ Vol.2: p.233

CYCLOS DESIGN
JUTTA SCHNIEDERS,
FRANK SEEPE

*— Our passion:
brand communication.*

cyclos design GmbH was founded in 1995 in Münster by graduate designers Jutta Schnieders and Frank Seepe and today employs a permanent staff of 34 people. The studio develops corporate identities, corporate images and brand strategies, realised as cross-media communication and design concepts, and through distinctive designs, intelligent communication and consistent brand management ensures the quality and continuity of the messages.

As a strategic partner for their clients, cyclos design commits itself to the long-term success of a brand. Their clients include AOK, ago dental, blomus, Dometic WAECO, microsonic, Royal Garden and UKV.

What has been your greatest challenge in a project so far?

It has always been and will remain the creative perfectionism that is so typical of cyclos.

What inspires you?

Every impression, no matter how tiny, can be the key to a new insight, a new idea. Sometimes finding an idea is a long process; sometimes it is a flash of inspiration.

Which trends do you currently recognise in your field?

Communication is becoming omnipresent. All channels, media, devices and target groups have to be fed with a clear message in a cross-media and individualised manner. The type of communication is not determined by the brand but by those who love the brand.

Awarded works
→ Vol.1: p.349,
p.350—351

DESIGNBOLAGET
CLAUS DUE
— *Will work for art!*

Claus Due established Designbolaget in Aarhus, Denmark, in 2002. He studied graphic design in New York and moved to Copenhagen in 2004 where the company today is located in a former antique store. The studio counts three designers and one intern and primarily works in the fields of art, culture and fashion, book design, corporate identity, packaging and web design.

Their work ranges from designing to creating entire visual concepts and art direction. Designbolaget received numerous awards, among them the Danish Agency of the Year at Creative Circle Awards, and has been published in books and magazines throughout the world.

What inspires you?

Our main inspiration comes – without any doubt – from the art scene. No matter what kind of job we are working on we always end up looking at artists' work or referring to exhibitions we have seen somewhere.

Which trends do you currently recognise in your field?

There is a font-driven trend in contemporary books and catalogues at the moment, which is nice for designers to look at but totally uninteresting for everybody else.

What do you understand by good communication design?

Good communication design is when you put effort in telling your clients' story instead of just doing "the flavour of the month".

DIEGUTGESTALTEN
ANDREAS ENNEMOSER,
GORAN POZNANOVIC
— *A simple and incisive appearance.*

DIEGUTGESTALTEN is a Düsseldorf-based agency for strategic design headed up by graduate designers Andreas Ennemoser and Goran Poznanovic. Their work stands for high-quality corporate communications, image building and brand design. They aim to develop a corporate identity that creates added value and is sincere.

DIEGUTGESTALTEN focuses on the interplay of design and strategy under the motto "identity, brand, emotions, success". Since its creation in 2009, the agency has already been awarded several renowned national and international prizes.

What inspires you?

*Every day in itself, every person, every culture –
in fact everything!*

Which trends do you currently recognise in your field?

*Good design has a value. An increasing number of
companies recognise the importance of good design
and make it the focal point of their communication.*

What do you understand by good communication design?

*Good communication design must be able to be
used in a multi-disciplinary way.*

Awarded works
→ Vol.1: p.293, p.376, p.377, p.391

E-DESIGN+COMMUNICATION
CHRISTIANE BÖRDNER, MARCUS GAAB

— *Meaning is created by difference, not by identity. (Ferdinand de Saussure)*

Agentur E, newly known as The Gaabs, are a leading creative studio run by photographer and art director Marcus Gaab and his wife, art director and stylist, Christiane Bördner. The couple has 15 years of experience in the business, making this boutique agency an eminent authority in lifestyle communication.

Founded in 1996, they defined multimedia design with award-winning projects in interactive design, print media and advertising. Their self-published magazine "I love you" created a huge fan readership in 15 countries within one year. The Gaabs work for brands such as Nike, Joop!, René Lezard and Stone Island, as well as the New York Times Magazine, Vogue, Wallpaper and Zeit Magazin.

What has been your greatest challenge in a project so far?

Our first real budget in 1996.

What inspires you?

Travelling, work, films, art, music and life.

Which trends do you currently recognise in your field?

Brands currently recognise, thanks to the Internet, that their customers are more imaginative and educated than they thought.

What do you understand by good communication design?

To communicate a good story in a consistent, targeted and engaging manner.

What kind of project would you like to realise once?

To shoot a film.

EIGA DESIGN
ELISABETH PLASS,
HENNING OTTO

EIGA Design is an interdisciplinary design agency founded by communication designers Elisabeth Plass and Henning Otto in Hamburg in 2003. The purpose of their work is to make visible the strengths, aims and values of their clients and to convey brand and company messages via cross-media concepts.

Since 2006, the agency has published significant design and societal trends in the form of an award-winning design calendar series. The team brings together a variety of design disciplines which are integrated into communication concepts in a practical way and then realised under the guiding principles of strict quality criteria for design, creativity and implementation.

What has been your greatest challenge in a project so far?

We got goose-bumps when we managed to persuade 35 decision-makers from 35 European countries of our design concept after just one presentation.

Which trends do you currently recognise in your field?

Design concepts require an interdisciplinary approach to ideas and actions and must create the right pre-conditions for a message to develop a hold on the entire media landscape. Clients and consumers want veracity; with the result that design must make the digital appear analogue.

What do you understand by good communication design?

It makes the nature of an object apparent from the outside and strikes a tone that lingers for a long time.

EN GARDE
— *Thru the heart!*

EN GARDE was founded in 2006 in the Austrian town of Graz. The agency specialises in industrial design, typography, illustration, animation, software development, graphic design, information design, marketing, music and street art. The young team of more than 20 people brings together a very individual approach to design and a range of media disciplines. Six interlinked creative units plan, design and produce printed materials, digital applications, as well as interior and exterior spaces. The agency develops interdisciplinary concepts for the external and internal communication of its clients and also loves inventing products and implementing its own ideas.

What inspires you?

Other people, conversations, travel, visits to the flea market, beautifully printed materials from bygone days, photography, the town in which we live and work.

Which trends do you currently recognise in your field?

At long last people have understood that a medium cannot exist in isolation, without another. Online is dependent on offline and vice versa. That is an important step in a long overdue direction.

What do you understand by good communication design?

A design that gives pleasure and manages to attract and inform the target group in a natural, self-evident way while at the same time conveying a clear, unambiguous message.

FIREFLY BRANDING
JIWON SHIN
— *Ideas take flight.*

Jiwon Shin, a brand designer, is founder, global CEO and creative director of Firefly Branding, headquartered in New York City, with offices in Prague and Seoul. She has directed more than 50 major international branding programmes in a wide range of industries and worked for companies such as Samsung, Microsoft, Marriott Hotel, UPS, Amtrak, Kia, Japan Airlines, Thrivent Financial and Bahrain Bay. She created the exhibition "Connecting New York – Prague – Seoul", an initiative designed to connect different cultures by means of design. Her work is published in the leading design publications and received numerous international design awards.

What has been your greatest challenge in a project so far?

The rebranding of Amtrak, America's railway system, and the creation of its high-speed train brand, Acela.

What inspires you?

Great cities and great cultures. New York is the centre of creativity. There is energy and diversity that ignite my creativity more than any other place.

Which trends do you currently recognise in your field?

Design as a dynamic tool for innovation and progress as well as green and sustainable design.

What do you understand by good communication design?

Harmony between strategy, creativity and logic. Together, they create tangible flows and connections of understanding.

GOBASIL
OLIVER SCHWARTZ, EVA JUNG, NICO MÜHLAN

— Don't swim! Walk!

gobasil in Hamburg develops strategic communication design and creates identities for people, brands, institutions, companies, products and projects. Oliver Schwartz, Eva Jung and Nico Mühlan are three among a staff of 16 that believes in the motivational power of design that features a clear message and brilliant implementation. The agency's logo is ornamented by a Basiliscus iguana, which, possessing webbed feet and the ability to run as a biped at high speed, can walk on water. It speeds across the water surface faster than the surface can break. Thus the motto: Always gets across!

What has been your greatest challenge in a project so far?

"We have always done it like that."

What inspires you?

A new day.

Which trends do you currently recognise in your field?

Everything becoming faster.

What do you understand by good communication design?

Self-explanatory design.

What kind of project would you like to realise once?

More of them.

GRAPHIC DESIGN STUDIO BY YURKO GUTSULYAK
YURKO GUTSULYAK, ZORYANA GUTSULYAK
— *Time matters. Design matters.*

Yurko Gutsulyak is a professional designer who in 2005, together with his sister Zoryana, founded his own graphic design studio in Kiev. The studio specialises in graphic design, art direction, corporate identity, packaging and object design. Its projects have garnered more than 50 international and local awards and were published worldwide.

Yurko Gutsulyak is actively involved in both the local design scene and the advertising market. He is the president of the Art Directors Club Ukraine and represented Ukraine in the jury of different international advertising and design festivals. In 2010 he was invited to lecture at the European Design Conference in Rotterdam.

What inspires you?

I always try to fill my design with some poetry and philosophy. I love simple things, simple figures and simple lines with a clear message and a deep sense. I like to combine common products to get something quite new.

Which trends do you currently recognise in your field?

One of the recent trends I see is "stingy design". It is minimal and black-and-white, uses simple elements and has no decorations. The main peculiarity of this trend is a strong idea behind a simple graphic. Our Trash Calendar is a good example of this trend.

What do you understand by good communication design?

Good design is clear and fresh. And it leaves a good aftertaste.

Awarded works
→ Vol.1: p.180–181,
p.193, p.195
→ Vol.2: p.247

HÄFELINGER + WAGNER DESIGN

— *People experience the world in stories.*

häfelinger + wagner design, founded in Munich in 1995, is an interdisciplinarily oriented design agency, focusing on corporate design, corporate branding, corporate architecture and interactive design. The agency's works have garnered many prizes in national and international design awards, including ninth position in the 2011 PAGE creative ranking and among the top-ten in the "manager magazine" award "The best annual reports". Holding a climate neutral certificate, the agency works for clients such as BMW Group, Deutsche Bank, Deutsche Post DHL, Fresenius Medical Care, Munksjö, ThyssenKrupp, Siemens and Wacker Chemie.

What has been your greatest challenge in a project so far?

The greatest challenge in a project lies in realising it consistently. The better the realisation, the stronger the overall visual appearance.

What inspires you?

The exchange within the team and with the client as well as sounding out a topic in terms of content and associations.

Which trends do you currently recognise in your field?

The strong reductionist stance in treating typography as well as the cross-media forms of thinking and implementation.

What do you understand by good communication design?

As the individual and visual rendering of content so that it can be read, sensed and experienced emotionally.

HAKUHODO INC.
ATSUSHI MUROI,
HATTORI KIMITARO

*— Design should "visualise" or "materialise"
the clients' strategy in an ideal way.*

ATSUSHI MUROI

HATTORI KIMITARO

Atsushi Muroi, born in Hiroshima, Japan, in 1975, graduated from Tokyo University of Science with a bachelor degree in architecture. He works in the brand experience design department of Hakuhodo Inc. in the fields of, among others, space design, product design, web design and event design.

Hattori Kimitaro, born in Gifu, Japan, in 1977, graduated from Tokyo University of the Arts. He works in the brand experience design department of Hakuhodo Inc. in the fields of, among others, graphic design, corporate identity and visual identity design.

What inspires you?

The essence of Japanese architecture: the "Shōji", a sliding door made of latticed wood, into which Japanese paper is pasted and which, without using colours, enables soft light filtered through the paper to create a variety of atmospheres inside a room. We are inspired by this Shōji essence, as well as other Japanese architectural elements of horizontality and verticality, to realise our "minimal and neutral" designs.

Which trends do you currently recognise in your field?

It becomes increasingly important to effectively integrate "physical contact points" into "virtual contact points" through mobile devices, equipped with various functions such as GPS and payment services.

HESSE DESIGN
CHRISTINE HESSE, KLAUS HESSE
— *Knowing. Moving. Achieving.*

Christine Hesse studied design management at the University of Westminster in London (MBA). Since 1988 she has been co-owner and managing director of Hesse Design in Düsseldorf. From 1993 to 2000 she held a teaching position in design management at University of Applied Sciences in Düsseldorf. She is an advisory board member of the Design Management Institute in Boston.

Prof. Klaus Hesse studied photography and typography in Wuppertal, and since 1988 has been design director and co-owner of Hesse Design in Düsseldorf. Since 1993 he has been a professor of communication design and has been teaching at the Academy of Art and Design in Offenbach since 1999. He is editor-in-chief of "sushi", member of the Type Directors Club New York and the Art Directors Club Germany.

What has been your greatest challenge in a project so far?

We wouldn't want to tell.

What inspires you?

The unknown.

Which trends do you currently recognise in your field?

Boundaries are dissolving. Everything is in movement.

What do you understand by good communication design?

To relate and surprise.

What kind of project would you like to realise once?

The concept and design of a virtual world atlas.

TING-YI HSU

— I tried to overcome every visual and skill challenge, and conquered 13 different aspects of colour, line and contrast.

Ting-Yi Hsu, born in Banqiao City, Taiwan, received a bachelor degree from Ling Tong University and a master's degree from Beijing Film Academy. The work HIDE AND SEEK took her four years to finish. Its rights belong to Beijing Huaxia Innomedia Technology (BHIT) Co., Ltd., China, one of the biggest production and operation companies of animation, comic and picture books.

What has been your greatest challenge in a project so far?

Being innovative in my works all the time is the most challenging to me.

What inspires you?

Trying to always be professional and dedicated. The support all around me inspires most.

Which trends do you currently recognise in your field?

In my opinion, the biggest trend is that authors have to contact audiences face to face. In other words, there is a change from B2B to B2C.

What do you understand by good communication design?

The best communication design avoids visual reading obstacles and exactly matches the topic.

Awarded works
→ Vol.1: p.222,
p.428–429

HUFAX ARTS
FA-HSIANG HU
— *We create. We design. We imagine.*

Hufax arts, founded in 2005 in Taipei, is a team of senior creatives and designers aiming to offer illustrious advertisement solutions for a variety of clients with creativity, innovation and imagination. They believe in the striking conjunction of creativity, design and strategy, and provide their clients with the whole-scale application of media and design, leading to a long-term development and influential branding effects. Fa-Hsiang Hu is a creative and senior art director at Hufax arts.

Which trends do you currently recognise in your field?

We have stepped into the digital era, with a better accessibility to tools, software and information. Their accessibility and convenience make people believe that everyone can easily make an impact on the market.

What do you understand by good communication design?

Good communication design contains the most creative and most suitable visual language, a language that is able to deliver the core information clearly and adequately to the target audience. Besides the features of the brand, I also expect my design to deliver hopes, dreams, a wonderful festival of visual design and – most of all – have a positive impact on the world.

KAN & LAU DESIGN CONSULTANTS
FREEMAN LAU SIU-HONG
— I believe that the dynamics of differences stimulate ideas.

Freeman LAU Siu-hong, born in Hong Kong in 1958, has been working as a designer for over 30 years and received more than 300 national and international design awards. In 2004, he designed the Watsons Water Bottle, which was awarded the international Bottled Water World Design Award in 2004 and the Outstanding Greater China Design Award in 2006. He also creates artworks and sculptures that are collected by museums all over the world. He is currently the vice-chairman of the Board of Directors of Hong Kong Design Centre and the advisor of Beijing Creative Centre. His contribution to enhancing the identity of Hong Kong design was awarded the Bronze Bauhinia Star in 2006.

Which trends do you currently recognise in your field?

In the process of globalisation, sustainability is always a hot topic. In fact, sustainability does not only refer to environmental protection but also to the preservation of cultural heritage.

What do you understand by good communication design?

I believe that good communication design should be able to help convey sustainability as well as the preservation of cultural heritage. I constantly endeavour to promote my belief through reflecting upon Chinese culture in both service and product designs. Through my designs, I hope there would be a better understanding of my country.

Awarded works
→ Vol.1: p.126,
p.132–133,
p.282–283

KAZAKOFF DESIGN
IGOR KAZAKOV

— To design is to visualise the need of the customer in the market.

Igor Kazakov studied at the School of Fine Arts and the Russian University of Arts, Crafts and Design, where he received his MA, and at Berghs School of Communication in Stockholm. He contributed to the artwork of the redesign programme for Scandinavian Airlines System (SAS), designed a packaging programme for IKEA, and was among others responsible for the graphic design for Sweden's Television (SVT), for the Swedish Society of Crafts and Design's corporate identity programme and the redesign of the corporate design system for Stockholm's local traffic services.

His works received several awards, including AIGA 365, Art Directors Club of Europe, Creative Review Annual, D&AD Awards, Advertising Association of Sweden and the red rot design award.

What has been your greatest challenge in a project so far?

To get a client to invest in a project all the way through.

What inspires you?

Mistakes.

Which trends do you currently recognise in your field?

Modernism.

What do you understand by good communication design?

Design that you can explain via the phone.

What kind of project would you like to realise once?

Any project that allows you to realise your ideas 100 per cent.

AGNES KELTAI, IMRE LEPSENYI
— *Staying contemporary.*

Agnes Keltai is a communication and branding expert based in Budapest. She currently runs Majom, a boutique branding and graphic design agency. Previously, she founded the agency Social Branding. Her clients include Hungarian Public Radio, Hungarian Paralympic Committee, International Training Centre for Bankers and Israeli Cultural Institute Budapest.

Imre Lepsenyi, born in 1974 in Zalaegerszeg, Hungary, studied electrical engineering at the Budapest University of Technology and Economics. Currently he is a doctoral student at the Hungarian University of Fine Arts. As a designer he works for clients such as Coca-Cola London, Gabor Palotai Design, Israeli Cultural Institute Budapest and Kassák Museum Budapest.

What has been your greatest challenge in a project so far?

While working on the Israeli Cultural Institute project, we had to create a multilingual graphic solution in a way that would smoothly integrate into the current Hungarian visual environment.

What inspires you?

The complexity of the world around us.

Which trends do you currently recognise in your field?

The need for flexibility and the desire to be responsible.

What do you understand by good communication design?

Design that is as functional as it is contemporary.

What kind of project would you like to realise once?

Graphic identity design for the Embassy of Planet Earth in Mars City.

Awarded works
→ Vol.1: p.226,
p.276–277
→ Vol.2: p.297

DESIGNGRUPPE KOOP
ANDREAS KOOP
— *Hasta la vista victoria siempre!*

Andreas Koop, born in 1970, is a graduate designer and has a Master of Advanced Studies. Since 1995 he has run a renowned design agency in the mountainous Allgäu region. He has also for many years been working as a lecturer, author and columnist. These activities are linked to his intense involvement with the field of design research in which he focuses on the conflict between history, society, the economy and design. He has published numerous articles and books on topics such as these, which reflect his attempt to develop sustainable solutions for and with clients. As a result, he set up the "oekoop" business unit a few years ago.

What has been your greatest challenge in a project so far?

Creating an exhibition with a minimal budget which prohibited attaching anything to the ground, walls or ceiling.

What inspires you?

Our library, things I have seen, talking to others.

Which trends do you currently recognise in your field?

A more English influence, more show, more fancy frippery.

What do you understand by good communication design?

If information is designed to be understood intuitively and be aesthetically appealing and can achieve this using as few trimmings as possible, that is good communication design.

What kind of project would you like to realise once?

There would be many!

TOM LEIFER DESIGN
TOM LEIFER,
ALESSANDRO ARGENTATO,
JOHANNES HERMANN
— *Design leads! Above all, to decision.*

Tom Leifer, born in 1964, studied communication design in Augsburg, Germany. After working with several renowned design agencies in Hamburg, he became a partner and member of the management of Factor Design AG, working for brands such as Kabel Deutschland, Gardena, Deutsche Welle, Philip Morris and Karstadt. In 2006, he founded his own agency, under the name Tom Leifer Design, focusing on the main competencies of corporate design, editorial design and web design. The Leica team comprises Tom Leifer, Alessandro Argentato and Johannes Hermann.

What inspires you?

Travelling, exhibitions, books...

Which trends do you currently recognise in your field?

Apart from a long, sustained and uninterrupted stylistic tendency towards the handwritten, what we are facing is increasing complexity and accelerating dynamics. Designers are creating ever less finished products, but instead increasingly accompany processes in which others pick up on one's ideas and modify them. Many disciplines such as architecture, digital media, programming and print are interlocking

What do you understand by good communication design?

Good communication design explains, simplifies, guides, touches and entertains on a highly aesthetic and handicraft level.

Awarded works
→ Vol.1: p.378–379,
p.380–381

MAISON MODERNE
MAXIME PINTADU,
MIKE KOEDINGER
— *Design is just the tip of the iceberg.*

Maxime Pintadu, after having obtained his higher diploma in applied art in 2005, first worked in Paris in various communication agencies. Since 2006, he has been employed as artistic director at Maison Moderne. His work regularly receives prizes in international design competitions.

Initially founded in 1994 by Mike Koedinger, Maison Moderne is Luxembourg's leading independent media group. With 70 employees, it is specialised in self-initiated magazines, corporate publishing, books, digital media and a daily TV programme.

What inspires you?

For the time being, the cartography of the 1960s, animal photography and picture material from science, research and astronomy.

Which trends do you currently recognise in your field?

The grid remains at the centre, the typography alternates between ultra-functional sans serif and antiquated flourishes and ornaments, the contrast is black and white. The printed product seems to find inspiration in its very roots with the aim of establishing a new identity in contrast to the Internet – this makes current developments highly exciting.

What do you understand by good communication design?

One that does not change a project's basic philosophy, and which stays coherent, creates clarity and positions the project visually.

MIES_CONTAINER
JONG EUN AHN, CHANG HEE LEE, YONG HAN LIM
— Idea, do it!

MIES_container is a Korea-based design studio and is connected to a restaurant of the same name run by the designers. The studio specialises in brand design and advertisement marketing, following a philosophy of not placing too much emphasis on the looks of a brand, but instead focusing on the service to provide what people want.

The designers consult with their clients in order to make their service, marketing and design more satisfying and design new systems for their own employees to give them pride and loyalty working for MIES_container. Satisfying both customers and one's own employees: this is the motto of the three designers and should be the real objective of all communication design.

What inspires you?

We are definitely inspired by finding joy and contentment in the faces of the people who enjoy our designs and when facts verify this result.

What do you understand by good communication design?

Good communication design can be defined as a combination of proper articulation based on vivid concepts and artworks that reflect the customers' expectation. Regardless of how good a design is, if it cannot satisfy customer needs and fails to survive on the design market, it won't be successful. We need to satisfy the customers first and then, based on their needs, we as designers have to continuously invent creative products.

MORRIS PINEWOOD STOCKHOLM

— *Antique ideas in a modern context.*

Morris Pinewood Stockholm is an advertising and design studio based in Stockholm, Sweden, creating brand communication and identities through big ideas, stringent simplicity, thorough research, tangible visions and strong differentiation. The studio works cross-disciplinarily to effectuate this vision, ranging from creative direction, design strategies, product design, brand identities, brand strategies, brand communication, through to line concepts and ideas, art direction and advertising. By initiating a close relation with its clients and understanding their business, Morris Pinewood Stockholm helps them solve their communicative needs, grow their brands and increase their business.

What has been your greatest challenge in a project so far?

The toughest thing about success is that you've got to keep on being a success.

What inspires you?

Knowledge, clarity and honesty.

Which trends do you currently recognise in your field?

True craftsmanship.

What do you understand by good communication design?

Harmony and simplicity.

What kind of project would you like to realise once?

Any kind.

NEUE GESTALTUNG
— *A clear visual language.*

Awarded works
→ Vol.1: p.310,
p.394–395
→ Vol.2: p.438

The studio Neue Gestaltung has ten years of experience in the creation of corporate images and interface applications, representing the identities of companies, brands and cultural institutions and positioning them firmly in the consciousness of the target groups through positive associations. Clear forms, clear typography, clear colour schemes – beyond compromise and across all channels, these are the design principles followed by the studio. The studio has gained a reputation as an expert in the digital dissemination and automated implementation of corporate design definitions and is regularly acknowledged in competitions with awards for outstanding design achievements.

What inspires you?

Everything. Including nonsense. However, often those things that are realised in a particularly bad way or which are even downright ridiculous offer the best food for thought – that can be social events and special occasions that receive exuberant medial attention, lived stereotypes or the like.

Which trends do you currently recognise in your field?

As part of our close relations with clients, we found out how internal communication today has gained a much higher significance than it used to have. Today there are many tasks in internal communication that a designer can and has to undertake. Here we see a new and attractive market for Neue Gestaltung.

FABIAN NICOLAY
— *Curiosity threatens the familiar.*

Fabian Nicolay, designer and founder of a publishing house, runs the studio usus.kommunikation in Berlin and has many years of experience in the visual mediation of cultural and ecological contents. He was art director at the magazine natur, developed visual identities for opera houses and companies, and created concepts for illustrated non-fiction books, among them the scientific book "Life Counts – Eine globale Bilanz des Lebens" (Life Counts – A global balance of life) published in 2000. Neugier.de was created together with Dirk Maxeiner, a freelance publicist. He is author of non-fiction books, columnist for the newspapers Die Welt and Basler Zeitung, and together with Henryk M. Broder and Michael Miersch runs the publicist network "Die Achse des Guten" (The Axis of Good).

What has been your greatest challenge in a project so far?

Everybody wants it, but no one wants to pay for it.

What inspires you?

Curiosity.

Which trends do you currently recognise in your field?

Reduction to the mass.

What do you understand by good communication design?

Design is useless without real content. We developed the newspaper starting from the inside. In the beginning, there was an unconventional idea and position. Those who are curious automatically question all prefabricated world outlooks. This often provokes conflict and even rejection. So everybody involved needs a certain passion in order to bear up against that.

Awarded works
→ Vol.1: p.257, p.265,
p.269, p.284–285

OGILVY & MATHER
ADVERTISING GMBH
SANDRA PRESCHER
— *Always different – always me.*

Sandra Prescher was born in Düsseldorf in 1980. After graduating from high school, she first worked for a photographer. Subsequently, she trained as a design technical assistant in the fields of media and communication and, in 2002, began studying communication design at the University of Wuppertal. The student work "My favorite type in motion" was presented as a course project at the Typo 2006 in Berlin and the fmx 2006 in Stuttgart, and won an award from the Type Directors Club New York in 2007. Sandra Prescher graduated from Prof. Uwe Loesch's course in 2007. Even while still a student, she worked in renowned advertising agencies and today works as an art director in Düsseldorf.

What has been your greatest challenge in a project so far?

To not loose the thread – in the truest sense of the word. Sometimes it pays off to be persistent, even if you have almost given up on a project.

What inspires you?

People, moments, interesting stories, the unexpected.

Which trends do you currently recognise in your field?

Sustainable design through the reduction to the essential.

What do you understand by good communication design?

It appeals, it sticks, it touches, it inspires, it works.

What kind of project would you like to realise once?

One day I would like to develop the corporate design for my hometown of Hilden – and of course also for the Hilden Jazz Festival.

Awarded works
→ Vol.1: p.218–219,
p.245
→ Vol.2: p.267,
p.324–325,
p.368–369, p.390

OGILVY FRANKFURT
EVA STETEFELD
— *An ad is an ad is an ad.*

Eva Stetefeld, born in 1984 in Hanau, studied communication design in Darmstadt. During her degree course, she was already gathering experience in agencies and having a first shot at photography and web design. After graduating, she was employed by Ogilvy Frankfurt where she began working in 2008.

She has since become art director for customers such as Deutsche Bank, the state television channels ARD and ZDF, ImmobilienScout24, Vorwerk, MAN and latterly also Media Markt. This includes as much TV as print work, a lot of fun and many challenges.

Which trends do you currently recognise in your field?

The stories we tell are becoming much more multi-layered and complex. Through the exciting use of different channels, unusual story structures and novel techniques it is possible to create multiple experiences, no longer merely messages.

What do you understand by good communication design?

Good communication is not an end in itself. It should not just be well designed, interesting, aesthetically pleasing or appealing to look at. It should communicate something, tell a story – and design should simply support this in the best way possible.

What kind of project would you like to realise once?

Painting Schloss Bellevue, the official residence of the president of the Federal Republic of Germany, pink.

OLAF OSTEN
— *I succeed best in what is close to me.*

Olaf Osten, born in 1972 in Lübeck, studied graphic design at the University of Applied Sciences and Arts in Hildesheim and at Dun Laoghaire College of Art & Design in Dublin. Since 1999, he has been working as a self-employed designer in Vienna in shared offices with cultural manager and designer Claudia Dzengel under the name Dzengel + Osten.

Olaf Osten has many years of experience in creating books and print media, as well as three-dimensional works such as exhibitions and signage systems for museums, including the Kunsthalle Wien, the MUMOK and Wien Museum, as well as for other clients mainly in the areas of culture and science.

What has been your greatest challenge in a project so far?

To successfully defend an unconventional idea in a group of several cooks and see it through to implementation.

What inspires you?

Good music.

Which trends do you currently recognise in your field?

The industry is becoming ever more individualist. Therefore, it has become more difficult to surprise by creating something unprecedented. In the best case, this forces you to generate your own ideas and thus elevates the quality of the work.

What do you understand by good communication design?

Good communication design is thoroughly conceived, very well crafted and has strong emotional impact.

Awarded works
→ Vol.1: p.238, p.239,
p.434

PAARPILOTEN
— *Extraordinary, precise and with spirit.*

Paarpiloten is an interdisciplinary graphic design studio, creating communication media in the fields of print, online and 3D for national and international companies, cultural institutions and organisations. The studio's approach is to develop creative and effective solutions that match the commercial requirements; its works are functional, often innovative and at times even unconventional, but always appropriate. The studio has received many international awards – but always with a focus on achieving adequate and successful solutions for its clients and not to collect trophies.

What has been your greatest challenge in a project so far?

Our clients are from the most diverse branches of industry, including both global and locally acting businesses. Therefore, our projects are equally diverse: identifying with each single project, developing a sense for it and finding a suitable solution are always the greatest challenges.

What inspires you?

The key for us is to greet this world with curiosity and our senses wide open.

What do you understand by good communication design?

Communication design should convey contents precisely. In order to make this happen, the works have to have spirit and idea – that is, they should touch and move people. Only then does design turn into communication design.

Q KREATIVGESELLSCHAFT

— I have never met a pessimist who actually reached the goals he set himself. (Claude Juncker)

Q is a Wiesbaden-based creative agency specialising in design. The agency was founded in 1997 and, headed by company owners Thilo von Debschitz and Laurenz Nielbock as well as partner Matthias Frey, currently has a staff of 12 employees and several freelance designers. Active in the areas of corporate design, print and web, their work aims at making their clients' brands and products visible in the market, support them through image building, and thus differentiating them from the competition. Satisfied clients, long-term business relations and numerous awards are proof of Q's successful path.

What has been your greatest challenge in a project so far?

This year's awarded Zufallskalender (Calendar of Coincidence) has been one of our most challenging jobs: we left large parts of our work to chance. This was very difficult for us, because we are used to meticulously controlling all stages of the process. But in the end, even the bookbinder's dog helped out in arranging the page sequence of the calendar …

Which trends do you currently recognise in your field?

The extension of the creative value-adding chain into the area of classic business consultancy.

What do you understand by good communication design?

Relevant content, design innovation and a discernible love of detail.

RE-PUBLIC
— *Less is more. More or less.*

Re-public, a graphic design agency based in Copenhagen, Denmark, was founded in 1999 by Morten Windelev, CEO. The agency employs five senior designers, along with a varying number of project affiliates, and is specialised in visual identity and communication design, across a range of media and communication channels. It challenges ideas, values and communication issues and translates them into competent and characteristic design solutions. Re-public is an active member of the Danish Design Association.

What inspires you?

The simple things in life.

Which trends do you currently recognise in your field?

We generally try not to follow trends. We are of course influenced by our surrounding visual culture, but we don't find modernity to be a validating quality in itself. We aspire to maintain a contemporary and fresh style, and we think it is more interesting to always experiment and push the boundaries of visual language than to simply adapt to current trends.

What do you understand by good communication design?

Aesthetics and concept make up two halves of good communication design, and usually one will not work without the other.

ROEMER UND HÖHMANN
DANIELA HÖHMANN,
MARION ROEMER
— *Strategy, creativity and innovation.*

roemer und höhmann develop smart design concepts and sustainable communication strategies in the fields of corporate identity, communication and networking. In the exciting field of work between customers and target groups the agency creates the brands' faces and sharpens the profiles of companies, institutions and products. Its customer portfolio includes social and church institutions as well as media institutions and also international companies. The agency works with a permanent in-house team and a network of professionals from the fields of design, photography, architecture, software development, and production.

What has been your greatest challenge in a project so far?

The implementation of our dementia campaign: to change the perspective lightning the situation of the family carers. Posters with slogans like "I've shunt my mother into a home" broach the taboo and spark a dialogue.

What inspires you?

Audacious customers, for whom we can find exceptional solutions, and the happiness about the grey heron that dwells, every once in a while, on our waterside of the Wupper.

Which trends do you currently recognise in your field?

We are not really interested in trends but individual solutions instead.

What do you understand by good communication design?

Impetus to a dialogue.

Awarded works
→ Vol.1: p.186–187
→ Vol.2: p.450–451

SAS
— *Simple, Authentic, Special.*

The studio set up shop 22 years ago with simple aims: design some great stuff, work with some nice clients, have some fun. Today, SAS is all about using creativity to solve business issues and giving businesses a competitive edge. Working in the fields of talent communication, corporate communication, digital communication and business branding, clients like Coca-Cola, Ernst & Young, Diageo, Unilever and GSK want to know how to attract the right talent, build trust with key stakeholders, change the way their people work or the way the world perceives them. In 2007, SAS became part of Publicis Groupe – more specifically MSLGROUP, a network of specialist PR and communications agencies.

What has been your greatest challenge in a project so far?

Thinking first about the audience. Too often they are the forgotten part of briefs. When you look at the way communications are consumed, particularly in the digital age, you end up redefining the brief.

Which trends do you currently recognise in your field?

We don't follow trends, only our beliefs in a wider social perspective. By placing our work in this context, you stop thinking about fashion. That having been said, we are constantly sharing what we have seen from all walks of life. You have to have your radar up at all times.

What do you understand by good communication design?

Emotion is as important as logic. It's about keeping it simple, authentic and creating emotional responses.

SCHMIDT/THURNER/ VON KEISENBERG
PHILIPP VON KEISENBERG, TIMO THURNER, GERWIN SCHMIDT
— *The MKO is a wonder of a client.*

The studio of Prof. Gerwin Schmidt has been developing many award-winning communication designs for cultural institutions, companies and artists since 1997, including Gaggenau appliances and Revolver film magazine. Timo Thurner and Philipp von Keisenberg became junior partners of the studio in 2004 and full partners in 2010.

Gerwin Schmidt has been a professor at Stuttgart State Academy of Art and Design and a member of AGI since 2003. Philipp von Keisenberg is co-editor and designer of book bestsellers "Fussball Unser" and "Ein Mann – Ein Buch". Timo Thurner most recently designed the multiple award-winning branding for Fritz Müller Perlwein.

What has been your greatest challenge in a project so far?

The next project.

Which trends do you currently recognise in your field?

Ever more subjective communication solutions due to precision-tailored details.

What do you understand by good communication design?

It is a high achievement if the content that a communication concept aims to get across reaches the recipients without loss.

What kind of project would you like to realise once?

See answer No. 1.

SENSETEAM
HEI YIYANG
— *Less is more.*

Hei Yiyang, born in 1975, founded SenseTeam in 1999 and is their creative director. He works in the fields of branding, exhibition planning, environmental design and publishing and is one of the most active cultural exchange pioneers in China. He devotes himself to combining different media, such as graphic design, contemporary art, advertising, architectural space, cities and societies, to make the works interesting, meaningful and valuable. SenseTeam focuses on civility and sociality. Hei Yiyang received numerous awards, including Art Directors Club New York, Cannes Lions International Advertising Festival, One Show Design New York, D&AD Awards, ADFEST Design Lotus Awards and the red dot design award.

What has been your greatest challenge in a project so far?

How to communicate with our team of more than twenty, and complete projects together.

What inspires you?

I have always been attracted by a kind of unknown and unpredictable mystical power, and it constantly stimulates me to keep going.

What do you understand by good communication design?

For visual identity design in different languages, information transmission is very important; also, visual systems must play a key role. Whether using images or text, we believe that good works should not only meet the visual identification requirements but also achieve the purpose of information transmission that can be understood in different countries and cultures.

SERVICEPLAN
ANDREAS SCHRIEWER,
ROMAN BECKER
— *Happiness is a ride on a unicorn.*

Awarded works
→ Vol.1: p.119, p.248,
p.426–427, p.437
→ Vol.2: p.264,
p.320–321

Andreas Schriewer was born in Osnabrück, Germany. He studied film & tv sciences, communication and psychology at the Ruhr University Bochum, and currently works at Serviceplan Campaign in Hamburg.

Roman Becker was born in Wolfsberg, Austria. He studied communication design at the University of Wuppertal, and currently works at Serviceplan Campaign in Hamburg.

What has been your greatest challenge in a project so far?

It's always the deadline.

What inspires you?

Accident.

Which trends do you currently recognise in your field?

Social media. No matter if it makes sense.

What do you understand by good communication design?

The mouth (of a woman).

What kind of project would you like to realise once?

The Stuttgart 22 railway station.

STANDARD RAD.
KERSTIN AMEND, KATHARINA MANZ

— Self-explanatory results that provide their own evidence, perhaps with a gentle twist, is what we aim for.

Kerstin Amend studied at the Academy of Art and Design in Offenbach and worked with the company Braun and Otl Aicher, before becoming a founding member of STANDARD RAD. Under her leadership, the Frankfurt-based agency has won a string of international awards. Since 2006, she has also taught corporate design and typography at academy level.

Katharina Manz studied design at the University of Applied Sciences in Darmstadt. She has been with STANDARD RAD. as a project manager and art director since 2008, where she is responsible for a variety of clients.

STANDARD RAD. lives by the creed "As radical as necessary!" and thus creates communications that are consistently effective and to the point, based on clear statements and relevant, engaging concepts.

What has been your greatest challenge in a project so far?

RAD up! Challenge us!

What inspires you?

Joy.

Which trends do you currently recognise in your field?

A lack of attitude.

What do you understand by good communication design?

See above.

What kind of project would you like to realise once?

To be responsible for the brands of my childhood.

STRIKE COMMUNICATIONS
JANGWOO KIM, JUHWAN KIM
— I constantly ask myself whether I have understood the content and concept, and have considered form or plasticity?

Juhwan Kim graduated from Hansei University with a degree in visual design in 2002. After a stint at a small studio he has been managing his own design office Strike Communications since 2007.

What has been your greatest challenge in a project so far?

We strive to understand the essence of a project so that a design emerges intuitively and accurately. We don't want a design to only focus on artwork or one that is too aloof.

What inspires you?

The core content of a project, conversations with people who rush past me, and formative objects.

Which trends do you currently recognise in your field?

A trend towards accuracy yet simplicity.

What do you understand by good communication design?

Finding the contact point between design and communication.

What kind of project would you like to realise once?

We want to model projects for inferior environments, inferior due to social policies or infrastructures.

Awarded works
→ Vol.1: p.147,
p.150–151

STUDIO INTERNATIONAL
BORIS LJUBIČIĆ
*— A logo has to show
the services of a company.*

Boris Ljubičić, a recognised explorer of the visual in Zagreb, creates brands and logos for sports, culture, economy and politics. His first project was the visual identity of the VIII Mediterranean Games in Split in 1979, whose sign and flag have become a permanent standard in all sports games of Mediterranean countries.

Since 1990, his most important project has been the visual identity of the Republic of Croatia, and he has worked for clients such as Croatian Radio and Television, the Croatian Auto Club, the Croatian Tourist Board, the Ministry for European Integration and the Croatian Designers Society. His work is published in significant international magazines and has received numerous awards.

What has been your greatest challenge in a project so far?

To create a complete and new international communication design for the VIII Mediterranean Games in Split in 1979.

Which trends do you currently recognise in your field?

There are many works today defined by typography. But besides that they look empty. I think that the time of using only typography in visual communication will soon be over.

What do you understand by good communication design?

As design that has a concept, a philosophy or a story that makes it timeless, and that works well in the time it is conceived. I always try to make designs that are ahead of their time to ensure their longevity.

TGG HAFEN SENN STIEGER
DOMINIK HAFEN, BERNHARD SENN, ROLAND STIEGER

The designers Dominik Hafen, Bernhard Senn and Roland Stieger founded the TGG Hafen Senn Stieger agency for visual communication in St.Gallen, Switzerland, in 1993. They had met when they were all studying typographical design – students of the book designer Jost Hochuli at the School of Design in St.Gallen.

Alongside the work in their own design agency, which now numbers around a dozen designers, they also accept lectureships. In the area of visual communication, the agency focuses on book and editorial design, signage, exhibition design, corporate, web and type design.

What inspires you?

We inhabit the world with open eyes and let ourselves be inspired by what we discover and the people we meet. We also foster dialogue with other designers, by regularly making it possible for the whole office to travel abroad to visit other studios. Design is always a creative process. We discuss things as a team, question and argue each case and, in this way, search for the optimal solution.

Which trends do you currently recognise in your field?

Reduced design which is more human and haptic, often combined with manual technique.

What do you understand by good communication design?

Communication design should fulfil its aim. We value clearly structured content whose design is nonetheless touching and surprising.

Awarded works
→ Vol.1: p.438—439

CHIN-SHUN WANG

— *I consider myself a pursuer of beauty and Chinese surname character totems.*

Chin-Shun Wang, born in 1957 in Taiwan, has been special-ising in Oriental and Western art since his early twenties and started his journey in calligraphy almost 20 years ago. Presenting Chinese surname totems through the integra-tion of calligraphy, Western painting styles and contempo-rary visual arts, he aims to introduce Chinese surname to-tems to the world. He regularly participates in industry fairs such as the Xiamen Cultural and Creative Fair in China, the Cross-Strait Cultural and Creative Fair Expo in Taiwan, and the Licensing International Expo in Las Vegas, USA, as well as in exhibitions, including the international Art Exchange Exhibition, Japan, and solo exhibitions such as the "heart and mind of calligraphy" in Taiwan.

What has been your greatest challenge in a project so far?

It is really hard to say because every project has its own unique challenge.

What inspires you?

Everything in the world inspires me. But I especially enjoy the work of other great artists and travelling, which usually provides me with new thoughts and ideas for new creation.

Which trends do you currently recognise in your field?

The hybrid of Chinese and Western art and style will be more commonly seen in our field.

What do you understand by good communication design?

A good communication design should touch its audience's heart in its own unique way and should provoke the audience into spending more time experiencing the work.

WHITE CAT STUDIO
MICHAŁ ŁOJEWSKI

— *Before you create something,*
consider first what you shouldn't create.

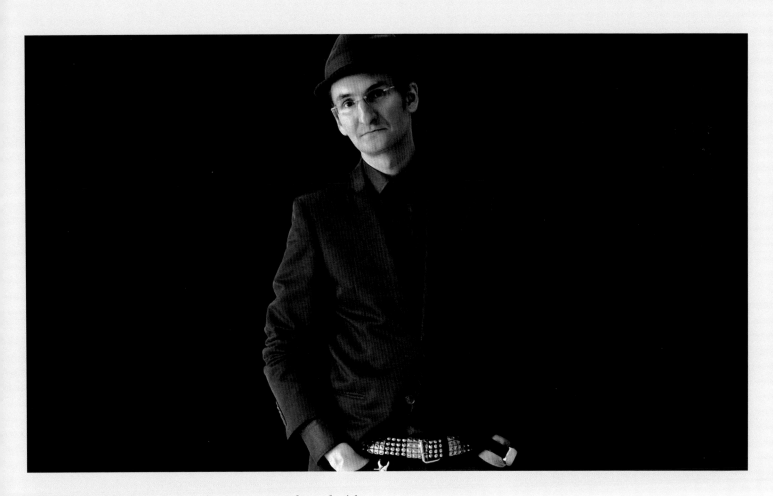

Michał Łojewski, born in 1974 in Warsaw, graduated with a master's degree in graphic art from the Academy of Fine Arts in Warsaw. In 2001, together with his brother, he started the brand development company White Cat Studio, which specialises in packaging design, brand design and corporate visual identity. In 2003, he co-founded the anti-fashion brand Usa e Getta (UEG), which he still manages today. In 2005, he became co-author and creative director of FUTU magazine, which, together with his other work, has received numerous international awards. He has lectured on packaging design at Poznan University of Economics and is repeatedly mentioned in prestigious publications.

What inspires you?

Life inspires me, especially change is inspiring.

Which trends do you currently recognise in your field?

Due to the dramatic changes in the media industry and their huge impact on consumers, many companies are moving towards a strategy of a total branding. This is the future.

What do you understand by good communication design?

I appreciate projects which show, besides a great design and typography, a coherent and strong concept of the whole system.

What kind of project would you like to realise once?

I would like to do a large-scale project in which graphic design would co-create the architecture.

XPLICIT GESELLSCHAFT FÜR VISUELLE KOMMUNIKATION

— Good communication design is when, at a glimpse, you cannot see how but that something has been created with joy.

The visual communication company xplicit was founded in 1994 by Alexander Branczyk, Thomas Nagel and Uwe Otto with offices in Frankfurt/Main and Berlin. The company and its staff of 20 works in the areas of corporate design and information design and, as a full-service agency, specialises in the realisation of product brochures – ranging from creation to pre-press production. As an expert in typography and fonts, xplicit creates exclusive corporate fonts for commercial enterprises and cultural institutions, as for example currently for Duravit AG, FEZ-Berlin, the Labyrinth Kindermuseum Berlin, as well as the new international Berlin Brandenburg Airport (BER).

What has been your greatest challenge in a project so far?

A particularly joyful one was the development of a font system for the "Christian Garden" in the "Gardens of the World" in Berlin. It consists of a square architecture built exclusively from fonts with its letters forming a colonnade of occidental Christian texts. Above all, when creating the statics we had to ensure that it had sufficient load-bearing capacity and achieved this through letters of various widths and in alternating shapes.

What inspires you?

Let's see what we can find in this weighty tome!

Which trends do you currently recognise in your field?

Thinking about trends, instead of taking the responsibility to create what you are convinced of is the right thing.

Awarded works
→ Vol.1: p.69, p.163,
p.188–189

ZUIDERLICHT
MELIANTHE WOUTERS,
ELINE DEKKER
— *Creating work that works.*
Communication by design.

Melianthe Wouters, senior designer, and Eline Dekker, copywriter and project manager, have been working for the Zuiderlicht design agency in Maastricht for more than ten years. The agency has 22 employees, all from different backgrounds, including art, photography, language, communication, information science and psychology.

Together they use smart concepts, good design and exciting, provocative text to reflect and promote the ambitions of their clients in annual reports, websites, brochures, working environments or give-aways. Zuiderlicht works for a range of clients, especially for cultural institutions including museums as well as universities.

What inspires you?

Inspired people, doers, culture, contact, cooperation, the city, music.

Which trends do you currently recognise in your field?

Everyone thinks that they understand design. You have to stand out from the mass though.

What do you understand by good communication design?

It must be distinctive, but most of all it has to appeal and therefore touch a nerve, stimulate and get people to act.

What kind of project would you like to realise once?

Variation is fun: big, small, it doesn't matter. The biggest surprises happen often in assignments that look uninteresting at first sight.

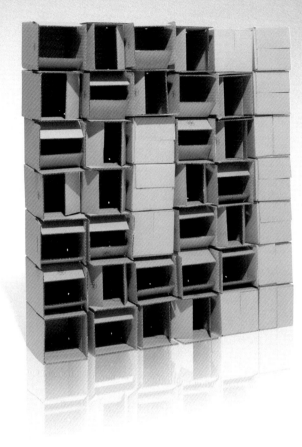

housemouse
Level 1
141 Flinders Lane
AUS-Melbourne, VIC 3000
www.housemouse.com.au
Vol. 1: 374

Ting-Yi Hsu
Room 1101, 11F, Trends
Building
No. 9, Guanghua Road
Chaoyang District
Beijing 100020
China
www.iamyunna.com
Vol. 1: 452, 481

hufax arts
13F-1, No. 17, Ln. 47, Sec. 1,
Baofu Road
Yonghe District
New Taipei 23444
Taiwan
www.hufax.com.tw
Vol. 1: 222, 428–429, 482

I
identis GmbH
design-gruppe joseph
pölzelbauer
Bötzinger Straße 36
D-79111 Freiburg
www.identis.de
Vol. 1: 118, 260–261
Vol. 2: 145

IlovarStritar
Trdinova 5
SLO-1000 Ljubljana
www.ilovarstritar.com
Vol. 1: 130, 137

Impulslabor
Martin-May-Straße 7
D-60594 Frankfurt/Main
www.impulslabor.de
Vol. 1: 61, 120

Interbrand
Weinsbergstraße 118a
D-50823 Cologne
www.interbrand.com
Vol. 1: 175

Interbrand
28 rue Broca
F-75005 Paris
www.interbrand.com
Vol. 1: 153

Interbrand
46–52 Mountain Street
Ultimo
AUS-Sydney, NSW 2007
www.interbrand.com
Vol. 1: 131, 134

Interbrand
Kirchenweg 5
CH-8008 Zürich
www.interbrand.com
Vol. 1: 79, 175

IRU Adcom
1744-5 Bisan-dong
Seo-gu
ROK-Daegu 703-825
www.iruad.com
Vol. 1: 56–57

Isabelle Illustration
Teckstraße 42
D-73119 Zell unter Aichelberg
www.isabelle-illustration.
de
Vol. 1: 421, 449

Ivity Brand Corp
Rua Dom Luís I 19, 3°
P-1200-149 Lisbon
www.ivity-corp.com
Vol. 1: 138–139

J
Jäger & Jäger
Heiligenbreite 52
D-88662 Überlingen
www.jaegerundjaeger.de
Vol. 1: 343

jangled nerves
Hallstraße 25
D-70376 Stuttgart
www.janglednerves.com
Vol. 1: 331

JUN Cooperation
18-2 Samdeok-dong 1-ga
Jung-gu
ROK-Daegu 400-411
www.ideadoit.com
Vol. 1: 56–57

Jung von Matt AG
Glashüttenstraße 38
D-20357 Hamburg
www.jvm.com
Vol. 1: 196–197

JUNO
Budapester Straße 49
D-20359 Hamburg
www.juno-hamburg.com
Vol. 1: 264

JWT Germany GmbH
Straßenbahnring 8
D-20251 Hamburg
www.jwt.de
Vol. 1: 421, 449

K
Kan & Lau Design Consultants
Room 416, InnoCentre
72 Tat Chee Avenue
Kowloon
Hong Kong
www.kanandlau.com
Vol. 1: 398–399, 483

Kazakoff Design
Vanadisplan 2, 6 tr
S-11331 Stockholm
www.kazakoffdesign.se
Vol. 1: 126, 132–133,
282–283, 484

Keim Identity GmbH
Schaffhauserstrasse 21
CH-8006 Zürich
www.keimidentity.ch
Vol. 1: 122–123

Keller Maurer Design
Baumstraße 4, Hof 1
D-80469 Munich
www.km-d.com
Vol. 1: 54–55

Agnes Keltai
Majom Pozsonyi út 43
H-1133 Budapest
www.majommajom.
blogspot.com
Vol. 1: 38–39, 485

kempertrautmann gmbh
Große Bleichen 10
D-20354 Hamburg
www.kempertrautmann.com
Vol. 1: 220–221, 267, 454–455
Vol. 2: 354–355, 454–455

Namoo Kim
S-604, 3rd Engineering
Building
Hankyong National
University
327 Chungang-ro
ROK-Anseong City, Gyeonggi
Province 456-749
www.golden-tree.kr
Vol. 1: 432

Klauser Design GmbH
Hardstrasse 69
CH-8004 Zürich
www.klauser-design.ch
Vol. 1: 326

KMS TEAM
Tölzer Straße 2c
D-81379 Munich
www.kms-team.com
Vol. 1: 88, 99, 101, 102
Vol. 2: 220–221, 362, 367,
486

Studio Marise Knegtmans
Brouwersgracht 42
NL-1013 GW Amsterdam
www.knegtmans.nl
Vol. 1: 336

KNSK Werbeagentur GmbH
An der Alster 1
D-20099 Hamburg
www.knsk.de
Vol. 1: 250, 252–253

köckritzdörrich GmbH
Agentur für Kommunikation
Obere Wässere 3
D-72764 Reutlingen
www.gokd.net
Vol. 1: 372, 373
Vol. 2: 412–413

Koeweiden Postma
Danzigerkade 9C
NL-1013 AP Amsterdam
www.koeweidenpostma.com
Vol. 1: 128

Kolle Rebbe GmbH
Dienerreihe 2
D-20457 Hamburg
www.kolle-rebbe.de
Vol. 1: 263
Vol. 2: 107, 269

Kolle Rebbe / KOREFE
Dienerreihe 2
D-20457 Hamburg
www.korefe.de
Vol. 1: 129

designgruppe koop
Obere Wank 12
D-87484 Nesselwang
www.designgruppe-koop.de
Vol. 1: 226, 276–277, 486
Vol. 2: 297

koržinekdizajn
Ilica 220
HR-10000 Zagreb
www.korzinekdizajn.com
Vol. 1: 67

Kuhn, Kammann & Kuhn
GmbH
Maria-Hilf-Straße 15–17
D-50677 Cologne
www.kkundk.de
Vol. 1: 213

KW Neun Grafikagentur
Neidhartstraße 24
D-86159 Augsburg
www.kw-neun.de
Vol. 1: 383

KW43 BRANDDESIGN
Platz der Ideen 1
D-40476 Düsseldorf
www.kw43.de
Vol. 1: 110–111, 124

L
labor b designbüro
Reinoldistraße 2–4
D-44135 Dortmund
www.laborb.de
Vol. 1: 94, 95, 333

Lambie-Nairn
Greencoat House
Francis Street
GB-London SW1P 1DH
www.lambie-nairn.com
Vol. 1: 100

Leagas Delaney Hamburg
GmbH
Eimsbütteler Straße 64
D-22769 Hamburg
www.leagasdelaney.de
Vol. 1: 402–403, 450–451
Vol. 2: 334–335, 338–339,
460–461, 490

Tom Leifer Design
Mittelweg 161
D-20148 Hamburg
www.tomleiferdesign.de
Vol. 1: 36–37, 487

gabriele lenz
büro für visuelle gestaltung
Turmburggasse 11
A-1060 Vienna
www.gabrielelenz.at
Vol. 1: 300
Vol. 2: 296

Fachhochschule Mainz
University of Applied Sciences Mainz
Lucy-Hillebrand-Straße 2
D-55116 Mainz
www.fh-mainz.de
Vol. 1: 288

Febrü
Büromöbel Produktions-
und Vertriebs-GmbH
Im Babenbecker Feld 62
D-32051 Herford
www.februe.de
Vol. 1: 117, 241

Fedrigoni S.p.A.
Viale del Piave, 3
I-37135 Verona
www.fedrigonicartiere.com
Vol. 1: 142–143

fiftyfifty
Obdachlosenorganisation
Jägerstraße 15
D-40231 Düsseldorf
www.fiftyfifty-galerie.de
Vol. 1: 420

File
Electronic Language International Festival
Rua Dona Veridiana 521/06
Consolação
BR-São Paulo,
SP 01238-010
www.file.org.br
Vol. 1: 360

Fish & More GmbH
Allmandstraße 8
D-88045 Friedrichshafen
www.fish-and-more.de
Vol. 1: 450–451
Vol. 2: 334–335

FLACC vzw
Casino Modern
André Dumontlaan 2
B-3600 Genk
www.flacc.info
Vol. 1: 301

Fluoro Publications Pty Ltd
Level 1
141 Flinders Lane
AUS-Melbourne, VIC 3000
www.fluorodigital.com
Vol. 1: 374

Forster & Uhl Architekten
GmbH
Hohlstrasse 169
CH-8004 Zürich
www.foruhl.ch
Vol. 1: 326

Forum Gestaltung e.V.
Brandenburger Straße 10
D-39104 Magdeburg
www.forum-gestaltung.de
Vol. 1: 323

Frankfurter Verein
für soziale Heimstätten e.V.
Große Seestraße 41–43
D-60486 Frankfurt/Main
www.frankfurter-verein.de
Vol. 1: 61

Fresenius Medical Care AG
& Co. KGaA
Else-Kröner-Straße 1
D-61352 Bad Homburg
www.fmc-ag.com
Vol. 1: 180–181

Fuenfwerken Design AG
Paul-Lincke-Ufer 42
D-10999 Berlin
www.fuenfwerken.com
Vol. 1: 112

Fuenfwerken Design AG
Taunusstraße 52
D-65183 Wiesbaden
www.fuenfwerken.com
Vol. 1: 112

Funen Art Academy
Brandts Torv 1
DK-5000 Odense C
www.detfynske
kunstakademi.dk
Vol. 1: 350–351

Porzellanmanufaktur
FÜRSTENBERG GmbH
Meinbrexener Straße 2
D-37699 Fürstenberg
www.fuerstenberg-
porzellan.com
Vol. 1: 175

G
Gärtner von Eden
Auf der Horst 34
D-33335 Gütersloh
www.gaertner-von-eden.de
Vol. 1: 109

Gas-Union GmbH
Theodor-Stern-Kai 1
D-60596 Frankfurt/Main
www.gas-union.de
Vol. 1: 75, 77

Jupp Gauchel
Graf-Eberstein-Straße 8
D-76199 Karlsruhe
www.juppgauchel.net
Vol. 1: 307

Gerstenberg Verlag
Rathausstraße 18–20
D-31134 Hildesheim
www.gerstenberg-verlag.de
Vol. 1: 446

GlaxoSmithKline Consumer
Healthcare GmbH & Co. KG
Bußmatten 1
D-77815 Bühl
www.gsk.com
Vol. 1: 284–285

Glückspilz Mode und Accessoires GmbH & Co. KG
Oelgasse 12a
D-41515 Grevenbroich
www.gluepi.de
Vol. 1: 92–93

Adrienne Goehler
Stiftung Forum der Kulturen zu Fragen der Zeit
Münzstraße 13
D-10178 Berlin
www.z-n-e.info
Vol. 1: 316

Görtz GmbH
Spitalerstraße 10
D-20095 Hamburg
www.goertz.de
Vol. 1: 227, 335
Vol. 2: 131

Graphopress
Sokratous 157
GR-17673 Athens
www.graphopress.com
Vol. 1: 165

Green at Heart
No. 3, G/F, Kowloonbay
International Trade & Exhibition Centre
1 Trademart Drive
Kowloon Bay
Hong Kong
www.greenatheart.com.hk
Vol. 1: 428–429

Griffin Theatre Company
10 Nimrod Street
Kings Cross
AUS-Sydney, NSW 2011
www.griffintheatre.com.au
Vol. 1: 131

großgestalten
kommunikationsdesign
Vondelstraße 29–31
D-50677 Cologne
www.grossgestalten.de
Vol. 1: 417

Ruth Gschwendtner-Wölfle
Im Buchholz 4
A-6820 Frastanz
www.kunstsalon.eu
Vol. 1: 347

GSK
GlaxoSmithKline
980 Great West Road
GB-Brentford TW8 9GS
www.gsk.com
Vol. 1: 186–187

GT Press
Daedong Apartment
103-1001 Deungchon-dong
Gangseo-gu
ROK-Seoul 157-031
www.golden-tree.kr
Vol. 1: 432

Graphic design studio by
Yurko Gutsulyak
App. 264
Urlivska 11/44
UA-02081 Kiev
http://gstudio.com.ua
Vol. 1: 321

H
HCBCzwei Verwaltung
UG & Co. KG
Große Elbstraße 279
D-22767 Hamburg
www.hoch3.cc
Vol. 1: 114

HDA
Haus der Architektur
House of Architecture
Mariahilferstraße 2
A-8020 Graz
www.hda-graz.at
Vol. 1: 300

Helmrinderknecht
contemporary design
Linienstraße 87
D-10119 Berlin
www.helmrinderknecht.com
Vol. 1: 293

HEMU
Haute École de Musique de
Lausanne
Rue de la Grotte 2
CH-1003 Lausanne
www.hemu.ch
Vol. 1: 83

HEWI
Heinrich Wilke GmbH
Professor-Bier-Straße 1–5
D-34454 Bad Arolsen
www.hewi.de
Vol. 1: 236–237

Hilfe für krebskranke
Kinder Frankfurt e.V.
Komturstraße 3
D-60528 Frankfurt/Main
www.hfkk.de
Vol. 1: 409

Hinz&Kunzt gGmbH
Altstädter Twiete 1–5
D-20095 Hamburg
www.hinzundkunzt.de
Vol. 1: 421, 449

HMS Management
Emmastraat 32
NL-2282 AR Rijswijk
www.hmsmanagement.nl
Vol. 1: 336

Hochschule für Gestaltung
Offenbach
Academy of Art and Design
Offenbach
Schlossstraße 31
D-63065 Offenbach/Main
www.hfg-offenbach
Vol. 1: 396–397

Holyfields Restaurant
GmbH & Co. KG
Breite Straße 1
D-40213 Düsseldorf
www.holyfields.de
Vol. 1: 53
Vol. 2: 155

HOME^Agentur für Kommunikation
Ückendorfer Straße 237h
D-45886 Gelsenkirchen
www.home-agentur.de
Vol. 1: 423

MIIN Design Co., Ltd.
3F-1, No. 34, Sec. 2, Ren'ai
Road
Zhongzheng District
Taipei 100
Taiwan
www.miingift.com
Vol. 1: 345

Dr. Gabriele Minz GmbH
Internationale
Kulturprojekte
Meierottostraße 6
D-10719 Berlin
www.minzgmbh.de
Vol. 1: 103

Bischöfliches Hilfswerk
MISEREOR e.V.
Mozartstraße 9
D-52064 Aachen
www.misereor.de
Vol. 1: 263

MKO
Münchener Kammer-
orchester
Oskar-von-Miller-Ring 1
D-80333 Munich
www.m-k-o.de
Vol. 1: 40–41, 406

Nils Holger Moormann
GmbH
An der Festhalle 2
D-83229 Aschau im Chiemgau
www.moormann.de
Vol. 1: 343

MorphoSys AG
Lena-Christ-Straße 48
D-82152 Martinsried/
Planegg
www.morphosys.de
Vol. 1: 190

Musikschule Allegro
Roßstraße 41
D-40476 Düsseldorf
www.musikschule-allegro.eu
Vol. 1: 265

N
n-tv
Nachrichtenfernsehen
GmbH
Richard-Byrd-Straße 4–6
D-50829 Cologne
www.n-tv.de
Vol. 1: 246
Vol. 2: 331

National Arts Council
90 Goodman Road
Block A, #01-01
Singapore 439053
www.nac.gov.sg
Vol. 1: 322

National Museum of
Contemporary Art
58-4 Makgye-dong
ROK-Gwacheon City,
Gyeonggi Province 427-701
www.moca.go.kr
Vol. 1: 168–169

NEC Mobiling, Ltd.
3-2-5, Kasumigaseki
Chiyoda-ku
J-Tokyo 100-6006
www.nec-mobiling.com
Vol. 1: 42–43

Netia S.A.
Taśmowa 7A
PL-02-677 Warsaw
www.netia.pl
Vol. 1: 170

NewRe
New Reinsurance Company
Zollikerstrasse 226
CH-8008 Zürich
www.newre.com
Vol. 1: 171

Nezu Institute of Fine Arts
6-5-1, Minami-Aoyama
Minato-ku
J-Tokyo 107-0062
www.nezu-muse.or.jp
Vol. 1: 136

Nike Inc.
1 Bowerman Drive, JR-1
USA-Beaverton, OR 97005
www.nike.com
Vol. 1: 391

Nordstrøms Forlag
Rådmandsgade 30
DK-2200 Copenhagen N
www.nrdstrm.dk
Vol. 1: 349

Notting Hill Editions Ltd
Newcombe House
45 Notting Hill Gate
GB-London W11 3LQ
www.nottinghilleditions.com
Vol. 1: 357

NTR
PO Box 29000
NL-1202 MA Hilversum
www.ntr.nl
Vol. 1: 106

O
Occhio GmbH
Wiener Platz 7
Rückgebäude
D-81667 Munich
www.occhio.de
Vol. 1: 287

OCI Company Ltd.
OCI Building
50 Sogong-dong
Jung-gu
ROK-Seoul 100-718
www.oci.co.kr
Vol. 1: 206

Ogilvy Deutschland
Darmstädter
Landstraße 112
D-60598 Frankfurt/Main
www.ogilvy.de
Vol. 1: 245

Adam Opel AG
IPC A3-01
D-65423 Rüsselsheim
www.opel.com
Vol. 1: 311, 413

Sal. Oppenheim jr. & Cie.
Unter Sachsenhausen 4
D-50667 Cologne
www.oppenheim.de
Vol. 1: 389

Orca
Acro Distribution Ltd
PO Box 74324
Greenlane
NZ-Auckland 1543
www.orca.com
Vol. 1: 297

Ospelt AG
Churer Strasse 32
FL-9485 Nendeln
www.ospelt-ag.li
Vol. 1: 155

OWL Optics
Sonnenburger Straße 63
D-10437 Berlin
www.owloptics.com
Vol. 1: 249

Kur- und Tourismusbüro
Oy-Mittelberg
Wertacher Straße 11
D-87466 Oy-Mittelberg
www.oy-mittelberg.de
Vol. 1: 226

P
Michael Pachleitner Group
Liebenauer Tangente 4
A-8041 Graz
www.michaelpachleitner
group.com
Vol. 1: 332

Palais 22
Interior Design
Julia Lee
Kennedyallee 70a
D-60596 Frankfurt/Main
www.palais22.com
Vol. 1: 224

Pan World Brands Limited
319 Ordsall Lane
GB-Salford, Manchester
M5 3FT
www.panworldbrands.com
Vol. 1: 251

Panasonic Energy
Europe N. V.
Brusselsesteenweg 502
B-1731 Zellik
www.panasonic.com
Vol. 1: 268

Verena Panholzer
Andreas Balon
Siebensterngasse 42/12
A-1070 Vienna
www.wortwerk.at
www.andreasbalon.com
Vol. 1: 344, 448

Parador GmbH & Co. KG
Millenkamp 7–8
D-48653 Coesfeld
www.parador.de
Vol. 1: 98, 234

Parque EXPO 98, S.A.
Avenida Dom João II
Lote 1.07.2.1
P-1998-014 Lisbon
www.parqueexpo.pt
Vol. 1: 121

Tony Petersen Film GmbH
Alter Wandrahm 11
Block W
D-20457 Hamburg
www.tpfilm.de
Vol. 1: 129

Pfizer Deutschland GmbH
Linkstraße 10
D-10785 Berlin
www.pfizer.de
Vol. 1: 370–371

Gemeinde Pfronten
Allgäuer Straße 6
D-87459 Pfronten
www.pfronten.de
Vol. 1: 276–277

Plus X
1F, Building 24
31-18 Cheongdam-dong
Gangnam-gu
ROK-Seoul 135-950
www.plus-ex.com
Vol. 1: 135

Dr. Ing. h.c. F. Porsche AG
Porschestraße 15–19
D-71634 Ludwigsburg
www.porsche.com
Vol. 1: 102
Vol. 2: 372, 373

Porzellanklinik
Kaiserstraße 28
D-40479 Düsseldorf
www.porzellanreparatur.de
Vol. 1: 257

PostNL
Prinses Beatrixlaan 23
NL-2595 AK The Hague
www.postnl.com
Vol. 1: 363

Alex Poulsen Arkitekter
Jagtvej 169B, 4. sal
DK-2100 Copenhagen Ø
www.alexpoulsen.dk
Vol. 1: 34–35

Pulchri Studio
Lange Voorhout 15
NL-2514 EA The Hague
www.pulchri.nl
Vol. 1: 415

Q
Qatar 2022
Bid Committee
PO Box 5333
Q-Doha
www.qatar2022bid.com
Vol. 1: 100

Stiftung
Berliner Philharmoniker
Herbert-von-Karajan-
Straße 1
D-10785 Berlin
www.berliner-
philharmoniker.de
Vol. 1: 172–173

Stiftung Sammlung Ziegler
Kunstmuseum
Mülheim an der Ruhr
Synagogenplatz 1
D-45468 Mülheim/Ruhr
www.sammlungziegler.de
Vol. 1: 174

Stiftung zur Erhaltung
der historischen
Altstadt Staufen
Hauptstraße 53
D-79219 Staufen
www.staufenstiftung.de
Vol. 1: 260–261
Vol. 2: 145

Stratley AG
Kaiser-Wilhelm-Ring 27–29
D-50672 Cologne
www.stratley.com
Vol. 1: 239

Strichpunkt Design
Krefelder Straße 32
D-70376 Stuttgart
www.strichpunkt-design.de
Vol. 1: 342

Studio Delhi
Rochusstraße 11
D-55116 Mainz
www.studiodelhi.de
Vol. 1: 327

SÜDWESTBANK AG
Rotebühlstraße 125
D-70178 Stuttgart
www.suedwestbank.de
Vol. 1: 122–123

T
Tango Mania Argentino
Landshut e.V.
Grillparzerstraße 18
D-84036 Landshut
www.tango-in-landshut.de
Vol. 1: 82

Tapwell AB
Renstiernas gata 31
S-11631 Stockholm
www.tapwell.se
Vol. 1: 132–133

Theater aan het Vrijthof
PO Box 1992
NL-6201 BZ Maastricht
www.theateraanhet
vrijthof.nl
Vol. 1: 163

Theater Biel Solothurn
Schmiedengasse 1
Postfach
CH-2500 Biel 3
www.theater-biel.ch
Vol. 1: 416

Theater Dortmund
Kuhstraße 12
D-44137 Dortmund
www.theaterdo.de
Vol. 1: 210

Theater Erlangen
Hauptstraße 55
D-91054 Erlangen
www.theater-erlangen.de
Vol. 1: 394–395

Theater, Oper und
Orchester GmbH Halle
Sparte Thalia Theater Halle
Universitätsring 24
D-06108 Halle
www.buehnen-halle.de
Vol. 1: 310

Municipality of
Thessaloniki
Department of Culture
and Youth
Venizelou 45
GR-54631 Thessaloniki
www.thessaloniki.gr
Vol. 1: 444–445

ThyssenKrupp
Postfach
D-45063 Essen
www.thyssenkrupp.com
Vol. 1: 193

ThyssenKrupp Uhde GmbH
Friedrich-Uhde-Straße 15
D-44141 Dortmund
www.uhde.com
Vol. 1: 204–205

Tinnitus-Hyperakusis-
Zentrum
Goethestraße 3
D-60313 Frankfurt/Main
www.tinnitus-frankfurt.de
Vol. 1: 255

Totaloil, LLC
Naschokinsky pereulok 14
RUS-119019 Moscow
http://total-oil.ru
Vol. 1: 51

Trademark Publishing
Westendstraße 87
D-60325 Frankfurt/Main
www.trademark
publishing.de
Vol. 1: 385

Transkulturelles Theater-
und Bildungsprojekt
„fremd?!"
Allemannengasse 25
CH-4058 Basel
www.projektfremd.ch
Vol. 1: 419

TÜV SÜD
Westendstraße 199
D-80686 Munich
www.tuev-sued.de
Vol. 1: 203

Typotron AG
Scheidwegstrasse 18
CH-9016 St.Gallen
www.typotron.ch
Vol. 1: 274–275

U
Prof. Andreas Uebele
Heusteigstraße 94a
D-70180 Stuttgart
www.uebele.com
Vol. 1: 337

Unicer Bebidas, S.A.
Via Norte
Leça do Balio
Matosinhos
P-4466-955 São Mamede
de Infesta
www.unicer.pt
Vol. 1: 211

University of Ljubljana
Faculty of Economics
Kardeljeva ploščad 17
SLO-1000 Ljubljana
www.ef.uni-lj.si
Vol. 1: 137

V
Van Gogh Museum
Stadhouderskade 55
NL-1072 AB Amsterdam
www.vangoghmuseum.nl
Vol. 1: 128

velonauten UG
Ortelsburger Straße 7
D-37083 Göttingen
www.velonauten.de
Vol. 1: 375

verbuendungshaus fforst e.V.
Forststraße 4
D-15230 Frankfurt/Oder
www.fforst.net
Vol. 1: 334

Verkehrsverbund Bremen/
Niedersachsen GmbH
(VBN)
Willy-Brandt-Platz 7
D-28215 Bremen
www.vbn.de
Vol. 1: 200

Verlag Hermann Schmidt
Mainz
Robert-Koch-Straße 8
D-55129 Mainz
www.typografie.de
Vol. 1: 433

Stadt Viersen
Stadtmarketing
Bahnhofstraße 23–29
D-41747 Viersen
www.viersen.de
Vol. 1: 86

Vlehan
PO Box 190
NL-2700 AD Zoetermeer
www.vlehan.nl
Vol. 1: 199

Volkswagen AG
Berliner Ring 2
D-38440 Wolfsburg
www.volkswagen.com
Vol. 1: 191
Vol. 2: 230

Volkswagen Zentrum
Freiburg
Tullastraße 82
D-79108 Freiburg
www.gehlert.de
Vol. 1: 118

Weingut von Othegraven
Weinstraße 1
D-54441 Kanzem
www.von-othegraven.de
Vol. 1: 44

Vorwerk & Co. KG
Mühlenweg 17–37
D-42270 Wuppertal
www.vorwerk.de
Vol. 1: 194

W
W'Law
Weber Wicki Partners Ltd.
Dufourstrasse 1
CH-8008 Zürich
www.wlaw.ch
Vol. 1: 152

Walser Privatbank
Walserstraße 61
A-6991 Riezlern
www.walserprivatbank.com
Vol. 1: 81

Wen-Cheng Tea Farm
No. 335, Yong'an Street
West District
Chiayi 600
Taiwan
Vol. 1: 50

Claus Wisser Verwaltungs-
und Beteiligungs GmbH &
Co. KG
Kennedyallee 76
D-60596 Frankfurt/Main
claus.wisser@cw-ivb.de
Vol. 1: 247

Woonpunt
PO Box 1112
NL-6201 BC Maastricht
www.woonpunt.nl
Vol. 1: 188–189

Y
Yeong Jin Furniture
Factory Corp., Ltd.
No. 360, Sec. 2, Nantun
Road
Nantun District
Taichung 408
Taiwan
www.macromaison.com.tw
Vol. 1: 231

Z
zgoll: Konferenzraum GmbH
Falkenweg 11
D-41468 Neuss
www.zgoll-konferenzraum.de
Vol. 1: 94

Zumtobel AG
Höchster Straße 8
A-6850 Dornbirn
www.zumtobel.com
Vol. 1: 178–179

Zürcher
Hochschule der Künste
Zurich
University of the Arts
Ausstellungsstrasse 60
CH-8005 Zürich
www.zhdk.ch
Vol. 1: 312–313
Vol. 2: 80–81